Intellectual Property Rights Issues in Vaccine Development

Edited by

Sachin Kumar Jain
Oriental College of Pharmacy & Research
Oriental University, Near Aurobindo
Hospital, Sanwer Road, Indore 453555, MP, India

Ravikant Gupta, Sudha Vengurlekar

&

Nidhi Bais
Faculty of Pharmacy, Oriental University
Near Aurobindo Hospital, Sanwer Road
Indore 453555, MP, India

&

Gajendra P. Choudhary
School of Pharmacy, Devi Ahilya Vishwavidhyalaya
Ring Road Takhshila Campus
Indore 452001, MP, India

Intellectual Property Rights Issues in Vaccine Development

Editors: Sachin Kumar Jain, Ravikant Gupta, Sudha Vengurlekar, Nidhi Bais & Gajendra P. Choudhary

ISBN (Online): 978-981-5274-76-9

ISBN (Print): 978-981-5274-77-6

ISBN (Paperback): 978-981-5274-78-3

First published in 2025.

need for a court order if at any point you breach any terms of this License Agreement. In no event will any delay or failure by Bentham Science Publishers in enforcing your compliance with this License Agreement constitute a waiver of any of its rights.

3. You acknowledge that you have read this License Agreement, and agree to be bound by its terms and conditions. To the extent that any other terms and conditions presented on any website of Bentham Science Publishers conflict with, or are inconsistent with, the terms and conditions set out in this License Agreement, you acknowledge that the terms and conditions set out in this License Agreement shall prevail.

Bentham Science Publishers Pte. Ltd.
No. 9 Raffles Place
Office No. 26-01
Singapore 048619
Singapore
Email: subscriptions@benthamscience.net

BENTHAM SCIENCE

CONTENTS

PREFACE

In the wake of the global COVID-19 pandemic, the spotlight has never shone brighter on the vital role of intellectual property rights in the realm of vaccines. As the world grapples with unprecedented challenges, from the rapid development of life-saving vaccines to the equitable distribution of doses, the intersection of innovation and accessibility has emerged as a defining issue of our time.

"Intellectual Property Rights: Role in Current Scenario for Vaccines" embarks on a timely exploration of this complex landscape, delving into the multifaceted dimensions of intellectual property and its profound impact on the development, production, and dissemination of vaccines.

Within these pages, we navigate through the intricate web of patents, trade secrets, and regulatory frameworks that underpin the global vaccine ecosystem. From the pioneering research laboratories to the corridors of power where policy decisions are made, we unravel the threads of innovation and entrepreneurship that drive progress in the field of vaccinology.

Yet, as we celebrate the remarkable achievements of science and technology, we confront the stark realities of inequity and access that threaten to undermine our collective efforts. The COVID-19 pandemic has laid bare the glaring disparities in vaccine distribution, exposing deep-rooted structural inequalities that demand urgent redressal.

In this context, the role of intellectual property rights looms large, shaping not only the pace of scientific innovation but also the contours of global health equity. Through a nuanced analysis of legal frameworks, ethical considerations, and socio-economic implications, this book seeks to illuminate the path forward, forging a more inclusive and sustainable future for vaccine development and delivery.

As we embark on this journey of exploration and introspection, we are reminded of the profound responsibility that comes with the stewardship of knowledge. In the quest for scientific advancement, let us not lose sight of our shared humanity, or the imperative to ensure that the fruits of innovation are accessible to all.

This preface serves as a call to action, inviting readers to join us in a dialogue that transcends disciplines and borders. Together, let us navigate the complex terrain of intellectual property rights, charting a course toward a world where vaccines are not just a privilege but a fundamental human right.

Sachin Kumar Jain
Oriental College of Pharmacy & Research, Oriental University
Near Aurobindo Hospital, Sanwer Road
Indore 453555, MP, India

Ravikant Gupta
Sudha Vengurlekar
Nidhi Bais
Faculty of Pharmacy, Oriental University
Near Aurobindo Hospital, Sanwer Road
Indore 453555, MP, India

&

Gajendra P. Choudhary
School of Pharmacy, Devi Ahilya Vishwavidhyalaya
Ring Road Takhshila Campus
Indore 452001, MP, India

List of Contributors

Aarti K. Thakre	Dadasaheb Balpande College of Pharmacy, Besa, Nagpur, India
Ashwini Ingole	Dadasaheb Balpande College of Pharmacy, Nagpur 440037, Maharashtra, India
Ashish Jain	Shri D. D. Vispute College of Pharmacy and Research Center, New Panvel, Mumbai, India
Dolly Rani	Amity Institute of Pharmacy, Amity University, Noida 201303, India
Dakshesh Goel	SGT College of Pharmacy, SGT University, Gurugram, Haryana, India
Gurpreet Bawa	Shri D. D. Vispute College of Pharmacy and Research Center, New Panvel, Mumbai, India
Gayatri Tiwaskar	Dadasaheb Balpande College of Pharmacy, Nagpur 440037, Maharashtra, India
Himanshu Vishwakarma	Oriental College of Pharmacy & Research, Oriental University Near Aurobindo Hospital, Sanwer Road, Indore 453555, MP, India
Khushi Jain	Oriental College of Pharmacy & Research, Oriental University Near Aurobindo Hospital, Sanwer Road, Indore 453555, MP, India
Kamal Singh Rathore	B.N. College of Pharmacy, B.N.University, Udaipur, Rajasthan, India
Megha Jha	Department of Biotechnology, School of Biological Sciences, Dr. Harisingh Gour Central University, Sagar, M.P. 470003, India
Manasi M. Choudhari	Dadasaheb Balpande College of Diploma in Pharmacy, Besa, Nagpur, India
Monali N. Dumore	Dadasaheb Balpande College of Pharmacy, Besa, Nagpur, India
Nitin G. Dumore	Dadasaheb Balpande College of Pharmacy, Besa, Nagpur, India
P. Bhide	Department of Pharmaceutics, Sri Aurobindo Institute of Pharmacy, Indore 453555, MP, India
Ruchi Shivhare	Dadasaheb Balpande College of Pharmacy, Nagpur 440037, Maharashtra, India
Sandhya Bagde	Dadasaheb Balpande College of Pharmacy, Nagpur 440037, Maharashtra, India
Sachin Kumar Jain	Oriental College of Pharmacy & Research, Oriental University, Near Aurobindo Hospital, Sanwer Road Indore 453555, MP, India
Shikha Jaiswal	Department of Pharmaceutics, Oriental University, Near Aurobindo Hospital, Sanwer Road, Indore 453555, MP, India
Sudha Vengurlekar	Department of Pharmaceutical Chemistry, Oriental University, Near Aurobindo Hospital, Sanwer Road, Indore 453555, MP, India
Simran Soni	Sri Aurobindo Institute of Pharmacy, Indore 453555, MP, India
Sonika Shrivastav	SGT College of Pharmacy, SGT University, Gurugram, Haryana, India
Umesh K. Patil	Department of Pharmaceutical Science, Dr. Hari Singh Gaur Vishwavidhyalaya, Sagar, MP, India

Vikas K. Jain	Department of Pharmacology, Acropolis Institute of Pharmaceutical Education and Research, Indore 453771, MP, India
Vaishali Raghuwanshi	Sri Aurobindo Institute of Pharmacy, Indore 453555, MP, India
V. Raghuwanshi	Department of Pharmaceutics, Sri Aurobindo Institute of Pharmacy, Indore 453555, MP, India
Y. Bhandari	Department of Pharmaceutical Chemistry, Sri Aurobindo Institute of Pharmacy, Indore 453555, MP, India

CHAPTER 1

Introduction of Intellectual Property Rights and Vaccines

Gurpreet Bawa[1,*] and **Ashish Jain**[1]

[1] *Shri D. D. Vispute College of Pharmacy and Research Center, New Panvel, Mumbai, India*

Abstract: The traditional discourse on the relationship between vaccines and intellectual property (IP) has primarily centered on patent rights. However, this conclusion advocates for a broader perspective that encompasses copyright, trademarks, patents, trade secrets, and potentially even plant breeders' rights in the context of vaccines. By recognizing the applicability of multiple IP rights to various facets of vaccines, a more comprehensive and robust protection framework can be established. This expanded discussion introduces novel considerations that have not been routinely addressed in relation to vaccines and IP rights. The argument emphasizes that the discourse should transcend the confines of a single IP right when discussing vaccines. Instead, it encourages a holistic approach, considering the integration and cooperation of multiple IP rights. Such an inclusive view not only broadens the scope of protection for vaccines but also facilitates the development of a strategic framework that leverages the synergies between different IP rights. The integrated perspective allows for a more nuanced strategy, enabling the evaluation of why specific IP rights should be included and how they contribute to the overall development and distribution of vaccines. In essence, the conclusion contends that a shift in the discussion from the application of individual IP rights to a comprehensive consideration of multiple rights is imperative. This evolved viewpoint enhances the productivity and conclusiveness of the strategy, emphasizing the need for a reformed discourse on vaccines and IP rights to adapt to the evolving landscape.

Keywords: Copyright, Intellectual property, Patents, Trademark, Vaccine.

INTRODUCTION

Vaccines come in a range of forms and components, including specific formulations, delivery systems, components, and distribution networks, and there are a variety of intellectual property (IP) rights available. Patent rights are frequently the starting and ending point of discussions over intellectual property

* **Corresponding author Gurpreet Bawa:** Shri D. D. Vispute College of Pharmacy and Research Center, New Panvel, Mumbai, India; E-mail: gurpreet_bawa@ymail.com

Sachin Kumar Jain, Ravikant Gupta, Sudha Vengurlekar, Nidhi Bais & Gajendra P. Choudhary (Eds.)

rights for vaccines. However, patent rights are not the sole form of intellectual property protection accessible to vaccinations. Other rights, including copyright, trademarks, plant breeders' rights, and trade secrets, may also apply to vaccinations.

For example, there is an ongoing debate about the ethical implications of awarding patent rights to innovations and items that improve public health, such as vaccines. This argument raises questions about whether patent rights have a good or detrimental impact on vaccine innovation and public access. Further doubts are raised about whether patent rights have a negative or good impact on the development of vaccine technology for diseases that primarily affect developing countries. This chapter admits that these discussions have been ongoing for many years and continue to be so. These are essential discussions; nevertheless, it is not the purpose of this chapter to add a voice to them.

This chapter explores how intellectual property rights impact vaccine development, use, and distribution. Right now, both ethical and practical discussions about intellectual property rights and vaccinations focus on patent rights. In the toolkit of intellectual property rights, patents provide owners with a major exclusive right, which has been utilised by various organisations to penalise those who attempt to imitate patented products. Patent rights have also been used to monopolise the market and justify exorbitant licensing costs for patent-protected products. These techniques can have a significant negative impact on the development of related technologies as well as access to patents. Thus, the scope and strength of patent rights have influenced the discussion of IP rights in general, so that the entire category of IP rights is considered as capable and culpable of the same exclusionary outcomes. In truth, patent rights are only one type of intellectual property right that may be applied to a vaccine, and the high prices and access constraints that result from the exercise of patent rights are only one option for an owner to use IP rights.

It is also noteworthy that the debate over intellectual property rights for vaccines is frequently overshadowed by the debate over pharmaceutical products and IP rights, which mostly focus on medications that do not contain vaccinations. Talking about vaccines in particular is crucial because they differ significantly from other medicinal products in terms of their characteristics and effects. Certain complications can arise in the formulation of vaccines (*e.g.*, expert input is required for some vaccines), in their distribution (*e.g.*, cold storage transit is required for many vaccines), and in their administration (*e.g.*, professional transmission is required for injected vaccinations). Because of these complications, debates on intellectual property rights in relation to other kinds of pharmaceutical items might not apply entirely to vaccines.

Vaccines offer huge societal benefits that other pharmaceutical treatments cannot match. According to the World Health Organisation, "much of the debate on [IP rights] and public health has focused on the possible impact that patents on final products have on the prices paid in developing countries, and thus their affordability." The nature of vaccine development and production, as well as the structure of the ultimate market, may necessitate a distinct type of argument [1]. The report goes on to cite distinctions between pharmaceuticals and vaccines, noting the following: vaccines have much smaller markets; the public sector has a greater involvement in the production, pricing, and marketing of vaccines; vaccines as biological products are more complex and costly to produce; clinical trials may also be much more expensive for vaccines; and it may be much more difficult to copy a vaccine [2]. Although these distinctions make it evident that discussions concerning the influence of patents on vaccine accessibility and affordability may differ from those surrounding pharmaceuticals, it is nevertheless true that both types of drugs play an important role in public health. It has been said that "despite the 1.5% share that vaccines have in global pharmaceutical turnover in dollars, vaccines represent much more than 1.5% of the capacity to deal with global health problems because they have positive externalities" [3].

Vaccines have provided significant societal benefits, including the elimination of diseases from entire communities [4]. This chapter will focus on the unique challenges of intellectual property (IP) rights in relation to vaccines, rather than the broader connection between IP rights and pharmaceuticals. Various types of intellectual property rights apply to vaccines, each offering distinct advantages to the proprietor.

This chapter will address the types of vaccines that seek protection, as well as the many types of intellectual property rights that are applicable to vaccinations. We will begin by looking at the features and aspects of vaccines that may be subject to various intellectual property rights, as well as the IP rights that are applicable to them. After we have established the nature of the specific IP rights that apply to vaccines, we can look at the motivations for pursuing IP rights and some of the specific elements that influence the application of IP rights to vaccines. IP rights can be used in tandem to implement an IP protection strategy for vaccines that benefits both vaccine development and public availability. There are numerous rights in the IP toolbox, and they should all be evaluated in the context of vaccine development and deployment.

Applying IP Protection to Vaccines

A prevalent misperception is that intellectual property rights apply to vaccinations in a 1:1 ratio manner. For example, such a viewpoint assumes that if patent rights apply to vaccinations, the discussion about IP rights pertaining to vaccines will end. However, because vaccination may contain several elements and characteristics, each may be protected by a different intellectual property claim.

Vaccines, for instance, may consist of components such as a formulation, a means of administering the vaccination to a subject, a brand name that helps the public recognise the vaccine, etc. A review of the IP toolbox's tools reveals that: (1) the combination of medicinal ingredients that make up the formulation may be protected by patent rights; (2) the device, which could be a capsule designed to release the vaccine in a specific area of the body or some other type of vaccine delivery system, may also be protected by patent rights; and (3) the vaccine's brand name may be protected by trademark.

Furthermore, additional intellectual property rights may be used to safeguard the vaccine's components and features, depending on its nature. A vaccination made from plants is one that is covered by additional intellectual property rights. Because early studies on this type of vaccination concentrated on administering it by the consumption of raw plant materials to achieve the immunisation effect, it was named an “edible vaccine.” Further investigation has revealed that it is challenging to ensure dose consistency in an edible vacuum-formed structure. As a result, researchers are now concentrating on using dried plant-derived vaccine ingredients to make a product that can be taken orally, like a tablet, capsule, or powder.

Vaccines generated from plants are produced by cultivating genetically modified plant material, which can be a leaf, fruit, or vegetable. Because of its genetic nature, the genetically engineered plant material functions as a vaccination when consumed. Potatoes, tomatoes, and bananas are among the plant materials that have been the target of these vaccinations. Plant materials have undergone genetic modifications to trigger an immune response against several illnesses, including cholera, rabies, and hepatitis B surface antigens [5].

In addition to the patent protections available to other vaccine types, plant-derived vaccines can also benefit from other intellectual property rights, including those related to plant breeders. Plant breeders' rights extend to engineered plants, as will be covered in greater depth below. As such, they also apply to the genetically modified plant component of vaccines made from plants. Some vaccinations might also benefit from specific intellectual property rights that do not apply to all vaccines because of their unique components and features. Thus, a vaccine's nature, components, and features should all be taken into account to guarantee that it is covered by any applicable intellectual property rights.

Furthermore, it should be acknowledged that there are numerous ways to enjoy and make use of these intellectual property rights, much as various IP rights may apply to certain parts and characteristics of a vaccination. When a vaccine is protected by intellectual property, the owner(s) of such rights can choose how the vaccine will be used and disseminated. Although intellectual property rights are exclusive, they do not always have to be used to prevent others from using or receiving vaccines. In actuality, a vaccine's broad usage and distribution rights can be granted through the utilisation of IP rights. Thus, contrary to popular belief, intellectual property rights may not always imply restricted rights. Intellectual property rights can guarantee an owner a range of rights that enable the formulation of a public distribution and vaccine development strategy specific to the type of vaccine. IP rights, for instance, can be used to enable the widespread and inexpensive distribution of vaccination without facing opposition from any third parties that might otherwise impede or block such a plan.

Intellectual property owners are free to use their rights however they see fit for their innovation. Therefore, intellectual property laws have several advantages for both the public and IP owners. Identifying which intellectual property rights might be relevant to vaccination is the first step (Fig. **1**).

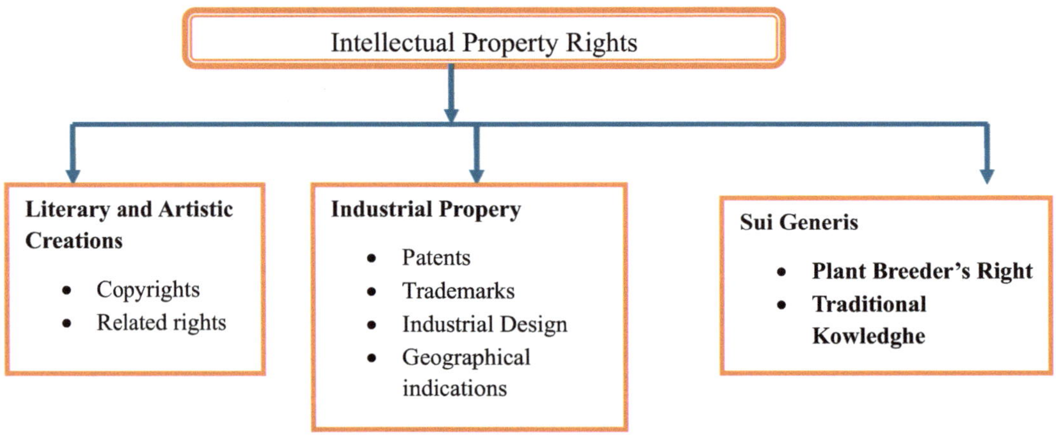

Fig. (1). Intellectual property rights.

Types of IP Protection

Every kind of IP right is different and might provide different possibilities for vaccinations as well as certain protections. This section will examine the applicability of patents, trademarks, copyrights, plant breeders' rights, and trade secrets to vaccinations. Notably, this chapter's remarks on IP rights are particularly relevant to Canadian IP laws. Since IP laws are typically jurisdiction-specific, the IP rights that apply in various states and locations may differ. For instance, there may be jurisdiction-specific variations in the duration of a copyright's enforcement and the kinds of subjects covered by patent rights. As a result, it should be acknowledged that the data in this chapter offers general observations about the relevance of various IP rights to vaccines. It is advisable to consult a legal expert before attempting to obtain intellectual property rights for vaccinations in any particular jurisdiction.

Patents

Inventions are protected by patents. However, not every invention qualifies for patent protection. In general, inventions that fall under the category of new and useful arts, processes, manufactures, compositions of matter, or any new and useful improvement in any of these categories are protected by patent laws [6]. These inventions also have to fall under the categories of inventions whose subject matter has been determined to be patentable. For instance, inventions that are either higher life forms or abstract theorems are not patentable under Canadian law [7].

Three more requirements must be satisfied before patent rights are awarded for a product, technique, composition, or improvement that has been determined to be an invention and to be directed toward patentable subject matter. The invention needs to be novel, useful, and concealed from someone who is experienced in the field in which it is being used. Patentability may be granted to vaccine inventions (*i.e.*, vaccine-related products, methods, formulations, or enhancements) that satisfy certain requirements.

The sole authority to create, construct, and utilise the invention, as well as to market it for usage by third parties, is conferred upon the patent holder [8]. The exclusive rights are valid for a predetermined amount of time. Many nations have committed, by treaty, to implementing a universal patent term of 20 years from the date of application filing [9]. (In particular, the member states of the World Trade Organization-governed Trade-Related Aspect of Intellectual Property Rights (TRIPs) accord have agreed to apply this twenty-year term.)

The timing of a patent application is a significant concern for inventors, particularly in the highly competitive field of vaccine development. In many countries, including Canada, patent rights follow the first-to-file rule, meaning that the first inventor to file a patent application for innovation will be granted patent protection, even if others independently develop the same idea. This rule underscores the importance of filing a patent application as early as possible to secure exclusive rights and prevent competitors from claiming the same invention. In the fast-paced vaccine development landscape, where multiple parties may be working on similar technologies, filing promptly is critical to protecting intellectual property and maintaining a competitive edge.

Some legal systems follow the principle of first to invent. When two or more parties file separate patent applications for the same invention, the party that can demonstrate it was the first to invent the invention will be awarded the patent rights to the innovation. This is known as the first-to-invent rule. The first-to-file criteria must be taken into account when deciding when to file patent applications because the market for films frequently spans several jurisdictions.

Another thing to keep in mind is that patents can be utilised to grant exclusive rights for many components and features of vaccines since the scope of innovations can include items, techniques, formulations, and improvements. Patent rights, for instance, can shield a vaccine's formulation, content, manufacturing process, and delivery system. A patent application that claims the components that are combined to generate the vaccine, such as adjuvants and immunogenic response-invoking factors, can protect the composition or formulation of the vaccine. A platform for vaccine manufacturing may be the target of a patent to protect vaccine-related processes. (For instance, some vaccinations must be prepared by an egg-culture procedure involving a specific kind of manufacturing.) Additionally, patent rights may be used to protect a vaccination delivery mechanism. A non-needle delivery system or a tool for administering a vaccine to a human could be examples of such a device [10]. These are only a few instances of the components and features of vaccines that could be covered by patent rights.

Interestingly, administering a vaccine as a medical therapy alone is not enough to protect a person in a number of countries. Patent rights are not given in these countries for inventions that are medical procedures or treatments. Interestingly, not every nation imposes this restriction in the same way. It is possible to obtain protection for administering vaccines in certain nations that recognise therapeutic or preventive procedures as patentable subject matter.

In conclusion, it is critical to examine a vaccination from a perspective that emphasizes its unique components and features while evaluating the patent rights that may be granted to it. The relationship between vaccines and patent rights can involve patent protection for many elements or aspects of the vaccine, just as the relationship between IP rights and vaccines is not a 1:1 ratio.

Trademark

A trademark could consist of any combination of the aforementioned, numbers, a word or words, a design, or a symbol. It is employed in order to link certain goods and services to a specific source company or individual that offers them. The fundamental purpose of a trademark, as stated by statute, is to set goods or services attributable to one source apart from those attributable to another [11].

The Latin name of a vaccine's main ingredient or any other relevant scientific phrase is rarely used when it is made available to the general public. Vaccines are commonly marketed and distributed to the general public under brand names. The public associates these brand names inextricably with the product. Public discussion on the human papillomavirus vaccine, for instance, is uncommon, although the same person may be aware of the GardasilTM vaccine. Another example is the TwinrixTM brand, which is widely recognised by the public as a hepatitis A and B vaccine.

Vaccine brand names are protected as trademarks. According to standard definitions, trademarks are symbols that are used by an individual or business to set itself apart from goods or services that are produced, sold, rented, hired, or performed by third parties [11]. The goodwill that is developed over time by the trademark's owner *via* the use of the mark constitutes the trademark's intrinsic worth. Many corporate entities view their trademark portfolios as their most valuable asset due to the value acquired through continual usage and goodwill connected with trademarks [12].

Brands can be either registered or unregistered. When it comes to protection, an unregistered mark is not as protected as when it is registered [13]. For instance, the protection might be restricted to the precise location where the unregistered mark was used and made public, and it might be necessary for the mark to be used in connection with the goods or services for a sufficient period of time to exhibit conventional trademark characteristics like distinctiveness and exclusivity [14]. Owners of registered trademarks typically have a wider range of rights, including the sole right to use the trademark for goods or services connected to the mark across national borders [15]. A registered trademark in Canada has an indefinite lifespan because it is renewable every 15 years [16]. Trademarks have a potential lifetime that sets them apart from other intellectual property (IP) types that have limited lifespans, such as patents and copyrights.

Certain marks will not be registrable, just as certain ideas will not be eligible for patent protection. A mark that is found to be confusingly similar to an already-registered trademark in Canada cannot be registered [17]. The test that should be used when comparing potentially confusing marks looks at a variety of factors, such as distinctiveness, length of use, type of goods, services, and trade the mark is used with, and similarity between the potentially confusing marks in terms of appearance, sound, or ideas they suggest [18]. Additionally, the ordinary consumer's perspective must be used to identify confusingly identical marks. Additionally, misleadingly deceptive marks are not allowed to be registered.

A trademark plays a significant role in the public's recognition of a vaccine. The trademark establishes a connection between the vaccination and its producer or other supplier. In the event that a trademarked vaccine's effectiveness is openly debated, it may also serve as a vehicle for the public to link a vaccine's level of quality or effectiveness. As a result, the trademark may come to represent the public's degree of support for the vaccine or lack thereof.

Furthermore, the owner of a vaccine can use trademark protection as a crucial tool to prevent others from misrepresenting their vaccination goods as coming from the owner of the branded vaccine [19, 20]. Through the use of trademark protection, a mark owner can also prevent third parties from misrepresenting who is offering vaccines to the public by using the registered trademark's name to promote their products. In this way, trademark protection can help significantly with vaccinations. In addition to protecting the public's impression of a vaccine's reputation, integrity, and quality, a trademark can be used to identify vaccines.

Copyright

Perhaps less evident than the tie between vaccines and patents or trademarks is the relationship between vaccines and copyright. Written and visual content that promotes vaccinations, such as articles, advertising, and promotional materials, is subject to copyright [21]. Notably, ideas expressed are protected by copyright rather than the ideas themselves [22]. When a work is protected by copyright, the owner has the exclusive right to create or reproduce the work or any significant portion of it in any kind of material form, to present the work or any significant portion of it in public, or, in the case of unpublished work, to publish the work or any significant portion of it.

Unlike other intellectual property rights, copyright is typically given at the time a work is created and does not need to go through an application procedure before being granted. The right to copyright is given to you automatically. Copyright protection can be obtained without registering the work or any other subject matter, even though there are a number of procedural advantages to doing so.

The fact that copyright is international in scope is another distinctive feature. While copyright will accompany a work wherever it goes, patent and trademark rights are exclusive to the jurisdictions in which they are awarded. For instance, Canadian copyright law will apply to written materials about a movie that is already in theatres, while US copyright law will apply to the same written materials that are already in theatres in the United States.

One significant distinction between the copyright laws of different nations and areas is that certain jurisdictions—such as Canada—expressly provide an author of a work “moral rights” [23]. In Canada, a performer's or author's moral right to the integrity of their work or performance is safeguarded only if it is not used in connection with a good, service, cause, or organisation, or if it is distorted, mutilated, or otherwise altered to the detriment of the performer's or author's honour or reputation [24]. The freedom to use a copyrighted work however one pleases is restricted by moral rights for assignees and licensees.

Any economic rights connected to copyright are not related to a moral right [25]. While moral rights belong exclusively to the work’s author, regardless of any arrangement or agreement between the author and any third party, economic rights are owned by the copyright holder. Moral rights, in contrast to economic rights, are non-assignable and may be partially or completely waived [26]. Therefore, merely assigning a copyright does not imply a relinquishment of moral rights [27]. The duration of moral rights is equivalent to the duration of copyright in the work [28]. For example, in the case of COVID-19 vaccines, pharmaceutical companies such as Pfizer and Moderna hold patents for their vaccine technologies, which are protected under intellectual property law. These economic rights allow them to control the production and distribution of the vaccines, but they cannot waive or assign moral rights related to the integrity and authorship of the vaccine development itself, as seen in the public debates around patent licensing and access to vaccines during the global pandemic.

A copyright owner should be informed, nonetheless, that the duration of their protection may fluctuate depending on the nation. In Canada, copyright generally lasts for the lifetime of the author plus fifty years afterward [29]. If an author of a work that is protected by copyright is not a living person, the copyright period is typically 50 years. In Canada, there is no way to prolong the duration of a copyright. It is possible for a work to have copyright protection in one nation while it has expired in another due to the diverse ways that different countries implement copyright laws.

The copyright granting standards used in different nations have an impact on whether a work is covered by copyright. Only original works—those that are: (1) more than mere copies of other works; and (2) the expression of an idea that is an intellectual endeavor attained through the use of skill and judgement in a manner that is more than a mechanical exercise—are eligible for copyright protection in Canada. In this context, judgement refers to the application of one's capacity for judgement or ability to make an opinion or evaluation by weighing several viable possibilities in generating the work, whereas skill refers to the application of one's knowledge, acquired aptitude, or trained ability in producing the work [30].

A "sweat of the brow" or "industriousness" criteria of originality is used in other nations [31]. This leads to the possibility that a work may be copyright-protected in some nations while not being in other nations. The level of copyright protection that is imposed in each nation determines whether or not copyright protection is present.

In order to prevent unauthorised use or theft of materials and designs related to vaccines, copyright can be useful. This protection can help the owner of a vaccine maintain and oversee the distribution of materials related to the vaccination, enabling public to get consistent and trustworthy information about the vaccine. A copyright holder can exercise control over others by using their rights to prevent them from duplicating their works and designs. Copyright can be a useful instrument when it comes to vaccines, as it is crucial that public communications and information about them be accurate and dependable.

Plant Breeders' Rights

Vaccines containing plant components may qualify for protection under plant breeders' rights, which apply to plant varieties that are unique, stable, uniform, and new. These rights grant the holder exclusive rights for 20 years (25 years for tree and vine varieties) to produce, reproduce, sell, export, or import the variety's propagating material [32]. They also allow the holder to use the protected variety for developing new varieties, such as hybrids, and to license these activities to others [33].

Canada's plant breeders' rights legislation was established following the Supreme Court's decision in Pioneer Hi-Bred Ltd. v. Canada, which ruled that plants created through crossbreeding were not patentable under the Patent Act. Amendments to the Act in 2015 improved plant breeders' rights by offering protection, although short of a full patent. Notably, the legislation covers only the propagating material, not the plant itself. Farmers, for instance, may save seeds from a protected crop for replanting, and breeders may use protected varieties to develop new ones. Additionally, compulsory licenses may be issued if a protected variety is not widely available, reasonably priced, or if royalty rates are excessive [34].

Protecting the intellectual property of plant breeders can be essential for vaccines made from genetically modified plants, as it prevents others from replicating and using the plant material in competing products [35]. This type of IP can complement other rights associated with the vaccine, offering comprehensive protection for innovation [36].

Trade Secret

The owner of a vaccine may want to keep some details and components about the vaccination private. Reverse engineering could be challenging or perhaps impossible. Since vaccination cannot be duplicated without the knowledge of certain components or characteristics, they may therefore be especially valuable. One well-known trade secret is the formula for Coca-Cola, for instance. Coca-Cola serves as an example of how maintaining trade secret confidentiality and safeguards might result in a competitive advantage and possibly an endless market monopoly [37]. This illustration shows the potential market value of goods with formulas or compositions that are hard to precisely duplicate and can, therefore, be successfully safeguarded by maintaining compositional confidentiality. Therefore, for some vaccinations, trade secrets might be a crucial kind of IP protection.

Exclusively sensitive information is safeguarded using trade secrets. Trade secrets are a type of intellectual property right that is statutorily protected in Canada [38]. The secret will be subject to protective measures. The very sensitive nature of the trade secret material must be made known to those who have access to it. Many business owners enforce confidentiality agreements on those who enter into a contract containing proprietary information, such as staff members, associates, clients, licensees, and business partners.

Trade secrets are seen as a subclass of IP rights that is related to patent rights. A contract known as a patent represents an agreement between the public and an inventor in which the creator grants public access to the innovation in exchange for the public receiving exclusive rights to the invention. Withholding knowledge from the public and refusing to disclose it in order to maintain a competitive advantage in the marketplace are known as trade secrets. A trade secret is a more delicate right than a patent since, once revealed, its value is gone and the only sort of compensation available to the owner of the secret is damages [38].

Trade secrets and patents are sometimes utilised in tandem to safeguard certain facets and components of inventions in specific businesses. For instance, a vaccination patent may reveal several possible formulations, yet the best and most efficient formulation might be kept under trade secret. This can give a producing party a competitive edge since, even after a patent expires, they might not be able to manufacture a vaccination that is exactly the same as the formulation made by the trade secret owner's company. Specifically, the vaccination copy could be less effective or of worse quality.

Trade secrets are extremely delicate and should be handled with extreme caution. Trade secret holders occasionally reserve the right to keep their secrets a secret for a limited amount of time, such as during the early stages of research and development. The trade secret method ought to be evaluated in the context of the various intellectual property rights that are accessible for vaccination. Commercial exploitation may support trade secret maintenance in situations when information is closely guarded, protected, and resistant to reverse engineering [39]. Therefore, for some vaccine kinds, trade secrets can effectively safeguard intellectual property.

Why Protect Vaccines with IP Rights?

Determining why any of the existing IP rights should be used to protect components and parts of vaccines is just as important as taking into account the kinds of IP rights that may be applicable to vaccines. The financial justification for vaccine protection is mostly due to the high cost of producing vaccines, and securing temporary exclusive protection for a vaccine can help offset some of the development expenses. This financial rationale has additional ramifications because it is probable that some of the money is made for the vaccine's owner through exclusive intellectual property rights or that it is reinvested in further product development and research.

As was previously said, another justification for using intellectual property rights to protect a vaccine is to exert some degree of control over how the vaccine is used, distributed, and perceived by the public in terms of its efficacy and quality as well as its market share. The effectiveness of vaccination in reducing the incidence of disease within a community can be influenced by factors such as public acceptance and widespread adoption. A prime example is the polio vaccine, which has been widely embraced and has significantly contributed to the near-eradication of polio in many regions. While intellectual property rights can protect the vaccine and its components, ensuring control over its production, distribution, and use, they are not directly responsible for community-level efficacy. Achieving high vaccination rates and public trust, alongside accessible distribution, are key factors in realizing the full public health potential of a vaccine.

This is not to say that the proprietor of a vaccine will be able to completely dictate how vaccinations are discussed and used. Intellectual property rights, however, can have certain advantages. For instance, it is becoming more common to pass off illegal prescription items as name brands. Not all vaccines need to be administered by a trained individual, but many do, and this helps prevent some of the issues that unregulated pharmaceutical goods. Immunisations are susceptible to counterfeiting, including needle-free immunisations and vaccines in capsule form. Trademark rights can be used as a tool to stop the use of a brand name in connection with a specific vaccine by a party that does not have the right to do so in order to oppose unregulated pharmaceutical products. For instance, trademark laws can be used to prevent the mark from being used in connection with a vaccination duplicate made by a company that is not the mark's owner and does not have permission from the mark's owner. Furthermore, the manufacture of counterfeit medical goods, such as vaccinations, can be outlawed through the utilisation of patent rights.

Negative public opinions of vaccines that have been observed in regard to school students serve as an example of the potential consequences of failing to battle counterfeit vaccines and mislabeled vaccines [40]. While these instances pertain to a dispute amongst research papers, it is also plausible that a rise in the number of fake and incorrectly labelled vaccinations might negatively impact public opinion. A community's child population is more likely to see an increase in the prevalence of infectious diseases as a result of these public attitudes. This includes illnesses that have been long thought to be completely eradicated in a community. These circumstances have a negative impact on people's health both individually and collectively.

"Intellectual property (IP) protections for vaccines can help facilitate their distribution and increase accessibility within various communities and regions. Ensuring access to vaccines is critical for improving public health. IP rights allow vaccine developers to implement strategies that support this goal. Such strategies might include expanding vaccine distribution and accessibility in both developed and developing countries. Overall, IP rights can play a significant role in vaccine development, distribution, accessibility, and public acceptance, given vaccines' potential to enhance community health."

IP Considerations for Vaccines

It is wise to develop a plan for IP rights protection for a vaccine in addition to deciding what kinds of intellectual property rights can be pursued in connection with a vaccine and why such rights should be sought. There are further concerns with vaccines related to the planning of intellectual property rights to be sought and how these will be utilised. In the section that follows, a few of these factors are discussed. Notably, this discussion only touches on a few examples of these pertinent factors: when to submit a patent application; provisions meant to make vaccines more accessible in developing nations; policies that support the use of intellectual property for humanitarian purposes; public health precautions; and harmonisation of laws pertaining to intellectual property rights and pharmaceuticals.

When to File a Patent Application and Sound Prediction

Determining the appropriate timing for filing a patent application is crucial if patent rights are to be pursued for vaccination in countries where first-to-file laws are in effect. A vaccine owner must file a patent application before its rivals before they can obtain a patent; this is the prerequisite for obtaining a patent for an innovation. The owner of the vaccination must, however, be sufficiently certain that the invention is, in fact, new, nonobvious, and useful. In the race to the patent office, the usefulness component of patentability is especially important. This implies that the patent application must include enough details to demonstrate the invention's functionality. Thus, an application that is filed too early may be denied for lack of utility, making it unpatentable.

Some countries, like Canada, allow inventors to apply for a patent as soon as they have good reason to believe that their vaccination method will work for a certain purpose. This means they can apply for a patent even before the vaccine is completely developed. Canadian law requires that this belief, called a "sound prediction," is not just a guess. To meet the standard, three things are needed: (1) there must be factual evidence supporting the prediction; (2) there should be clear, logical reasoning based on these facts that show how the vaccine is likely to work; and (3) the patent application must include enough information to support this prediction. This approach allows inventors to share their work early, balancing their rights with the public's benefit of getting information sooner, even if the vaccine's effectiveness is not fully proven yet [41].

Vaccine IP and Accessibility in the Developing World

Certain vaccinations may include unique qualities or applications that make them especially useful in underdeveloped nations. For instance, a number of features of plant-derived vaccines, in particular, make them advantageous for developing countries in particular. These include the ability to produce vaccine components quickly, in large quantities, affordably, and conveniently, even in remote places. These characteristics imply that these vaccinations may be able to address problems, such as access and pricing, that impede the use of many current medications, particularly in the surroundings of developing nations. Despite being owned by organisations and researchers in the rich world, plant-derived vaccine breakthroughs may eventually be used mostly in environments found in developing countries.

Strong intellectual property rights, particularly patent rights, have raised concerns that they may have a negative impact on vaccination accessibility in underdeveloped countries by encouraging the monopolisation of certain market sectors, which raises prices [42]. While infrastructure and investment are important factors that also hinder access to films in poor countries, patent holders' actions might make the situation worse [43]. Supporting innovation is "a leap of faith for investors in industrialised countries; imagine how hard it is in countries where R&D expenditures may be only a fraction...of gross national product, skilled and educated labour is at a premium, intellectual turf wars stifle collaboration, economic difficulties and inflation are rampant, venture capital investors are an unknown species, intellectual property protection is murky, and political turmoil is a frequent backdrop," according to one commentator [44]. It is estimated that, in the case of a hepatitis B vaccine, "from first licensure in a developed country, it can take an additional 10–15 years or more and substantial financial resources to introduce such a vaccine into significant numbers of developing country national immunisation programmes" [45]. This is because the exact cost of introducing a new vaccine into the public sector in developing countries has not been determined. This implies that long-term, committed support is needed. The strength of the patent rights that must be awarded is not apparent, but many observers concur that they must be part of the answer [46].

Numerous collaborations [47] and significant international grants [48] have been established to address the challenges associated with vaccination implementation in impoverished countries. In view of worries about the possibility of pandemics, developed nations' activities on vaccine development have become more important at the same time as these developing nations' programmes [49]. The argument surrounding the most effective way to deploy vaccinations internationally has not yet produced any definitive answers, but the main worry is IP rights. This is especially true in developing countries where diseases that can be prevented are common. The TRIPS rules for least-developed countries (or "LDCs") are a factor that could have a significant impact on any resolution pertaining to the enforcement of intellectual property rights over-vaccination products.

TRIPs and LDCs

The application of IP rights in LDCs is specifically covered by Article 66 of the TRIPs. In particular, the article states that because of "their economic, financial, and administrative constraints, and their need for flexibility to create a viable technological base," LDCs are excluded from most TRIPs regulations [50]. This exemption is only valid for a period of ten years following the state's admission as a member nation, and it can be extended longer upon request [51]. In tandem with the TRIPs exception for LDCs, industrialised countries are advised to establish incentives for domestic firms to participate in technology transfers to LDCs, "to enable [LDCs] to create a sound and viable technological base" [52].

Article 66 so effectively grants LDCs a temporary exemption from enforcing national IP regimes. This has benefits and drawbacks for LDCs. Market monopolies may be avoided and invention replication is allowed since an LDC is not required to offer intellectual property protection. Nonetheless, the fact that LDCs lack the scientific and financial capacity to generate and support innovation on their own is one of the reasons they have been given an exemption from TRIPs. As a result, LDCs must import innovations from other nations [45]. If the LDC is unable to provide market returns—which are often obtained as a result of a market monopoly made possible by exclusive patent rights—it may be challenging to draw in national investment. There is a vicious cycle as a result. Because they lack the infrastructure—laboratories, skilled scientific personnel, advanced equipment, etc.—to generate innovation, LDCs are exempted from the need for patent systems [53]. Because they do not provide investors with the advantages of national patent rights, LDCs are unable to draw the capital required to construct an internal infrastructure [54]. The pattern repeats itself.

Therefore, while national patent rights cannot prevent access to vaccines in low-income countries (LDCs) because they do not exist, their absence could nevertheless make access difficult because vaccines must be imported from developed countries where patent rights are available. The patent rights probably mean that the imported vaccines are sold for a higher price. Furthermore, there is no incentive for pharmaceutical corporations to support the production of vaccines in LDCs because they cannot get patent rights for their goods and procedures there. Although it may be acceptable in LDCs, the absence of advanced infrastructure makes it impossible for LDCs to launch an initiative to duplicate a vaccine [55]. In conclusion, patent rights are not worthless for LDCs even with the TRIP exemption.

Vaccines and Humanitarian Purposes

Various nations have endeavoured to tackle the potential adverse effects that pharmaceutical product exclusivity may have on public health. For instance, the Canadian patent legislation was amended to include provisions that establish a compulsory licencing mechanism in order to address the use of patents for pharmaceutical products to address public health issues facing developing and least-developed countries, particularly those resulting from HIV/AIDS, tuberculosis, malaria, and other epidemics. This system was designed to handle extreme emergency situations or national emergencies in nations lacking the pharmaceutical capacity to produce pharmaceutical products in large enough quantities to meet emergency needs. Under the proposed framework, pharmaceutical goods that are only intended to treat emergencies would be able to be produced and protected by patents in Canada. Vaccines are pharmaceutical items by definition, and the products that are generated would not be used for profit.

One technology that is being studied to treat these kinds of health problems is vaccinations. Consequently, with regard to a vaccine, mechanisms included in the Canadian patent legislation may be activated. A patented medication has not yet been distributed under a compulsory license thanks to this method. As a matter of fact, the public list of apps to call the technique shows only two efforts to use it. The manufacturer of generic drugs Apotex initially submitted an application in 2007 and had it renewed in 2009, seeking permission to manufacture and export a patented pharmaceutical product under the mechanism. The World Trade Organisation member states' issues, among other obstacles, have made the implementation of the obligatory license difficult, which may be the reason for the mechanism's low utilisation. This has hindered the regime's aspirations. As a result, as of the publication date, the mechanism has not been able to fulfill its intended purpose of generating allegations of humanitarian issues through the provision of pharmaceutical products under a compulsory license.

Another illustration is the IP application procedure that the USA established, which enables owners of intellectual property intended for humanitarian purposes to be eligible for rewards. In particular, the Patents for Humanity Programme is available through the US Patent and Trademarks Office. Applications detailing the application of patented technology or product to humanitarian concerns for the underprivileged are encouraged to be submitted under this programme [56]. The applicants can compete in five different categories of global challenges. Recipients receive a certificate that they can use to expedite certain processes with the US Patent Office. The Patent Trial and Appeal Board may expedite an ex parte appeal, an ex parte reexamination, or a patent application by using the certificate. As a result, the initiative encourages patent holders to apply their rights to address humanitarian issues. Interestingly, one of the categories of global issues that have been highlighted is medicine, and this group is specifically designated to include vaccinations.

Protection of Public Health

International treaties have been signed by nations, and among their terms are some aimed at protecting public health. Pharmaceutical items, such as vaccines, and their application to public health are topics of discussion in both developed and developing countries. TRIPs have clauses aimed at implementing the compulsory licensing remedy in "national emergency or extreme urgency" situations, when the invention will be used for "public noncommercial use" [57].

In order to preserve public order or morality, Article 27.2, which recognises exclusions from patentability or commercial exploitation, may be upheld. It is understood that this clause specifically covers health protection. A nation may decide, based on Article 27.2, that some subjects are not patentable in order to safeguard public health. This topic area may encompass pharmaceutical medications or vaccinations. Because it permits substantial changes to the scope of patentable subject matter in the interest of health protection, this clause is noteworthy.

Furthermore, "measures necessary to protect public health" are specifically addressed in section 8 of TRIPs. Articles 8 and 27.2, at the very least, leave open the possibility that any patent pertaining to medical treatment may be exempted due to ordre public or morals. If a vaccine invention is excluded from these restrictions, the patent holder's rights might be severely curtailed, if not completely eliminated. Notably, if these clauses are applied widely, it could reduce the strength of the IP protections for vaccine patents' presumption of exclusive rights.

Links between Patent and Drug Legislation

Some countries have adjusted their drug and patent regimes to work in harmony with one another, addressing particular difficulties related to pharmaceutical items, including vaccines. In particular, vaccines fall into the injectable and biologic categories under such a system. Vaccines stand apart from other forms of medical treatments, including chemically composed drugs, mostly due to their biological makeup. The US Food and Drug Administration classifies vaccines as biologics, stating that they are obtained from living sources (people, animals, and microorganisms), as opposed to pharmaceuticals that are chemically synthesized. The majority of biologics are complicated mixes that are difficult to define or identify, and biotechnology is frequently used in their production. In the future, biological products might provide the most efficient ways to treat a range of diseases and ailments for which there are now no alternative treatments accessible. They frequently represent the state-of-the-art in biomedical research [58].

The Food and Drugs Act (the "F&D Act"), the Patent Act, and the Patented Medicines (Notice of Compliance) Regulations (the "NOC Regulations") are three pieces of cooperative legislation that were previously separate but are now linked to help reduce fears and calm emotions that are inextricably linked to health issues in Canada [59, 60]. Exclusive patent rights for novel vaccines related to a particular disease or practical use may be granted under the Patent Act [61]. Before releasing the medication on the market, a further procedure needs to be completed after a vaccine patent is approved. It needs to be authorized in line with the F&D Act. After the vaccination is determined to be safe and effective, the minister will issue a notice of compliance (or "NOC") to facilitate this process and to support the integration of the food and drug regime with the patent regime. In Canada, a vaccination cannot be promoted or sold until a NOC is issued. A new vaccine application needs to be accompanied by a comprehensive collection of data, information, and research—including details regarding any vaccine-related patents—in order to be granted an NOC.

A patented vaccine's term is respected when the Food and Drug Administration and the Patent Administration work together. Specifically, it is against the law for producers of generic drugs to try to release a substitute product onto the market while the patent is still pending [62]. "The NOC Regulations introduce patent considerations into the regulatory approval process" [62], which is the result of the collaborative work. IP protection decisions for vaccines will be influenced by the relationship between the food and drug regulatory agencies and the patent regime.

CONCLUSION

While patent rights have generally dominated discussions regarding the relationship between vaccines and intellectual property rights, other topics that fall under this umbrella include copyright, trademarks, patents, trade secrets, and perhaps even the rights of plant breeders. Furthermore, this expanded conversation brings up issues related to IP rights and vaccinations that were not previously regularly discussed. In addition to potentially giving vaccines a wider scope of IP protection in the long run, a perspective that acknowledges the applicability of multiple IP rights to the different components and aspects of vaccines can also facilitate the development of a strategy that benefits from the cooperation and integration of IP rights for vaccines.

The discussion of IP rights and vaccines should go beyond focusing on a single IP right applied to a vaccine. It should address the variety of intellectual property rights that apply and how they can work together to aid in vaccine creation and dissemination. This integrated approach allows for the development of a more comprehensive strategy, considering which IP rights should be included and the factors that might influence different protections for vaccines. Acknowledging the full range of IP rights vaccines can significantly shape the approach to their development and distribution, leading to a more effective and definitive plan.

REFERENCES

[1] WHO, "Intellectual Property Rights and Vaccines in Developing Countries" WHO/IVB/04.21, 2004at4.

[2] WHO, "Intellectual Property Rights and Vaccines in Developing Countries" WHO /IVB/04.21, 2004at4-5

[3] WHO, "Intellectual Property Rights and Vaccines in Developing Countries" WHO /IVB/04.21,2004at6

[4] Griffith Greene, Megan, "Vaccines: Busting commonmyths", CBC, (27 Nov 2014) at: http://www.cbc.ca/news/health/vaccines-busting-common-myths-1.2851270

[5] Canadian Patent Application No. 2,321,260, filed October 12,2000

[6] Patent Act, R.S.C.1985,cP-4,s.2

[7] Patent Act, R.S.C. 1985, c P-4, s. 27(8);Harvard College v. Canada (Commissioner of Patents), [2002] 4SCR45;Monsanto Canada Inc .v. Schmeiser, [2004] 1SCR902

[8] Patent Act, R.S.C.1985,cP-4,s.42

[9] Patent Act, R.S.C.1985,cP-4,s.43

[10] http://www.vaxxas.com/nanopatch-technology/benefits. Nanopatch™ is an exam-ple of a non-needle vaccine delivery system, comprising a patch incorporating an array of nano projections that directly delivers a vaccine to immune cells

[11] Trade-marksAct, R.S.C.1985,c.T-13,s.2

[12] Kirkbi AGv. Ritvik HoldingsInc.,2005 Carswell Nat3631atpara.30

[13] Kirkbi AGv. Ritvik HoldingsInc.,2005 Carswell Nat 3631; see also Kirkbi AG v. Ritvik Holdings Inc.,2003

[14] Carswell Nat2175 Trade-marks Act, R.S.C.1985,c.T-13,s.19

[15] Trade-marksAct,R.S.C.1985,c.T-13,s.46

[16] Trade-marks Act, R.S.C. 1985, c. T-13, s.12(1)(d)

[17] MattelU.S.A.Inc.v.3894207CanadaInc., 2006 Carswell Nat 1400 at para. 51; see also Canadian Tire Corp.v. Accessoires d'autos Nordiques Inc., 2007 Carswell Nat3988atpara.25.Trade-marksAct,R.S.C.1985,c.T-13,s.6(5)

[18] Perry v. Truefitt (1842),6Beav.66,49E.R.749 cited with approval in Ciba-Geigy Canada Ltd.v.Apotex Inc.,1992 Carswell Ont 007,Supreme Court of Canadaat30

[19] Ciba-Geigy Canada Ltd. v. Apotex Inc., 1992Carswell Ont 1007, Supreme Court of Canadaat33 Copyright Act,R.S.C.1985, c.C-42,s.2

[20] CCH Canadian Ltd. v. Law Society of Upper Canada, 2004 SCC 13, [2004] 1 S.C.R. 339atpara.8

[21] Copyright Act, R.S.C. 1985, c. C-42, s. 2,s.14.1ands.17.1

[22] CopyrightAct,R.S.C.1985,c.C-42,s.28.2(1)

[23] Thé bergev. Galeried'Art duPetit Champlaininc., [2002]2S.C.R.336

[24] CopyrightAct,R.S.C.1985,c.C-42,s.14.1(2)ands.17.1(2)

[25] CopyrightAct,R.S.C.1985,c.C-42,s.14.1(3)ands.17.1(3)

[26] Copyright Act, R.S.C.1985,c.C-42,s.14.2(1),s.14.2(2),s.17.2 (1)ands.17.2(2)

[27] Copyright Act,R.S.C.1985,c.C-42,s.6

[28] CCH Canadian Ltd. v. Law Society of Upper Canada, 2004 SCC 13, [2004] 1 S.C.R. 339 atpara.16

[29] CCH Canadian Ltd. v. Law Society of Upper Canada, 2004 SCC 13, [2004] 1 S.C.R. 339 atparas.22 to 25.

[30] Morin E (1997) of mice and men: the ethics of patenting animals. Health Law J 5:147–197; Plant Breeders' Rights Act, R.S.C. 1990, c. 20 ats.4

[31] Plant Breeders' Rights Act, R.S.C. 1990, c. 20ats.6

[32] Plant Breeders' Rights Act, R.S.C. 1990, c. 20ats.5.2

[33] Pioneer Hi-Bred Ltd. v. Canada (Commissioner for Patents) [1989] 1S.C.R.1623.

[34] Calgon Carbon Corporation v. City of NorthBay, [2005] F.C.838

[35] AFX International Focus. The Week's Business: Coca Colacaper, 7 July 2006

[36] Lac Minerals v. International Corona Resources, [1989] 2S.C.R.574

[37] Isaacs R (2004) How not to tell all: Find out how to preserve the company's competitive edge by preventing proprietary information from being given away. Security Mgmt 102

[38] Johnson L (2015) Mandatory childhood vaccinations supported by majority in B. C. And Alberta: poll" (9 June 2015) CBC at http://www.cbc.ca/news/canada/british-columbia/ mandatory-childhoo--vaccinations-supported-by-majority-in-b-c-and-alberta-poll-1.3106259

[39] Apotex Inc.v.Wellcome Foundation Ltd., [2002] 4S.C.R.153, 2002SCC77

[40] Mahoney RT, Pablos-Mendez A, Ramachandran S. The introduction of new vaccines into developing countries III. The role of intellectual property. Vaccine 2004; 22(5-6): 786-92.

[41] Kapczynski A, Samantha , Yochai B, Zachary K. Addressing Global Health Inequities: An Open Licensing Approach for University Innovations. Berkley Tech Law 2005; 20:1031.

[42] Marshall A (2004) Opensecrets. Nat Biotechnol 22:DC1

[43] Mahoney RT, Maynard JE. The introduction of new vaccines into developing countries. Vaccine 1999 Feb 26;17(7-8):646-52

[44] MorelCetal (2005) Health innovation in developing countries to address diseases of the poor. Innov Strat Today 1.1 15, Mahoney RTet al (2004) The introduction of new vaccines into developing countries III. The role of intellectual property. Vaccine 22:787; and Royal Society of London etal (2000)

[45] Transgenicplants and world agriculture. National AcademyPress,p12,http://books. nap.edu/html/transgenicat29

[46] International AIDS Vaccine Initiative, the International Partnership for Microbicides, the Medicines for Malaria Venture, Malaria Vaccine Initiative, and the Global Alliance for TB Drug Development; Morel Cetal (2005) Health innovation in developing countries to addressed is eases of the poor. Innov Strategy Today1:1–15

[47] See, e.g., Trials Show Inactivated Zika Virus Vaccines is Safe and Immunogenic, NAT'L INST. OF ALLERGY AND INFECTIOUS DISEASES (Dec. 4, 2017), https://www.niaid.nih.gov/news-events/trials-show-inactivated-zika-virus-vaccinesafe-and-immunogenic [https://perma.cc/6HPK-LEBL].

[48] See id; see also Rutschman, supra note 84, at 654. For a timeline of this particular R&D project see Rutschman, supra note 84.

[49] Public Health Emergency Declaration, U.S. DEP'T. OF HEALTH & HUM. SERVS., https://www.phe.gov/Preparedness/legal/Pages/phedeclaration.aspx [https ://perma.cc/JBL4-TDYH] (last updated Nov. 26, 2019).

[50] IHR Procedures Concerning Public Health Emergencies of International Concern (PHEIC), WORLD HEALTH ORG., https://www.who.int/ihr/procedures/pheic/en/ [https://perma.cc/X4AH-A3TN] (last

visited Jul. 10, 2020).

[51] As opposed to property rules, in the Calabresi-Melamed formulation. See Calabresi G, Melamed AD., Property Rules, Liability Rules, and Inalienability: One View of the Cathedral, HARV. L. REV 1972; 85(6): 1089-1128.

[52] Balkin JM, Ayres I. Legal Entitlements as Auctions: Property Rules, Liability Rules, and Beyond, 106 Yale L. J 1996; 106, 703: 707.

[53] Mallapaty S. India's massive COVID surge puzzles scientists. Nature. 2021; 592(7856): 667–668.

[54] Twohig KA, Nyberg T, Zaidi A, *et al.* Hospital admission and emergency care attendance risk for SARS-CoV-2 delta (B.1.617.2) compared with alpha (B.1.1.7) variants of concern: a cohort study. Lancet Infect Dis. 2021.

[55] Madhi SA, Baillie V, Cutland CL, *et al.* Efficacy of the ChAdOx1 nCoV-19 COVID-19 Vaccine against the B.1.351 Variant. N Engl J Med. 2021 May 20;384(20): 1885–1898.

[56] Sabino EC, Buss LF, Carvalho MPS, *et al.* Resurgence of COVID-19 in Manaus, Brazil, despite high seroprevalence. Lancet. 2021; 397(10273): 452–455.

[57] Krause PR, Fleming TR, Longini IM, *et al.* SARS-CoV-2 Variants and Vaccines. N Engl J Med. 2021; 385(2): 179–186.
[PMID: 34161052] [PMCID: PMCPMC8262623]

[58] Hotez PJ, Narayan KMV. Restoring Vaccine Diplomacy. JAMA. 2021; 325(23): 2337–2338.

[59] Davies NG, Jarvis CI, Group CC-W, *et al.* Increased mortality in community-tested cases of SARS-CoV-2 lineage B.1.1.7. Nature. 2021; 593(7858): 270–274.

[60] Wouters OJ, Shadlen KC, Salcher-Konrad M, *et al.* Challenges in ensuring global access to COVID-19 vaccines: production, affordability, allocation, and deployment. Lancet. 2021; 397(10278): 1023–1034.
[PMID: 33587887]

[61] Erfani P, Binagwaho A, Jalloh MJ, Yunus M, Farmer P, Kerry V. Intellectual property waiver for COVID-19 vaccines will advance global health equity. BMJ. 2021; 374: n1837.

[62] Khan MI, Ikram A, Hamza HB. Vaccine manufacturing capacity in low- and middle-income countries. Bull World Health Organ. 2021; 99(7): 479–479A.

CHAPTER 2

Historical Perspective on Vaccines and IP Rights

Sandhya Bagde[1,*], **Ruchi Shivhare**[1], **Ashwini Ingole**[1], **Gayatri Tiwaskar**[1] and **Sachin Kumar Jain**[2]

[1] *Dadasaheb Balpande College of Pharmacy, Nagpur 440037, Maharashtra, India*

[2] *Oriental College of Pharmacy & Research, Oriental University, Near Aurobindo Hospital, Sanwer Road Indore 453555, MP, India*

Abstract: As an efficient means for the prevention and management of infectious diseases, vaccines are the most notable achievements in the field of public health. This chapter explores the relationship between intellectual property (IP) rights and vaccines, including their historical development and current implications for global health. The chapter also discusses the importance of vaccinations for public health, highlighting how they can prevent disease and save lives. Simultaneously, it presents intellectual property and its significant impact on vaccine development in the pharmaceutical sector. A history of vaccines is presented, starting with important events like Edward Jenner's ground-breaking research on the smallpox vaccine. The 20th century witnessed the development of contemporary vaccines, which indicated a turning point in medical research and advances against illnesses including influenza, measles, and polio. Early IP strategies in the vaccine industry that focused on collaboration and information exchange enabled quick advancement. The contribution of intellectual property to pharmaceutical innovations and how IP rights act as vital inducements to investment in and innovation within the field of vaccine development. The impact of vaccination accessibility under the Trade Related Aspects of Intellectual Property Rights Agreement (TRIPS) is examined. Difficulties and disputes about vaccine patents and intellectual property rights are further explored, focusing on negotiating the complicated intellectual property environment for vaccine distribution. Public-private partnerships and collaborative techniques are two recent developments in vaccine research that are also covered. Lastly, a case study is provided for examining the function of intellectual property in the creation, manufacturing, and distribution of vaccines. The pandemic's effect on how the world views intellectual property rights related to vaccines highlights the continuous discussion about fair access to vaccines during public health emergencies. Overall, this chapter offers a thorough analysis of the historical viewpoint on vaccinations and their beneficial association with intellectual property rights, highlighting the difficulties and complexities present at the junction of public health, science, and innovation.

* **Corresponding author Sandhya Bagde:** Dadasaheb Balpande College of Pharmacy, Nagpur 440037, Maharashtra, India; E-mail: sandhyahadke90@gmail.com

Sachin Kumar Jain, Ravikant Gupta, Sudha Vengurlekar, Nidhi Bais & Gajendra P. Choudhary (Eds.)

Keywords: COVID-19, Intellectual property rights, Pharmaceutical innovations, TRIPS, Vaccines.

INTRODUCTION

Edward Jenner demonstrated in 1796 that vaccination against smallpox may be prevented by using material from a cowpox (vaccinia) lesion. Although the next vaccine (against rabies) was not released for another century, this marked the start of the vaccination era. In the 20th century, several innovative vaccines were developed and implemented, significantly lowering the prevalence of diseases. The Centers for Disease Control and Prevention (CDC) rank vaccinations as one of the top 10 public health innovations of the 20th century [1].

This chapter explores the early history of vaccinations, highlighting significant turning points that led to the development of contemporary immunization programs. It highlights human creativity, resilience, and the pursuit of healthier communities, spanning from prehistoric practices to groundbreaking discoveries that transformed modern medicine [2].

During the early stages of civilization, prehistoric societies faced significant infectious diseases, leading to the development of strategies like variolation, which involved intentionally exposing people to smallpox to build immunity, providing hope against sickness [3].

In the late 1700s, Edward Jenner made a groundbreaking discovery in rural England that led to the development of modern immunization. He used cowpox sore material to inoculate a child, illustrating cross-immunity and confirming centuries of anecdotal evidence, marking the beginning of vaccine research [4].

The word "vaccine" originates from the Latin word "vacca," meaning "cow," and was named after Jenner discovered the smallpox vaccine, a significant breakthrough in the fight against infectious diseases [5].

The World Health Organization (WHO) played a role in international immunization campaigns, leading campaigns to eradicate smallpox and preventable diseases. The successful eradication of smallpox in 1979 exemplifies the effectiveness of vaccinations. Today, the WHO continues to prioritize immunization and ensure universal access to vaccines [6].

Intellectual property (IP) is an original work of human thought, be it artistic, literary, scientific, or technological. Intellectual property rights, or IPR, are the legal privilege that allows an innovator or creator to keep their creation or idea confidential for a set period [7]. These legal rights give the inventor/creator or his assignee the exclusive right to utilize their innovation to its fullest extent for a predetermined amount of time. It has long been known how important intellectual property is to the modern economy.

Furthermore, it has been conclusively demonstrated that for innovation to benefit the public good, the intellectual labour that went into it must be acknowledged. The costs associated with research and development (R&D) have increased sharply, which has resulted in a rise in the equivalent investments required to bring new technologies to market [8]. The stakes for technology developers are now very high, thus knowledge must be protected from unauthorized use, even only temporarily, to recover R&D costs and other associated expenses and to create enough cash to support continued R&D expenditures [9]. Since it gives the creator/inventor an exclusive right to use his creation for a set period, intellectual property rights (IPRs) are an effective tool for protecting the time, money, and effort that the creator/inventor has invested in creating an intellectual property. IPR thus supports a nation's economic development by fostering healthy competition, industrial progress, and economic prosperity.

ANCIENT PRACTICES AND VARIOLATION

Throughout history, Asia and Africa have developed strategies to protect against the smallpox virus, including early immunization methods like variolation, despite potential risks and serious illness [10]. This practice dates back to prehistoric societies, with records from China describing "wenyi" in the 10th century. Traditional methods in Africa involved scarification or inhalation of smallpox particles [11]. In the 18th century, Lady Mary Wortley Montagu, a British ambassador, witnessed the practice of variolation in Constantinople, which spread throughout Western Europe. Despite its effectiveness in boosting immunity, it posed serious risks, including smallpox infection and death [12].

EARLY HISTORY OF VACCINES

Edward Jenner and the Smallpox Vaccine

Edward Jenner's 1796 discovery of cowpox-induced immunity against smallpox marked a significant shift in medical history. Inspired by legends of milkmaids becoming immune to smallpox, Jenner conducted a risky experiment using cowpox sore material to inoculate a young child. This groundbreaking experiment demonstrated cross-immunity, representing that exposure to a less pathogenic disease could protect a more pathogenic one, which in turn, transformed disease prevention and introduced the term "vaccine" from the Latin word "Vacca," meaning "cow" [11 - 15].

Global Efforts in Smallpox Eradication:

The World Health Organisation (WHO) led international efforts to eradicate smallpox in the 20th century, focusing on vaccination campaigns and surveillance. The WHO's success in 1979 demonstrates the effectiveness of immunization and global cooperation. The WHO's multipronged strategy includes mass vaccination, which targeted susceptible populations in endemic areas [11].

KEY ELEMENTS OF THE SMALLPOX ERADICATION CAMPAIGN INCLUDED

Surveillance

The World Health Organisation (WHO) played a crucial role in the global campaign to eradicate smallpox in the 20th century. A robust surveillance system was established, consisting of trained medical professionals, epidemiologists, and laboratory staff. These professionals were responsible for identifying potential cases, investigating outbreaks, and gathering information on the spread of the disease. The WHO's surveillance network functioned on a national and international scale, enabling cross-border information sharing and coordination. Epidemiologists conducted epidemiological investigations to determine the source of infection and identify potential contacts. Laboratory workers confirmed suspected cases, providing crucial information for monitoring transmission and evaluating containment strategies. This data-driven approach allowed health authorities to efficiently distribute resources and respond to new challenges [16].

Vaccination

The smallpox eradication campaign was a global effort by the World Health Organization (WHO) in the 20th century, focusing on mass immunization campaigns. Teams of volunteers and local health professionals carried out door-to-door immunization campaigns in endemic areas, ensuring equal access to vaccine supplies. The WHO provided millions of doses of the vaccine at no cost, ensuring the efficacy and security of these programs. The goal was to achieve herd immunity, preventing smallpox from spreading. Special vaccination campaigns were also conducted in high-risk areas to reach specific demographics. The sharp drop in smallpox cases during the eradication campaign demonstrated the effectiveness of vaccination as a public health measure. The lessons learned from the smallpox eradication campaign continue to guide future efforts to prevent other diseases [11, 17].

Containment

The World Health Organization (WHO) used containment techniques and vaccination campaigns to manage smallpox epidemics. Quarantine and vaccination teams were sent to isolate infected individuals and their close contacts, preventing the virus from spreading. Despite challenges like political unpredictability, logistical difficulties, and vaccination resistance, the WHO and its allies successfully eradicated smallpox worldwide. The World Health Assembly formally declared that smallpox was eradicated on May 8, 1980, marking the first and only time that a human infectious illness was successfully eradicated through vaccination. Containment measures included isolating sick people, tracking their contacts, and immunizing the local community. The ring vaccination method aimed to establish a buffer of immune people around the outbreak location. Collaboration between health officials, local communities, and foreign partners was crucial for the effectiveness of containment efforts. The WHO and its allies persevered despite obstacles, demonstrating the success of vaccinations and the combined efforts of the international community to combat contagious illnesses [11, 16, 18].

GLOBAL VACCINE INITIATIVES IN THE 21ST CENTURY

The World Health Organization (WHO) is leading international efforts to combat new disease risks through vaccination programs. The Global Vaccine Action Plan (GVAP) and the Access to COVID-19 Tools Accelerator (ACT-A) aim to promote equitable access to vaccines and achieve universal access to immunization. The GVAP aims to enhance vaccine delivery networks, boost research and development, and advocate for long-term funding for immunization initiatives. The ACT-A, introduced in April 2020, aims to ensure fair access to COVID-19 vaccines, diagnostics, and treatments. The WHO recognizes that inequities in vaccine accessibility can worsen health disparities and prolong poverty and illness cycles. Initiatives are being made to remove obstacles to immunization, such as supply chain limitations and vaccine reluctance. The WHO's commitment to vaccination programs reflects its commitment to improving health equity and the universal right to health [19, 20]. The vital milestones in the journey of vaccine development are shown in Fig. (**1**).

VACCINE AND THE PHARMACEUTICAL INDUSTRY

The pharmaceutical industry has played a crucial role in the development and distribution of vaccines, which are essential for preventing infectious diseases and improving public health. The history of vaccinations and the pharmaceutical industry is intertwined, with the first vaccine developed by Edward Jenner in 1796. The 19th and early 20th centuries saw significant advancements in vaccine research, with new vaccines for cholera, typhoid fever, and rabies reducing fatality rates. The establishment of regulatory bodies like the EMA and FDA in the mid-20th century ensured the security and effectiveness of vaccines. International health programs like the Expanded Program on Immunization have also accelerated vaccine production and distribution [21, 22].

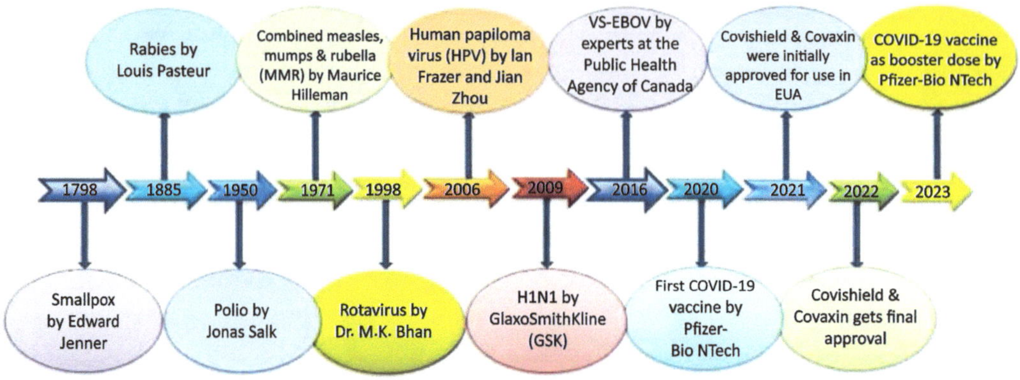

Fig. (1). The vital milestone in the journey of vaccines.

The pharmaceutical industry has been instrumental in developing vaccines against emerging infectious diseases like COVID-19, Ebola, and HIV/AIDS, aided by government financing, public-private collaborations, and biotechnology advancements. Despite these advancements, challenges like vaccine nationalism, supply chain limitations, and reluctance persist, particularly in low- and middle-income nations. Despite these obstacles, the pharmaceutical sector continues to drive innovation and progress in vaccine research, saving lives and improving global health outcomes [22].

THE ROLE OF IP IN THE PHARMACEUTICAL INDUSTRY

Europe is where the rules and regulations about intellectual property originated. The fourteenth century saw the beginning of the patent-granting trend. However, England was more advanced and thus became favorable for applicants to apply for IP with their desirable terms. Italy gave the origination and recognition of copyrights. Venice became the birthplace of IP system with different laws and processes for the rest of the world [4]. In India, the Patent Act was activated more than 150 years back since 1856. The First Act was established with the 14-year patent period during the British patent system which was then modified several times [7].

TYPES OF INTELLECTUAL PROPERTIES AND THEIR DESCRIPTION

The phrase "Intellectual Property" currently refers to much more than patents, trademarks, and industrial designs which were the only types of properties under the phrase. Technology advancement is enhanced by IPR in the following ways [7 - 9, 23]. It helped to protect these properties from violations, piracy, and unapproved use. These properties are made available for the public access to help them increase their wealth of knowledge.

A range of intellectual endeavors can be followed for IP protection, such as:

• **Patents:** A patent is a legal right to exclude others from making, using, or selling an invention for a limited period of time [24].

When an invention meets the requirements of worldwide uniqueness, non-obviousness, and industrial or commercial applicability, it is granted a patent. Patents may be issued for both goods and procedures. A patent had a 14-year duration from the date of filing under the Indian Patent Act of 1970, except for procedures for making drugs and food, for which the period was either 7 years from the date of filing or 5 years from the date of the patent, whichever came first. Food and medicine products did not receive any product patents. Without the requirement for registration, a copyright created in one of the Berne Convention's member nations is immediately protected in all of the member nations. India has excellent copyright laws on par with those of any other nation, and it is a signatory to the Berne Convention. However, in nations that are not signatories to the Berne Convention, copyright will not always be granted. As a result, copyright might not strictly speaking be regarded as a territorial right. IPR can be given, sold, or transferred just like any other property [25, 27, 28].

IP RIGHTS INCENTIVE INNOVATION AND INVESTMENT IN VACCINE RESEARCH

Challenges in Encouraging Vaccine Production

The vaccines are not very profitable in comparison to different medications, thus only the government sector is indulged in its production and not the private sector [29].

Several issues are responsible for the lower profitability of vaccines as compared to their medicine counterparts. One is the reason that they are going to be used for prophylaxis and preventive measures due to which the consumers become reluctant to pay their high prices [26].

They are long-lasting and need less reproduction which is not favorable for companies in terms of profit [29]. Though the vaccines are administered to a majority of people for preventative measures, it is not a profitable earning for the manufacturer. On the other hand, the facilities required for vaccine production, and approval are the same. However, these investments are at risk if the distribution approval is not granted.

Vaccines represent substantial at-risk investments, as manufacturing facilities must be constructed before vaccine approval, which entails the potential loss of significant funds if the vaccine does not receive distribution approval [28].

- Push and Pull incentives.
- The incentive schemes are offered by the public sector to increase vaccine production and R and D in that sector for the enhancement of public health. Vaccine innovation policy encompasses two approaches
- Pull incentives: obtained from patent protections and
- Push Incentives: Grants/ funds from the government.

These incentives complement each other and help private companies to increase their participation in vaccine development and manufacturing. Several global and national funding organizations push incentives for vaccines R & D [29]. The National Institute of Health (NIH) contributes 2 billion dollars to vaccine R &D in 2018 [30]. This funding from NIH helps for the innovation and manufacturing of vaccines. In addition, the Defence Advanced Research Projects Agency (DARPA), administered by the US Defence Department, contributed to RNA vaccines in 2010 [31]. The Global Influenza Surveillance and Response System (GISRS) also received 56 million dollars for the development of vaccines for WHO [32].

The Canadian government funded phase I clinical trials for VSV-EBOV Ebola Vaccine [33]. Under the Bayh-Dole and Stevenson-Wydler Acts in US legislation, Private companies receive additional incentives for patentable invention [34].

The incentives which were given earlier were based on the pre-investments of the companies. And only private companies could avail of them. However, the government sector can also reap the benefit in the form of potential rewards not just in monetary form but also in terms of improved public health and getting more protected citizens in the long term [35].

THE TRIPS AGREEMENT'S EFFECT

With 164 member states, the World Trade Organization (WTO) is an international organization whose mission is to set trade regulations and provide a framework for economic relations among its members. Members of the WTO are bound by several agreements upon joining, with the Agreement on Trade-Related Aspects of Intellectual Property Rights (TRIPS) having a major impact on the pharmaceutical industry [36]. WTO members are required to integrate the minimum criteria outlined in the TRIPS Agreement into their national laws to safeguard and enforce a variety of intellectual property rights.

Adopted in 1995, the TRIPS Agreement allowed countries varying transition periods based on their economic development and pre-existing intellectual property protection. Before TRIPS, each country addressed patent issues differently, with diverse approaches to safeguarding intellectual property, including patents, tailored to their unique requirements [37, 38].

The topic of intellectual property (IP) and patents has been a subject of extensive debate regarding access to medicines since the establishment of the World Trade Organisation (WTO) and the implementation of the Agreement on Trade-Related Aspects of Intellectual Property Rights (TRIPS). While patents are not the sole impediments to accessing lifesaving medications, they can significantly impact or even decisively influence the situation. A significant percentage of people in underdeveloped nations may become financially unable to afford important medicines due to the patent holder's power to set prices for the duration of the protection, in the absence of market competition. There are drawbacks to using patent protection as the main mechanism of incentive for creating life-saving medications. Little incentive has been offered by the system for research and development aimed at diseases that are common in underdeveloped nations. The WHO Commission on Intellectual Property Rights, Innovation, and Public Health (CIPIH) recognized these difficulties and emphasized the weak incentive effect of IPRs in solving health issues that largely affect developing countries. Therefore, different financial structures and incentives are required [36].

TRIPS IMPACT ON VACCINES

Patent Protection and its Access

The TRIPS requirement for patent protection has an impact on vaccine pricing and accessibility globally. Pharmaceutical companies are able to maintain monopolies on the production of vaccines through the patents granted under TRIPS, which could result in high costs that restrict access, particularly in low- and middle-income nations [39].

Access to Medicine and Public Health

Compulsory Licensing: To encourage competition and drive down costs, different countries can approve the production of generic vaccines without the permission of patent holders due to TRIPS provisions on compulsory licensing. In areas where cost is a major obstacle to immunization, this has made vaccines more accessible [40].

Global Health Crises

In order to guarantee fair access to vaccines in times of global health emergency, such as the COVID-19 pandemic, TRIPS flexibilities are essential. The pandemic has brought to light inequalities in vaccine distribution and the significance of policies like compulsory licensing to increase vaccine manufacturing and alleviate the world's vaccine deficit [41].

ACCESS TO VACCINES AND GLOBAL HEALTH

Access to vaccines is a critical aspect of global health, as it helps prevent the spread of infectious diseases and lower mortality rates around the world. Vaccine availability and equitable distribution are critical for achieving optimal public health outcomes and reducing health disparities across populations [42 - 44].

There are multiple important aspects that make up the concept of vaccine access:

Vaccines must physically be present in a certain area or nation in order to be considered available. To meet the immunization needs of populations, particularly in low and middle-income nations where access to healthcare resources may be limited, it is imperative to ensure an adequate supply of vaccines.

The accessibility of vaccines is crucial for promoting their widespread use among communities, governments, and individuals. High prices may operate as an impediment to access, especially in environments with limited resources. Making vaccines more accessible to those in need is the goal of a number of initiatives, including government subsidies, international aid initiatives, and collaborations with pharmaceutical companies.

Vaccine accessibility is influenced by several variables, including geographic location, the availability of transportation, and healthcare delivery systems. To reach underserved populations, innovative strategies like outreach programs, mobile clinics, and community health workers are often needed in rural and remote areas where access to vaccination services is often limited.

Acceptability: Culture, religion, and vaccine reluctance can all have an impact on people's and communities' willingness to accept vaccinations. To create acceptance of immunization programs, it is necessary to address misinformation, improve vaccine literacy, and interact with local stakeholders.

Adaptability: New infectious diseases and developing vaccination technologies bring with them both new opportunities and challenges in the ever-changing global health landscape. To effectively address new health risks and guarantee that everyone has access to life-saving vaccinations, vaccine development, production, and distribution processes must be adaptable and versatile.

Coordination and cooperation between governments, international organizations, the private sector, and civil society are necessary to increase vaccine accessibility and improve global health outcomes. To remove obstacles to vaccine access and boost everyone's health and well-being, stakeholders should prioritize equity, sustainability, and unity.

VACCINATION'S IMPACT ON GLOBAL HEALTH: PAST, PRESENT, AND FUTURE

Global health has greatly improved as a result of vaccination. Serious diseases like smallpox have been eradicated. Global vaccine coverage against several important infectious diseases that affect children has significantly increased since the World Health Organization's Expanded Programme of Immunization in 1974 and the Global Alliance for Vaccine and Immunization was established in 2000. Polio has nearly totally disappeared thanks to measles control initiatives that have made it feasible to target the pathogen for eradication. Notwithstanding these successes, 6.6 million children still die annually, and almost half of these fatalities are related to diseases like pneumonia and diarrhea that may be prevented with immunization. Consequently, enhanced rotavirus immunization combined with the recently developed pneumococcal conjugate vaccines ought to result in low childhood mortality [45 - 47].

THE VACCINATIONS OF THE FUTURE GENERATION

A human vaccine for rabies was created in 1885, almost a century after Jenner's experiments, and was the next to be developed using the attenuation principle [48]. Pasteur developed the vaccine. The basis for this vaccine was material from an infected rabbit brain that had been dried, an unpredictable process that frequently resulted in serious side effects in vaccines made this way. The majority of human rabies vaccinations currently rely on tissue-grown, inactivated viruses [49]. The 1950s and 1960s saw the development of attenuated vaccinations against poliomyelitis and measles as a result of the ability to grow viruses on tissue culture for a prolonged length of time [50].

Among malaria vaccines, RTS, S/AS01 (Mosquirix) is the most popular and the first vaccine to be approved on a global scale. The WHO endorsed it for children in areas of moderate to high malaria incidence after successful pilot projects were undertaken in Ghana, Kenya, and Malawi [51, 52].

R21/ Matrix-M: A relatively new malaria vaccine, produced by the University of Oxford and the Serum Institute of India, has just been registered for use in Ghana and Nigeria. According to the results of clinical trials of the R21/Matrix-M vaccine, its efficacy is high, and it is likely to be mass-produced which would make malaria control cheaper and more effective [53, 54].

Whole-Cell, Attenuated Pneumococcal Vaccine:

Immunogenic and non-toxic inactivated or attenuated cells of Streptococcus pneumoniae are the focus of a whole-cell pneumococcal vaccine that is currently in clinical trials. This strategy would enhance the ability to target several serotypes of the pneumococcus and hence it may be able to deliver broader immunity than current conjugate vaccines (e.g. PCV13, PCV20) that are designed to acknowledge specific pneumococcal serotypes [55].

The study of additional attenuated pneumococcal vaccines is being conducted by several research groups with the purpose of mounting strong immune responses while minimizing the danger of using live bacteria. Some of these candidates are able to reach the immune induction level and are currently undergoing clinical trials phase I [56, 57].

Because young children have a high death rate, vaccination programs in developing nations initially concentrated on protecting them against potentially fatal infections. It is becoming more widely acknowledged, nevertheless, that vaccinations have far wider-ranging benefits for public health than just the first year of life. For instance, immunizing older children against HPV infection [58] and more seasoned children and young grown-ups against meningococcal infection within the African meningitis belt [59] can prevent cancer in adults.

The Vaccination's long-term Prospects

Even though major infections like HIV, TB, and malaria cannot be completely eradicated, effective vaccines against them will likely be developed in the future, even though it is troublesome to foresee when this will happen. A worldwide high-level reconnaissance framework is essential to recognize modern, possibly perilous diseases and to rapidly distinguish the rise of vaccine-resistant strains so that preventative measures can be taken. Only then will vaccination be able to protect against infectious diseases to the fullest extent possible.

Chronic condition management is difficult in communities with limited access to healthcare. The development of vaccines that alter the course of diabetes and hypertension is making some progress [60]. Vaccination against addiction, such as smoking, is possible but requires high antibody concentrations to be effective [61]. Additionally, early studies suggest that vaccination against Alzheimer's disease may slow its progression [62].

CONTROVERSIES AND CHALLENGES

Recent available data from WHO and UNICEF based on estimates of national immunization coverage indicate that more than one out of four children in middle-income countries (MICs) fails to complete the basic vaccine schedule. As a result, about 25 million children, more than 60 percent of them living in just 10 countries (India, Nigeria, Indonesia, Ethiopia, the Philippines, the Democratic Republic of the Congo, Brazil, Pakistan, Angola, and Myanmar), were un- or under-vaccinated in 2021. Worse still, in the same year, more than 18 million children did not receive any vaccines (zero-dose children), hence an increase of 5 million from 2019, and the situation worsened by the pandemic when many children were not properly vaccinated [63].

Restricted Accessibility of Intellectual Property Rights (IPR) understanding:

Developing nations frequently lack the knowledge and resources needed to successfully negotiate the complicated world of intellectual property. This involves negotiating license agreements, upholding intellectual property rights, and comprehending patent laws.

- High Costs of Licensing and Royalties: Upfront fees, royalties, and technology transfer costs are only a few of the high costs associated with licensing patented technologies for vaccine development. Developing nations with low financial resources may find these costs excessive, which would limit their access to and utilization of exclusive technologies.
- Intellectual Property obstructions to Technology Transfer: Critical vaccination technology can be prevented from being transferred from developed to developing countries by intellectual property hurdles like trade secrets and patents. As a result, attempts to combat public health emergencies like pandemics may be hampered and vaccine manufacture may be delayed [64].
- Lack of Local Manufacturing Capacity: Developing nations frequently lack the infrastructure and manufacturing capability needed to manufacture vaccines in their own country. This dependence on imported vaccinations may increase supply chain weaknesses and restrict the availability of necessary vaccinations in emergency situations [65].

- Uneven Access to Vaccines: Patent monopolies and exorbitant costs imposed by pharmaceutical companies make it difficult for developing countries to obtain reasonably priced vaccines. This is one way that intellectual property rights can lead to unfair access to vaccines. This makes health inequities worse and makes it harder to attain global health equity.
- Pressure to Uphold Intellectual Property Rights: Developed countries and multinational companies may exert pressure on developing governments to reinforce the protection of intellectual property rights, which may further impede access to reasonably priced vaccinations and necessary medications [66].

RECENT DEVELOPMENTS AND TRENDS

An overview of recent trends in vaccine development, including the role of public-private partnerships

- Advancements in Vaccine Technology: Newer vaccine platforms including mRNA and viral vector vaccines have been developed, among other revolutionary vaccine technologies. In comparison to conventional vaccination strategies, these technologies provide quicker development schedules and higher efficacy [67].
- Expansion of Vaccine Pipeline: A wide range of vaccines have been developed to combat a variety of infectious diseases, including newly emerging threats such as the Zika virus, SARS-CoV-2 (the virus that causes COVID-19) and Ebola virus. The pipeline for vaccines is being expanded as part of continuous attempts to address global health issues [68].
- Public-Private Partnerships (PPPs): By combining the advantages of public and private sectors, PPPs have been vital in speeding up the development of vaccines. These collaborations make it easier for governments, universities, businesses, and nonprofit organizations to work together to finance studies, carry out clinical trials, and ensure everyone has access to vaccines.
- Funding and Investment: Infrastructure for production and delivery, as well as financial assistance for vaccine research and development, are provided via PPPs. The Global Alliance for Vaccines and Immunization (GAVI) and the Coalition for Epidemic Preparedness Innovations (CEPI) have raised a significant amount of money to promote the development of vaccines for infectious illnesses.
- Emerging illnesses: By investing in vaccination platforms that can be quickly implemented in response to outbreaks, PPPs have significantly improved global preparedness for emerging infectious illnesses. The goal of this proactive strategy is to stop the spread of infectious diseases and lessen the effects of potential pandemics.

A review of programs encouraging collaborative and open science methods in vaccine research is shown in Table **1**.

Table 1. Initiatives promoting open science and collaborative approaches to vaccine research.

Sr. No.	Initiative	Description	Source
01	COVAX	COVAX is an international program that emphasizes international cooperation in order to provide COVID-19 vaccines to all people equally.	Gavi, the Vaccine Alliance. (2022). COVAX.
02	Vaccine Research and Development (VRD)	A cooperative forum bringing together scientists, decision-makers, and business partners to promote the development of vaccines.	World Health Organization. (2021). Vaccine Research and Development (VRD).
03	Global Vaccine Action Plan (GVAP)	The goal of the GVAP is to achieve universal access to vaccines through sector-wide collaboration.	World Health Organization. (2020). Global Vaccine Action Plan (GVAP)
04	Open-Vaccine	An open-source platform that makes it easier to collaborate on vaccine development initiatives by publicly sharing resources and research data.	OpenVaccine. (n.d.). OpenVaccine: An Open-Source Platform for Vaccine Development.
05	CEPI (Coalition for Epidemic Preparedness Innovations)	CEPI encourages cooperative efforts to create vaccines against newly emerging infectious illnesses in keeping with the values of open science principles.	Coalition for Epidemic Preparedness Innovations (CEPI). (2021). About CEPI.

THE COVID-19 PANDEMIC AND VACCINE IP

In Wuhan, Hubei province, China, an outbreak of a novel coronavirus appeared in December 2019 as a worldwide health crisis. On January 30, 2020, the World Health Organization (WHO) declared it a public health emergency of global concern, and on March 11, 2020, it was declared a pandemic [69].

Early in the pandemic, WHO recommended that health workers and high-risk individuals in all countries should receive vaccinations first; however, HICs, such as the US, the UK, and EU states, chose to prioritize their populations, including those who were comparatively low-risk and did not follow through on this recommendation. Developed countries like the UK and several EU members have double-vaccinated 70–75 percent of their adult populations as of February 2022; meanwhile, 85 percent of Africans have not received a single shot. Note. Furthermore, billions of people in LMICs—including vulnerable healthcare workers—are still waiting for their first dose, while Israel, the US, the UK, and Germany have given the residents their third or fourth "booster" dose.

The development of the world's most effective vaccines has been centralized in a relatively small number of Western companies, including Johnson and Johnson (J&J), Oxford-AstraZeneca, Pfizer-BioNTech, and Moderna. The issue of insufficient worldwide production was made worse in 2021 by the fact that there were so few voluntary licensing arrangements developed to boost vaccine production capacity. For instance, J&J and Merck reached a partnership to increase J&J vaccine production in the US, and J&J also agreed to a limited "fill and finish" cooperation with Aspen in South Africa. AstraZeneca (AZ) agreements with Serum Institute of India (Serum)Footnote28 and Fiocruz in Brazil; BioNTech's joint venture with Fosun Pharmaceuticals in China (different from BioNTech's agreement with Pfizer); and Pfizer-BioNTech's narrow fill and finish agreement with Biovac in South Africa. Apart from the moral discrimination, production and distribution disparities could be visibly obvious: in the absence of adequate vaccination supply, fair worldwide dispersal, and long-term dose administration, novel COVID-19 variations, like Omicron, might keep emerging. Variants like this could make current vaccines less effective. Everyone must battle COVID-19 in a fair and long-lasting way.

Efforts to boost production capacity for producing vaccines in LMICs have collided with the economic motive and the concomitant emphasis on upholding IP limitations rather than sharing IP or related technology transfer. To put it briefly, the existing intellectual property structure has not been able to provide proper incentives to address vaccination inequities promptly [70].

CONCLUSION

In conclusion, vaccinations are essential for protecting the public's health since they prevent the spread of dangerous diseases. The development of vaccines from their earliest forms best represented by Edward Jenner & groundbreaking to their most advanced versions in today's world highlights the importance of ongoing innovation and teamwork in the field. Access to and affordability of vaccines have changed globally since the Agreement on Trade-Related Aspects of Intellectual Property Rights (TRIPS) was established. It is still difficult to strike a careful balance between defending intellectual property rights and guaranteeing everyone has access to immunizations. The intricacies involved in striking this balance are highlighted by several disputes involving vaccination patents and intellectual property rights, which call for sophisticated strategies to meet the interests of both global health equality and inventors. Increased public-private partnerships and open science efforts are two recent developments in vaccination research that present promising paths for boosting innovation while reducing access restrictions. However, the COVID-19 pandemic has made clear how urgently existing IP frameworks need to be reevaluated, as the search for vaccinations against the novel coronavirus has brought to light both the advantages and disadvantages of these systems. We must steer clear of the COVID-19 pandemic and steer clear of other challenges by prioritizing global health equity and encouraging innovation and investment in vaccine research. This necessitates coordinated efforts to find a middle ground between defending intellectual property rights and guaranteeing that everyone, regardless of location or socioeconomic background, has access to life-saving vaccinations. Ultimately, we may work toward a future in which vaccines act as rays of hope, safeguarding the health and welfare of people everywhere by encouraging cooperation, supporting open science, and rethinking IP frameworks.

REFERENCES

[1] Malone KM, Hinman AR. Vaccination mandates: the public health imperative and individual rights. Law in public health practice 2003; 338: 339-40.

[2] Fenner F, Henderson DA, Arita I, Jezek Z, Ladnyi ID. Smallpox and its eradication. Geneva: World Health Organization 1988; 6: pp. 1371-409.

[3] Plotkin SA, Orenstein WA, Offit PA, Edwards KM. Plotkin's Vaccines. 7th ed., Philadelphia, PA: Elsevier 2018.

[4] Hopkins DR. The greatest killer: Smallpox in history. Chicago: University of Chicago Press 2002. [http://dx.doi.org/10.7208/chicago/9780226189529.001.0001]

[5] Offit PA. Vaccinated: One Man's Quest to Defeat the World's Deadliest Diseases. Washington, D.C.: Smithsonian Books 2007; 3.(11).

[6] World Health Organization. Immunization: Vaccines and Biologicals - History of Vaccines. Geneva: World Health Organization. Available from: https://www.who.int/teams/health-product-and-policy-standards/immunization/policy/history-of-vaccines

[7] Singh DR. Law relating to Intellectual property: a complete comprehensive material on intellectual property covering acts, rules, conventions, treaties, agreements, digest of cases and much more. Universal Law Publishing Company 2008.

[8] Delhi N. Department of Science and Technology (DST), Government of India; 2002. Anonymous. Research and development statistics.

[9] New Delhi: Department of Scientific and Industrial Research, Government of India; 2002. Anonymous. Research and development in industry: An overview.

[10] Hopkins DR. The Greatest Killer: Smallpox in History. Chicago: University of Chicago Press 2002. [http://dx.doi.org/10.7208/chicago/9780226189529.001.0001]

[11] Fenner F, Henderson DA, Arita I, Jezek Z, Ladnyi ID. Smallpox and Its Eradication. Geneva: World Health Organization 1988.

[12] Rando HM, Lordan R, Kolla L, *et al.* The coming of age of nucleic acid vaccines during COVID-19. mSystems 2023; 8(2): e0092822.

[13] Offit PA. Vaccinated: One Man's Quest to Defeat the World's Deadliest Diseases. Washington, D.C.: Smithsonian Books 2007.

[14] Centers for Disease Control and Prevention. Epidemiology and Prevention of Vaccine-Preventable Diseases. Atkinson W, Hamborsky J, McIntyre L, Wolfe S, eds. Sth ed. Washington DC; Public Health Foundation, 2006, p. 548.

[15] Bennett M. War against smallpox: Edward Jenner and the global spread of vaccination. Cambridge

University Press, 2020.

[16] World Health Organization. Smallpox Surveillance. Geneva: World Health Organization. Available from: https://www.who.int/csr/disease/smallpox/surveillance/en/

[17] World Health Organization. Smallpox Vaccination. Geneva: World Health Organization. Available from: https://www.who.int/csr/disease/smallpox/vaccination/en/

[18] World Health Organization. Expanded Program on Immunization (EPI). Geneva: World Health Organization. Available from: https://www.who.int/teams/health-product-and-policy-standards/immunization/policy/expanded-program-on-immunization

[19] World Health Organization. Global Vaccine Action Plan 2011-2020. Geneva: World Health Organization. Available from: https://www.who.int/publications/m/item/global-vaccine-action-p-an-2011-2020

[20] World Health Organization. Access to COVID-19 Tools (ACT) Accelerator. Geneva: World Health Organization. Available from: https://www.who.int/initiatives/act-accelerator

[21] Montero DA, Vidal RM, Velasco J, et al. Two centuries of vaccination: historical and conceptual approach and future perspectives. Front Public Health: 11: 1326154.

[22] World Health Organization. Immunization: Vaccines and Biologicals - History of Vaccines. Geneva: World Health Organization. Available from: https://www.who.int/teams/health-product-and-pol-cy-standards/immunization/policy/history-of-vaccines

[23] Bainbridge DI. Intellectual property. Pearson Education 2007.

[24] New Delhi: Commercial Law Publisher (India) Pvt. Ltd; 2005. Anonymous. The Copyright Act 1957 as amended up to 1999 along with Copyright Rules 1958 and International Copyright Order 1999.

[25] New Delhi: Universal Law Publishing Co. Ltd; 2004. Anonymous. The Geographical Indications of Goods (registration and protection) Act, 1999 along with Geographical Indications of Goods (registration and protection) Rules 2002.

[26] New Delhi: Universal Law Publishing Co. Ltd; 2004. Anonymous. The Design Act. 2000 along with Design Rules 2001.

[27] Xue QC, Ouellette LL. Innovation policy and the market for vaccines. J Law Biosci 2020; 7(1): lsaa026.
[http://dx.doi.org/10.1093/jlb/lsaa026] [PMID: 32733687]

[28] Sampat BN, Shadlen KC. The COVID-19 Innovation System: Article describes innovations that emerged during the COVID-19 pandemic. Health Aff (Millwood) 2021; 40(3): 400-9.
[http://dx.doi.org/10.1377/hlthaff.2020.02097]

[29] Xue and Ouelette, "Innovation Policy," 16.

[30] INDIA'S PP. Padmashree Gehl Sampath.

[31] Lalani HS, Avorn J, Kesselheim AS. US taxpayers heavily funded the discovery of COVID-19 vaccines. Clin Pharmacol Ther 2022; 111(3): 542-4.
[http://dx.doi.org/10.1002/cpt.2344] [PMID: 34243221]

[32] Plummer FA, Jones SM. The story of Canada's Ebola vaccine. CMAJ 2017; 189(43): E1326-7.
[http://dx.doi.org/10.1503/cmaj.170704] [PMID: 29084758]

[33] Xue and Ouelette, "Innovation Policy," 17.

[34] Velásquez G. Vaccines, Medicines and COVID-19: How Can WHO Be Given a Stronger Voice?. Springer Nature 2022.
[http://dx.doi.org/10.1007/978-3-030-89125-1]

[35] Overview: the TRIPS Agreement, World Trade Organization. Available from: https://www.wto.org/english/tratop_e/trips_e/intel2_e.htm

[36] Smith RD, Correa C, Oh C. Trade, TRIPS, and pharmaceuticals. Lancet 2009; 373(9664): 684-91. [http://dx.doi.org/10.1016/S0140-6736(08)61779-1] [PMID: 19167054]

[37] World Trade Organization (WTO). (n.d.). TRIPS Agreement: Part I – General Provisions and Basic Principles. Available from: https://www.wto.org/english/tratop_e/trips_e/t_agm0_e.htm

[38] UNAIDS. (2001). TRIPS and Access to Medicines. Available from: https://www.unaids.org/sites/default/files/media_asset/trips-and-access-to-medicines_en

[39] World Health Organization (WHO). (2021). TRIPS and Public Health. Available from: https://www.who.int/phi/implementation/trips/tripstext/en/

[40] World Health Organization. Immunization, vaccines and biologicals: Vaccine supply and quality. Geneva: World Health Organization; 2020. Available from: https://www.who.int/teams/immunization-vaccines-and-biologicals/procurement-and-supply-chain/vaccine-supply-and-quality

[41] United Nations children's fund (UNICEF), (2020), UNICEF; Immunization. Available from: https://www.unicef.org/immunization

[42] World bank (2019), Immunization. Available from: https://www.worldbank.org/en/topic/health/brief/immunization

[43] Greenwood B. The contribution of vaccination to global health: past, present and future. Philos Trans R Soc Lond B Biol Sci 2014; 369(1645): 20130433. [http://dx.doi.org/10.1098/rstb.2013.0433] [PMID: 24821919]

[44] Henderson DA. Smallpox: the death of a disease: the inside story of eradicating a worldwide killer. Prometheus Books; 2009.

[45] Youde J. Cattle scourge no more: The eradication of rinderpest and its lessons for global health campaigns. Politics Life Sci 2013; 32(1): 43-57. [http://dx.doi.org/10.2990/32_1_43] [PMID: 24047090]

[46] Geison GL. The private science of Louis Pasteur. Princeton University Press; 1996. [http://dx.doi.org/10.1515/9781400864089]

[47] Wu X, Smith TG, Rupprecht CE. From brain passage to cell adaptation: the road of human rabies vaccine development. Expert Rev Vaccines 2011, 10(11). 1597-608. [http://dx.doi.org/10.1586/erv.11.140] [PMID: 22043958]

[48] Wilson JR. Margin of safety. No Title 1963.

[49] Nuttall JJ, Eley BS. BCG vaccination in HIV-infected children. Tuberculosis Research and Treatment. 2011.

[50] Lu YJ, Leite L, Gonçalves VM, *et al.* GMP-grade pneumococcal whole-cell vaccine injected subcutaneously protects mice from nasopharyngeal colonization and fatal aspiration-sepsis. Vaccine 2010; 28(47): 7468-75. [http://dx.doi.org/10.1016/j.vaccine.2010.09.031] [PMID: 20858450]

[51] Duffy PE, Patrick Gorres J. Malaria vaccines since 2000: progress, priorities, products. NPJ Vaccines 2020; 5(1): 48. [http://dx.doi.org/10.1038/s41541-020-0196-3] [PMID: 32566259]

[52] World Health Organization. WHO recommends groundbreaking malaria vaccine for children at risk. Geneva: World Health Organization; 2021. Available from: https://www.who.int/news/item/06-1--2021-who-recommends-groundbreaking-malaria-vaccine-for-children-at-risk

[53] Halbroth BR, Draper SJ. Recent developments in malaria vaccinology. Adv Parasitol 2015; 88: 1-49. [http://dx.doi.org/10.1016/bs.apar.2015.03.001] [PMID: 25911364]

[54] Adu-Gyasi D, Asante KP, Owusu-Agyei S. Malaria control and vaccine development: prospects and challenges. In: Gyasi RM, Phillips DR, Eds. Aging and Health in Africa. Cham: Springer 2021; pp. 163-83.

[55] Malley R, Anderson PW. Serotype-independent pneumococcal experimental vaccines that induce cellular as well as humoral immunity. Proc Natl Acad Sci USA 2012; 109(10): 3623-7. [http://dx.doi.org/10.1073/pnas.1121383109] [PMID: 22308483]

[56] Wang Y, Anderson PW, Malley R. Whole-cell pneumococcal vaccination: prospects and challenges. Curr Opin Immunol 2020; 65: 87-93. [http://dx.doi.org/10.1016/j.coi.2020.04.001]

[57] Feldman C, Anderson R. New pneumococcal vaccines: developments, indications, and future prospects. Front Immunol 2020; 11: 1850. [http://dx.doi.org/10.3389/fimmu.2020.01850]

[58] Crosignani P, De Stefani A, Fara GM, *et al.* Towards the eradication of HPV infection through universal specific vaccination. BMC Public Health 2013; 13(1): 642. [http://dx.doi.org/10.1186/1471-2458-13-642] [PMID: 23845195]

[59] Daugla DM, Gami JP, Gamougam K, *et al.* Effect of a serogroup A meningococcal conjugate vaccine (PsA–TT) on serogroup A meningococcal meningitis and carriage in Chad: a community study. Lancet 2014; 383(9911): 40-7. [http://dx.doi.org/10.1016/S0140-6736(13)61612-8] [PMID: 24035220]

[60] Bachmann MF, Jennings GT. Therapeutic vaccines for chronic diseases: successes and technical challenges. Philos Trans R Soc Lond B Biol Sci 2011; 366(1579): 2815-22. [http://dx.doi.org/10.1098/rstb.2011.0103] [PMID: 21893545]

[61] Maurer P, Bachmann MF. Vaccination against nicotine: an emerging therapy for tobacco dependence. Expert Opin Investig Drugs 2007; 16(11): 1775-83. [http://dx.doi.org/10.1517/13543784.16.11.1775] [PMID: 17970637]

[62] Winblad B, Andreasen N, Minthon L, *et al.* Safety, tolerability, and antibody response of active Aβ immunotherapy with CAD106 in patients with Alzheimer's disease: randomised, double-blind, placebo-controlled, first-in-human study. Lancet Neurol 2012; 11(7): 597-604. [http://dx.doi.org/10.1016/S1474-4422(12)70140-0] [PMID: 22677258]

[63] UNICEF. Immunization. UNICEF Data. Updated July 2023. Available from: https://data.unicef.org/topic/child-health/immunization

[64] Azam M. Intellectual property and public health in the developing world. Open Book Publishers 2016. [http://dx.doi.org/10.11647/OBP.0093]

[65] Maskus KE, Reichman JH. The globalization of private knowledge goods and the privatization of global public goods. J Int Econ Law 2004; 7(2): 279-320. [http://dx.doi.org/10.1093/jiel/7.2.279]

[66] Hoen E. TRIPS, pharmaceutical patents, and access to essential medicines: a long way from Seattle to Doha. Chi J Int'l L 2002; 3: 27.

[67] Plotkin SA, Gilbert PB. Nomenclature for immune correlates of protection after vaccination. Clin Infect Dis 2012; 54(11): 1615-7. [http://dx.doi.org/10.1093/cid/cis238] [PMID: 22437237]

[68] Plotkin SA, Orenstein W, Offit PA. Vaccines E-book. Elsevier Health Sciences; 2012.

[69] Tietze F, Vimalnath P, Aristodemou L, Molloy J. Crisis-critical intellectual property: findings from the COVID-19 pandemic. IEEE Trans Eng Manage 2022; 69(5): 2039-56. [http://dx.doi.org/10.1109/TEM.2020.2996982] [PMID: 35938060]

[70] Thambisetty S, McMahon A, McDonagh L, Kang HY, Dutfield G. Addressing vaccine inequity during the COVID-19 pandemic: The trips intellectual property waiver proposal and beyond. Camb Law J 2022; 81(2): 384-416. [http://dx.doi.org/10.1017/S0008197322000241]

CHAPTER 3

Intellectual Property Rights and Vaccine Innovation

Dolly Rani[1] and **Megha Jha**[2,*]

[1] *Amity Institute of Pharmacy, Amity University, Noida 201303, India*

[2] *Department of Biotechnology, School of Biological Sciences, Dr. Harisingh Gour Central University, Sagar, M.P. 470003, India*

Abstract: Intellectual Property Rights (IPR) play a pivotal role in the realm of vaccine innovation, shaping the global landscape of healthcare. This abstract explores the intricate interplay between IPR and vaccine development, shedding light on its multifaceted implications. As vaccines hold the key to combating infectious diseases, protecting the intellectual property associated with them has become a contentious issue. This paper delves into the advantages and challenges that IPR poses to vaccine innovation, discussing the impact on accessibility, affordability, and equitable distribution of vaccines worldwide. The analysis highlights the delicate balance required to incentivize research and development through IPR while ensuring that vaccines remain accessible to all, particularly in the face of global health crises. Key considerations include patents, trade agreements, licensing, and technology transfer, which can either foster or hinder vaccine development and distribution. Understanding these dynamics is critical in the context of the ongoing COVID-19 pandemic and future disease outbreaks. This abstract underscores the need for global collaboration and innovative solutions that safeguard IPR while prioritizing public health, emphasizing the importance of balancing innovation and accessibility.

Keywords: Intellectual Property Rights (IPR), Vaccine Innovation, Infectious Diseases, Global Healthcare, Equitable Distribution, Patents, Trade Agreements, Licensing, Technology Transfer.

INTRODUCTION

Overview of Vaccine Innovation-

A vaccine is a substance containing either a weakened or inactivated pathogen or a part of a pathogen, like its genetic material or proteins. When this substance is

* **Corresponding author Megha Jha:** Department of Biotechnology, School of Biological Sciences, Dr. Harisingh Gour Central University, Sagar, M.P. 470003, India; E-mail: meghajhabtbpl@gmail.com

Sachin Kumar Jain, Ravikant Gupta, Sudha Vengurlekar, Nidhi Bais & Gajendra P. Choudhary (Eds.)

given to a person, it triggers a defensive reaction from the immune system's cells. This response helps protect individuals from a specific disease the vaccine is designed for. This entire process of giving a vaccine to someone is called vaccination. In simpler terms, vaccination is the method of safeguarding people who are vulnerable to diseases by introducing a living or altered agent (for example, the oral polio vaccine), a suspension of killed organisms (like in the case of pertussis), or an inactivated toxin (as seen in tetanus) into their bodies [1]. Vaccination is a remarkable achievement in medicine, with ongoing progress driven by multidisciplinary knowledge and substantial investments. Modernizing clinical vaccine evaluation is crucial, but challenges persist. Efforts concentrate on enhancing vaccine efficacy and safety. Advances in immunology and microbiology are swiftly applied to vaccine development. To succeed, those involved need a grasp of recent trends in vaccination and relevant diseases. Key factors include pathogen understanding (life cycle, epidemiology), immune response dynamics, antigen selection, and rigorous preclinical and clinical testing [2].

Vaccine Innovation

Vaccine innovation encompasses progress in the creation, enhancement, and dissemination of vaccines aimed at thwarting and managing diseases. This entails pioneering methods such as mRNA and vector vaccines, as well as refinements in vaccine preservation and dissemination. These innovations play a vital role in bolstering global health by elevating the effectiveness and availability of vaccines for the prevention of infectious diseases. The core components of vaccine innovation encompass the formulation of novel and improved vaccines to combat communicable illnesses, a journey that frequently integrates a variety of scientific, technological, and medical breakthroughs [3]. Here, are the key aspects of vaccine innovation:

Antigen Identification

Scientists identify specific substances known as antigens that can trigger the immune system's response against a particular pathogen. Recent advancements in genomics and bioinformatics have improved this process. The process of pinpointing vaccine antigens can be more or less complex depending on whether the entire pathogen or materials derived from the pathogen are used. When it comes to using the pathogen itself for developing vaccines, the complexity of the materials can vary. This might involve using entire viruses or bacteria in different forms, such as reassortant, attenuated, or inactivated microbes. Attenuated pathogens are still alive and capable of replicating, but they have been modified in some way to reduce their ability to cause diseases in the host. Inactivated pathogens, on the other hand, are no longer capable of causing disease, as they are either dead or, in the case of viruses, rendered unable to replicate. Reassortant pathogens are a specific type of attenuated organisms, containing genetic material from at least two different strains of the same pathogen, and they express proteins from all the contributing strains [2]. In situations where it's not possible to use the entire pathogen, alternative approaches come into play, like using split, subunit, or recombinant antigens. The choice of which type of antigen to use depends on what delivers the best balance of safety and the ability to stimulate an immune response, as well as what is technologically feasible. Another avenue for vaccine antigens involves recombinant DNA techniques. This method involves isolating the gene responsible for encoding the antigen and then either producing it and purifying it from a protein-production system (like yeast or insect cells) or having the vaccine recipient's body produce it directly after receiving an engineered plasmid or a live vector. It is worth noting that DNA-based candidate vaccines are still in the early stages of development compared to vaccines that use the whole pathogen as a basis [4].

Technological Platforms

Different vaccine platforms, such as mRNA, viral vectors, subunit vaccines, and inactivated vaccines, are continually evolving and are discussed below:

mRNA

mRNA vaccines are remarkable because they have strong immunological properties, a great safety track record, and the unique ability to adapt like genetic vaccines. These vaccines work by generating proteins inside the body, which in turn trigger a comprehensive immune response, involving both cellular and antibody-based defenses, without being limited by specific genetic factors. Moreover, mRNA acts as a safe carrier of genetic information, being minimal and temporary, so it does not interfere with the body's genetic code. The standout feature of mRNA vaccines is their capacity to produce nearly any protein without requiring extensive adjustments to the production process, giving them significant flexibility in development. In essence, mRNA has the potential to revolutionize vaccine technology, and this article explores various aspects to consider when creating mRNA-based vaccines. When it comes to making mRNA, you start with a cDNA template, often plasmid DNA (pDNA), and use bacteriophage RNA polymerase in an in vitro transcription process. Initially, it might seem more challenging to produce mRNA compared to pDNA. However, raw pDNA comes with issues like traces of bacterial genomic DNA and exists in different forms (supercoiled, relaxed circle, or linear) in varying proportions [5]. This makes consistently generating pure and uniform pDNA, which is crucial for vaccine development, a demanding task. On the other hand, using linearized pDNA for transcription with bacteriophage RNA polymerase circumvents problems related to bacterial DNA remnants and pDNA variability. In this process, all DNA is removed during subsequent steps. Synthetic mRNA includes a protein-encoding open reading frame (ORF) surrounded by essential elements for mature eukaryotic mRNA functionality: a "cap," which is a 7-methyl-guanosine residue connected to the 5'-end *via* a 5'-5' triphosphate, and a poly(A) tail at the 3'-end. Therefore, a pDNA template for in vitro transcription should include at least a bacteriophage promoter, an ORF, and optionally a poly[d(A/T)] sequence that becomes poly(A), along with a unique restriction site for plasmid linearization to ensure well-defined transcription termination (note that the cap is not encoded by the template) [6]. The linearized pDNA template is transcribed into mRNA using recombinant RNA polymerase (T7, T3, or SP6) and nucleoside triphosphates. To produce capped mRNA, a cap analog-like "regular cap analog" can be included in the reaction. If the cap analog is more abundant than GTP, transcription begins with the cap analog rather than GTP, resulting in capped mRNA. Alternatively, the cap can be added enzymatically after transcription. If the pDNA template lacks a poly(A) tail, it can be added post-transcription. After transcription, both the pDNA template and any contaminating bacterial DNA are broken down by DNase. When it comes to purifying mRNA, the sample contains not only the desired mRNA transcript but also a mix of undesired elements, including different nucleotides, short abortive transcripts from incomplete initiation, and proteins. To clean this up, a combination of precipitation and extraction steps is employed to remove these contaminants [7]. However, there are still other unwanted RNA species that can't be easily separated from the correct transcript. Some are shorter due to early termination during elongation, others are longer because of linearized template DNA with a 3'-overhang or remnants of unlinearized template DNA. Undesirable transcripts can also arise from the RNA-dependent RNA polymerase activity of bacteriophage polymerases. For mRNA to be suitable as a drug substance, further purification is necessary to get rid of these problematic transcripts. This is achieved through a single chromatographic step that separates the mRNA based on its size, effectively removing both shorter and longer transcripts and producing a pure, single mRNA product [8]. Implementing this chromatographic purification during Good Manufacturing Practice (GMP) production significantly enhances the activity of mRNA molecules in terms of in vivo protein expression. This increase in protein expression is also observed when purifying transcripts for proteins like luciferase or erythropoietin using high-performance liquid chromatography (HPLC). The boost in protein expression after HPLC purification goes beyond what would be expected just by eliminating incorrect transcripts. The study's authors demonstrated that this improved protein expression post-purification is also due to the removal of contaminants, like double-stranded RNA, which can activate innate immune sensors and consequently reduce protein expression [9].

Viral Vectors

Viral vectors constitute a vital cornerstone of vaccine development, capitalizing on the unique capability of viruses to transport genetic material into host cells, thereby inciting immune responses. In the quest for effective vaccines, a diverse array of viral vectors has been harnessed, each boasting its distinct advantages and attributes. Among these, adenoviruses stand out as one of the most prominent viral vectors. These versatile entities can be genetically engineered to carry harmless portions of a pathogen's genetic material, thus facilitating the development of vaccines that trigger an immune response without causing the disease itself. Adenoviral vectors are prized for their remarkable efficiency in infecting human cells, culminating in the elicitation of robust immune responses [10]. Lentiviruses, a different class of viral vectors, have also carved a niche in the vaccine development landscape. What sets them apart is their capacity to infect both dividing and non-dividing cells, making them a promising choice for ensuring long-lasting immunity. In parallel, retroviruses, akin to lentiviruses, have demonstrated their potential by integrating their genetic material into the host's genome. This integration feature empowers the sustained expression of vaccine antigens, ultimately contributing to a prolonged and robust immune response [11]. Expanding the roster of viral vectors, vesicular stomatitis viruses (VSV) and measles viruses are additionally enlisted in vaccine development efforts. These vectors are prized for their favourable safety profiles and their ability to provoke potent immune reactions. These attributes make them compelling options when constructing vaccines for a variety of infectious diseases. In a remarkable stride toward innovation, the relatively recent emergence of mRNA vaccines has shifted the landscape of vaccination [12]. These vaccines, exemplified by those developed for COVID-19, employ lipid nanoparticles as vehicles for delivering mRNA encoding the target antigen directly into host cells. This groundbreaking approach eliminates the necessity for traditional viral vectors, offering a more streamlined and versatile path to vaccination. The mRNA vaccines have demonstrated remarkable efficacy and speed in addressing global health challenges, and their development has notably contributed to the ongoing fight against the COVID-19 pandemic [13]. The availability of this diverse spectrum of viral vectors provides vaccine developers with a versatile toolkit, allowing them to tailor vaccine platforms to the unique demands of various infectious diseases. By leveraging the strengths and characteristics of these viral vectors, scientists can engineer vaccines that not only safeguard against specific pathogens but also ensure safety, efficacy, and adaptability in the face of ever-evolving health threats [14]. As we continue to witness breakthroughs in vaccine research and development, the role of viral vectors remains pivotal in the quest to enhance global health and protect against infectious diseases.

Subunit Vaccines

Subunit vaccines represent a category of vaccines used in the development of immunization strategies, harnessing specific components or subunits of a pathogen to stimulate an immune response without the need to use the whole pathogen. These subunits typically include proteins, peptides, or other molecular structures that are recognized by the immune system. One of the primary advantages of subunit vaccines is their safety profile. Since they do not contain live or inactivated pathogens, there is no risk of causing the actual disease in the recipient. This makes subunit vaccines particularly attractive for vulnerable populations and individuals with compromised immune systems [15]. Additionally, subunit vaccines are highly specific, targeting only the most critical components of the pathogen, which reduces the risk of side effects. This precision also allows for the design of subunit vaccines for a wide range of diseases, from bacterial infections like pertussis to viral threats like hepatitis B. A classic example of a subunit vaccine is the hepatitis B vaccine, which has been instrumental in reducing the incidence of this potentially life-threatening viral infection. The vaccine contains a subunit of the hepatitis B virus surface antigen (HBsAg). When administered, this subunit elicits a protective immune response that generates antibodies against the HBsAg, thus preventing hepatitis B infection [16]. Notably, this subunit vaccine has an outstanding safety record and is a crucial component of routine immunization programs worldwide. Another subunit vaccine of significance is the human papillomavirus (HPV) vaccine. HPV is a group of viruses responsible for various cancers, including cervical cancer. The vaccine comprises virus-like particles (VLPs), which are subunits mimicking the outer shell of the virus. These VLPs are non-infectious, but they trigger a strong immune response. By vaccinating against these specific subunits, individuals are protected from HPV infection and the associated risks of cancer. Furthermore, subunit vaccines have played a pivotal role in the fight against bacterial infections [17]. The acellular pertussis vaccine, an essential component of the DTP (diphtheria, tetanus, pertussis) vaccine, is a notable example. It contains purified, inactivated subunits of the pertussis bacterium, including various toxins. This subunit vaccine approach offers an effective way to protect against pertussis while minimizing the risk of adverse reactions that were associated with whole-cell pertussis vaccines used in the past. As vaccine research advances, subunit vaccines continue to evolve, adapting to the demands of emerging infectious diseases. For instance, subunit vaccines are being explored in the development of vaccines against the novel coronavirus, SARS-CoV-2, which causes COVID-19. Multiple COVID-19 subunit vaccines are in various stages of development, utilizing key proteins or components of the virus, such as the spike protein, to induce an immune response. These subunit COVID-19 vaccines hold the promise of being safe, efficacious, and amenable to rapid production and distribution, which is crucial in the face of a global pandemic [18]. In summary, subunit vaccines represent a versatile and promising approach to vaccine development. Their safety and specificity make them valuable tools in the prevention of infectious diseases, from viral threats like hepatitis B and HPV to bacterial infections like pertussis. With ongoing research and development, subunit vaccines are poised to continue contributing significantly to the protection of global health, even in the face of novel and challenging pathogens [19].

Inactivated Vaccines

Inactivated vaccines, also known as killed vaccines, are a vital category of vaccines used in the development of immunization strategies against a wide array of infectious diseases. These vaccines are formulated by using pathogens that have been rendered non-viable, typically through chemical or physical processes, ensuring they can no longer cause disease. The main advantage of inactivated vaccines lies in their safety profile. Since the pathogen is no longer active, there is no risk of causing the actual disease in the vaccinated individual [20]. This makes them particularly suitable for individuals with weakened immune systems or those who cannot tolerate live vaccines. Inactivated vaccines have been instrumental in controlling and preventing numerous infectious diseases, including polio, hepatitis A, and influenza. One of the most iconic examples of an inactivated vaccine is the polio vaccine. The inactivated polio vaccine (IPV) played a pivotal role in the global effort to eradicate polio, a debilitating and potentially lethal disease caused by the poliovirus. The IPV contains inactivated poliovirus strains from each of the three serotypes. When administered, the immune system recognizes these non-infectious viral particles and generates an immune response. This equips the vaccinated individual with the necessary antibodies to fend off the live poliovirus should they encounter it in the future. Thanks to the widespread administration of the inactivated polio vaccine, the wild poliovirus has been nearly eradicated globally, with only a few remaining endemic regions [21]. Another critical inactivated vaccine is hepatitis A vaccine. Hepatitis A is a viral infection that primarily spreads through contaminated food and water. The inactivated hepatitis A vaccine contains inactivated hepatitis A virus particles, which, when introduced into the body, trigger an immune response, producing antibodies that protect against future exposure to the live virus. This vaccine has been invaluable in reducing the incidence of hepatitis A worldwide, particularly among travelers to regions with higher disease prevalence. Influenza vaccines are another notable example of inactivated vaccines. The flu virus is known for its rapid mutations, necessitating the development of new vaccines each flu season [22]. Inactivated influenza vaccines contain killed influenza virus strains, typically representing a combination of different subtypes. These vaccines are instrumental in reducing the severity and spread of seasonal influenza and provide essential protection against the flu's various strains. Continuous research and monitoring of circulating influenza strains allow for the timely update and formulation of effective inactivated vaccines. Inactivated vaccines have also played a critical role in the global response to emerging infectious diseases. In the midst of the COVID-19 pandemic, several inactivated vaccines for the SARS-CoV-2 virus, such as Sinopharm and Sinovac from China, have been developed and deployed to combat the spread of the virus. These vaccines rely on inactivating the virus with chemicals or heat to ensure safety while retaining its immunogenic properties [23]. Inactivated vaccines offer a well-established platform to quickly respond to emerging threats. In summary, inactivated vaccines are a cornerstone of modern vaccination programs, providing safe and effective protection against a broad spectrum of infectious diseases. Their track record in controlling polio, hepatitis A, and influenza, and their critical role in responding to emerging infectious diseases like COVID-19 underscores their importance in safeguarding global health. As research and technology continue to advance, inactivated vaccines remain a vital tool in our arsenal against infectious diseases [24].

For instance, the mRNA technology utilized in COVID-19 vaccines enables swift vaccine creation and manufacturing.

Adjuvants and Delivery Systems

Adjuvants and delivery systems are crucial components in the development of vaccines, enhancing their efficacy and ensuring a robust immune response. Adjuvants are substances added to vaccines to augment the body's immune response to the antigen (the specific component of the pathogen that the vaccine is targeting). These adjuvants serve as immunostimulants, kickstarting and amplifying the immune system's reaction to the vaccine. They work by increasing the longevity and strength of the immune response, ultimately leading to better protection against the targeted disease [25]. Some well-known adjuvants include aluminum salts, which have been used in vaccines for decades, and newer formulations such as AS03 and MF59, which are employed in influenza and COVID-19 vaccines. These adjuvants play a critical role in ensuring that vaccines are effective, especially for diseases that require a robust and long-lasting immune response. Delivery systems are another integral aspect of vaccine development. They are designed to transport the antigen or vaccine components to the target cells, ensuring they are presented to the immune system most effectively [26]. Liposomes, for example, are tiny lipid-based vesicles that can encapsulate antigens and deliver them to the immune cells, enhancing their recognition and uptake. Virus-like particles (VLPs) mimic the structure of viruses but are non-infectious and can serve as effective delivery systems. Nanoparticles, composed of various materials, can also carry antigens and stimulate potent immune responses. Furthermore, advances in mRNA vaccine technology, as seen in COVID-19 vaccines, have employed lipid nanoparticles to efficiently deliver the genetic information encoding the antigen into host cells. These innovative delivery systems are instrumental in optimizing the immune response and enabling the development of safe and effective vaccines [27]. Adjuvants and delivery systems are particularly crucial in the development of subunit and recombinant vaccines, which often contain purified antigens without the innate immunostimulatory properties of live attenuated or inactivated vaccines. By carefully selecting the appropriate adjuvant and delivery system, vaccine developers can fine-tune the immune response, ensuring it is robust, long-lasting, and specific to the targeted pathogen. Moreover, these components aid in reducing the required vaccine dosage, enhancing safety, and mitigating the need for frequent booster shots. In the context of emerging infectious diseases, adjuvants and delivery systems are key tools in accelerating vaccine development [28]. The rapid response to the COVID-19 pandemic showcased the importance of these components, as mRNA vaccines leveraged lipid nanoparticles for efficient antigen delivery, enabling the swift development of vaccines against a novel coronavirus. Additionally, they facilitate the production of vaccines that induce broader and more durable immunity, which is particularly relevant for diseases with constantly evolving strains, such as influenza. As vaccine research continues to advance, adjuvants and delivery systems play an increasingly pivotal role in tailoring vaccines for specific populations and optimizing their effectiveness. These components are integral in enhancing vaccine immunogenicity, reducing the risk of adverse effects, and providing rapid responses to emerging threats. Thus, their continued exploration and innovation are crucial for the development of vaccines that are not only safe but also highly effective in preventing a wide range of infectious diseases [29].

Improved vaccine delivery systems, including nanoparticle-based carriers, have revolutionized vaccine administration by enhancing their effectiveness. Nanoparticles, with their tiny size and versatile properties, serve as highly efficient delivery vehicles for vaccine antigens. They can protect antigens from degradation, target specific cells, and improve the presentation of antigens to the immune system, leading to a more robust and targeted immune response. These carriers are particularly valuable for subunit vaccines that contain purified antigens but lack the inherent immunostimulatory components found in live vaccines. Nanoparticle-based delivery systems have shown great promise in vaccines against a range of diseases, from cancer to infectious pathogens like influenza and COVID-19 [30]. As research in this field continues, nanoparticle technology is poised to play a pivotal role in creating more effective and specific vaccines, ensuring better protection against a variety of health threats.

Personalized Vaccines

Personalized vaccines, also referred to as precision vaccines, represent an exciting frontier in the field of vaccine development. These innovative vaccines are custom-tailored to an individual's distinctive genetic and immunological profile, ensuring a highly personalized and effective immune response. The concept of personalized vaccines has garnered significant attention in recent years, primarily due to their potential to address several challenges in the field of vaccinology. These challenges include vaccine hesitancy, the quest for more comprehensive protection, and the need for more effective strategies against fast-evolving pathogens. The driving force behind personalized vaccines is the acknowledgment that individuals do not all respond uniformly to vaccines [31]. Genetic variations, underlying health conditions, and prior immune history can significantly influence how an individual's immune system reacts to a vaccine. Consequently, the effectiveness of vaccines can exhibit substantial variation among the population. Personalized vaccines are designed to mitigate this variability by tailoring the composition and administration of the vaccine to each recipient's unique characteristics. Developing personalized vaccines involves exploring a range of innovative approaches. Advances in genomics and immunogenetics enable scientists to scrutinize an individual's genetic profile, identifying specific genetic markers that influence their immune response [32]. This understanding of genetic factors allows for the customization of vaccines to optimize an individual's immune reaction. Additionally, the application of systems biology and omics technologies offers a comprehensive understanding of how the immune system responds to vaccination, facilitating the development of vaccines that are precisely calibrated to provoke the desired immune response in each individual. One prominent application of personalized vaccines is in the context of cancer. Cancer immunotherapy, which often involves the creation of personalized cancer vaccines, harnesses the individual's tumor-specific antigens to activate the immune system. This approach stimulates the immune system to recognize and target cancer cells, demonstrating remarkable potential in treating various cancer types and representing a paradigm shift in cancer treatment [33]. The concept of personalized vaccines is also being explored in the field of infectious diseases. Particularly, in response to rapidly evolving viruses like influenza and HIV, personalized vaccine strategies aim to develop vaccines that can adapt to an individual's unique immune responses and the specific viral strains they may encounter. Despite the immense promise of personalized vaccines, there are notable challenges to their widespread implementation. The development and manufacturing of personalized vaccines are more intricate and resource-intensive compared to traditional vaccines, which are typically produced in large batches for mass distribution [34]. Furthermore, regulatory and ethical considerations need to be carefully addressed to ensure the protection of personal genetic information and the provision of informed consent. In conclusion, personalized vaccines represent a remarkable advancement in vaccine development. These vaccines have the potential to address the limitations of one-size-fits-all immunization and offer more effective protection against a variety of diseases, including cancer and infectious pathogens [35]. As our understanding of genomics and immunology continues to progress, personalized vaccines are poised to play a pivotal role in shaping the future of healthcare by offering tailored and highly efficient immune responses that are specifically designed to match each individual's unique profile. Enhanced comprehension of individual immune reactions paves the way for crafting customized vaccines that align with an individual's genetic composition. This holds the potential for more efficient and precisely targeted vaccination approaches.

Vaccine Thermostability

The importance of vaccine thermostability cannot be overstated in the realm of vaccine development, particularly when confronted with the multifaceted challenges of global vaccine distribution and the need to sustain a vaccine's efficacy over time. Thermostability encompasses the capacity of a vaccine to retain its potency and effectiveness under diverse temperature conditions, including exposure to heat or temperature fluctuations. This attribute carries profound significance, as it directly influences the vaccine's overall quality, safety, and performance [36]. To guarantee that vaccines maintain their viability and efficacy from production to administration, extensive endeavors are undertaken to design, formulate, and rigorously test vaccines that can withstand the rigors of extreme temperatures and various storage conditions. Preserving the structural integrity of a vaccine's active components, known as antigens, stands as a primary concern in the context of vaccine thermostability. These antigens serve as the vital constituents of the vaccine, responsible for eliciting the desired immune response within the vaccine recipient. When exposed to elevated temperatures, the structural integrity of these antigens is susceptible to compromise, potentially rendering the vaccine ineffective. To combat this issue, vaccine developers employ diverse strategies, such as the selection of stabilizing agents and the optimization of vaccine formulations. These measures are strategically implemented to safeguard the vaccine's antigens, ensuring the maintenance of their structural and functional properties, even when subjected to adverse temperature conditions [37]. Another pivotal facet of vaccine thermostability revolves around preventing the proliferation of harmful microorganisms within the vaccine. The contamination of vaccines can give rise to concerns regarding safety and a subsequent loss of vaccine potency. Consequently, vaccine formulations often incorporate preservatives and antimicrobial agents to deter microbial growth during the storage and transportation phases. The overarching objective is to guarantee the sterility and safety of vaccines for administration. In addition to vaccine formulation, the choice of storage conditions plays an instrumental role in preserving vaccine thermostability. Many vaccines necessitate cold chain storage, signifying that they must be stored and transported within a specified temperature range, typically between 2 to 8 degrees Celsius. Deviations from these stipulated conditions can result in a decline in vaccine potency [38]. Challenges frequently emerge in regions with limited access to dependable refrigeration infrastructure, underscoring the urgency of developing vaccines capable of withstanding temperature fluctuations without compromising their efficacy. This holds particular relevance in the context of vaccine distribution in remote areas and amid public health emergencies. Over the years, substantial research and innovation have been dedicated to enhancing vaccine thermostability. This has culminated in the development of groundbreaking technologies, such as heat-stable vaccines capable of enduring higher temperatures without suffering degradation [39]. For example, advancements in vaccine formulation techniques, such as lyophilization (freeze-drying), have enabled the creation of stable vaccine formulations that do not necessitate continual refrigeration. These innovations have significantly bolstered the practicality of vaccine storage and distribution, especially within resource-constrained settings. The concerted efforts to enhance vaccine thermostability bear wide-reaching implications, not only for routine vaccination programs but also in emergency response scenarios [40]. Amid a public health crisis, such as an outbreak of a contagious disease or a pandemic, the ability to swiftly deploy and distribute vaccines without strict temperature constraints is nothing short of life-saving. It facilitates the rapid immunization of vulnerable populations and plays a pivotal role in curbing the dissemination of infectious diseases [41]. In summation, the consideration of vaccine thermostability looms large in the development of vaccines. The capability of a vaccine to maintain its potency and safety under diverse temperature conditions is indispensable for the success of vaccination programs on a global scale. Advances in vaccine formulation, storage technology, and the creation of heat-stable vaccines stand as pivotal components in addressing the intricate challenges associated with global vaccine distribution, ultimately contributing to the enhancement of public health outcomes. Creating vaccines that remain stable at varying temperatures is crucial, especially for regions with limited access to refrigeration. Innovations in formulation and storage technologies aim to increase the shelf life and transportability of vaccines [42].

Reverse Vaccinology and Computational Approaches

Reverse vaccinology involves using genomics and bioinformatics to predict antigens for vaccine development. This accelerates the identification of potential vaccine candidates. Reverse vaccinology and computational methods have brought about a paradigm shift in the realm of vaccine innovation, introducing a potent means of swiftly and precisely identifying, designing, and creating vaccines. This innovative approach harnesses computational tools and bioinformatics to meticulously sift through the extensive genomic data of pathogens, with the primary objective of spotting potential vaccine targets or antigens. By thoroughly analyzing a pathogen's complete genome, researchers can zero in on genes responsible for encoding proteins crucial to the pathogen's survival and virulence, thus identifying prime candidates for vaccines. This novel approach has been pivotal in accelerating the development of vaccines, particularly in response to emerging infectious diseases [43]. The remarkable facet of reverse vaccinology lies in its capacity to circumvent the conventional, time-consuming methods of vaccine discovery. Instead of relying on laborious culturing and in vitro experiments, this approach expedites the identification of antigen candidates, resulting in significant time and resource savings. Computational tools are instrumental in forecasting the immunogenic potential of these antigens, heightening the chances of selecting those capable of eliciting a robust immune response [44]. Additionally, reverse vaccinology empowers scientists to customize vaccines for specific pathogen strains or variants, rendering them more adaptable and effective in the face of evolving threats. Furthermore, computational methodologies play an indispensable role in vaccine design and enhancement. Sophisticated modeling and simulation techniques facilitate the development of innovative vaccine formulations, adjuvants, and delivery systems. This streamlines the development process and concurrently enhances the safety and efficacy of vaccines. Computational models are adept at simulating the behavior of antigens within the human body, predicting their interactions with the immune system, and aiding in the design of vaccines capable of inducing the desired immune responses [45]. In addition, computational approaches contribute significantly to comprehending the immune response to vaccines, thereby facilitating the development of more effective and enduring immunization strategies. Systems biology and bioinformatics furnish valuable insights into how vaccines interact with the immune system at a molecular level. This knowledge enables the fine-tuning of vaccine regimens, encompassing the determination of the most appropriate dosages, intervals, and adjuvants to elicit robust and enduring protection. Computational tools also assist in forecasting potential adverse effects, thereby enhancing the overall safety of vaccines [46]. Reverse vaccinology and computational strategies played an instrumental role in the rapid development of vaccines during the COVID-19 pandemic. Researchers managed to decipher the genome of SARS-CoV-2 and identify prospective vaccine candidates within mere weeks. This groundbreaking achievement led to the expeditious creation and deployment of mRNA vaccines, exemplified by the Pfizer-BioNTech and Moderna vaccines, which have exhibited exceptional efficacy in safeguarding against COVID-19 [47]. Furthermore, the flexibility of computational methods is exemplified in the development of therapeutic vaccines, notably those designed to combat cancer and autoimmune diseases. Through the utilization of bioinformatics, scientists can craft personalized cancer vaccines that specifically target tumour antigens based on an individual's genetic profile. This precision-driven approach is profoundly reshaping the landscape of cancer treatment. Reverse vaccinology and computational methods have ushered in a new era of vaccine innovation [48]. By harnessing the capabilities of genomics, bioinformatics, and modeling, these techniques have expedited vaccine development, enriched vaccine design, and deepened our understanding of the immune response. As we confront evolving pathogens and intricate diseases, the integration of computational methodologies into vaccine research remains poised to propel progress and yield more effective, tailored, and versatile vaccines [49].

Global Collaboration and Data Sharing

International collaboration and data sharing stand at the forefront of vaccine innovation, marking a crucial shift in the way we combat global health threats. Initiatives such as the Coalition for Epidemic Preparedness Innovations (CEPI) have emerged as beacons of global cooperation, fostering collaborative endeavours that transcend geographical boundaries. In the realm of vaccine development, where time is often of the essence, such partnerships have proven instrumental in accelerating progress. By pooling resources, knowledge, and expertise from various corners of the world, we have witnessed remarkable advancements in vaccine research and development [50]. International collaborations enable scientists to work in tandem, leveraging diverse perspectives and sharing data that might otherwise remain siloed. This interconnected approach not only expedites the identification of vaccine candidates but also promotes transparency and accountability in the vaccine development process. Moreover, in the face of pandemics and emerging infectious diseases, it is increasingly evident that our global community must stand united, as the health and well-being of one nation are intricately linked to that of another. Thus, international collaboration and data sharing have transcended being mere strategies and have become imperative pillars of our collective defense against global health threats [51].

Disease Eradication and Elimination

Innovations in vaccine development have a dual objective, going beyond prevention to pursue the complete eradication or elimination of diseases. Demonstrating this potential, initiatives such as the Global Polio Eradication Initiative underscore the capacity of vaccines to globally eliminate specific diseases. Disease eradication and elimination represent ambitious yet attainable goals in the field of vaccine innovation. These strategies aim to permanently remove specific diseases from human populations or, at the very least, significantly reduce their prevalence [52]. Vaccines have played a pivotal role in this endeavour, offering a potent means of achieving these objectives. The most iconic example of disease eradication is smallpox, which was declared eradicated in 1980 thanks to a global vaccination campaign. Other diseases like polio and guinea worm disease are on the brink of eradication due to relentless vaccination efforts. In contrast, disease elimination targets specific geographic areas, such as regions or countries [53]. Malaria elimination programs, for instance, use vaccines to reduce the transmission of the disease in endemic areas. These efforts underscore the transformative power of vaccines in controlling and ultimately eliminating infectious diseases. While the road to disease eradication and elimination is challenging and demanding, vaccines are among our most potent weapons in this noble crusade, and ongoing research and innovation continue to pave the way for a healthier, disease-free world.

Vaccine Safety Monitoring

Vaccine safety monitoring is a fundamental component of vaccine development and plays a critical role in ensuring the efficacy and safety of vaccines. The safety of vaccines is a top priority for public health authorities, vaccine manufacturers, and healthcare professionals. The process of vaccine safety monitoring begins long before a vaccine reaches the market and continues throughout its use in the population. During the preclinical phase of vaccine development, extensive laboratory and animal testing is conducted to assess the safety of the vaccine candidate. This includes evaluating the vaccine's potential for adverse effects, its ability to stimulate an immune response, and its overall safety profile [54]. Only candidates that pass these rigorous preclinical assessments advance to human clinical trials. Clinical trials, conducted in multiple phases, are the next step in vaccine development. In these trials, vaccines are tested in human volunteers to evaluate their safety, efficacy, and appropriate dosage. Monitoring safety during clinical trials is a top priority, and rigorous procedures are in place to collect and analyze safety data. Any adverse events or side effects are thoroughly investigated, and the data are closely scrutinized by regulatory agencies, independent safety monitoring boards, and vaccine manufacturers. After a vaccine is licensed and approved for use, post-marketing surveillance and monitoring continue. This phase is critical for assessing the vaccine's safety in larger and more diverse populations. Vaccine safety surveillance systems, such as the Vaccine Adverse Event Reporting System (VAERS), are established to collect and analyze reports of adverse events following vaccination. These systems help detect and investigate potential safety concerns, enabling swift responses when necessary [55]. Vaccine safety monitoring also involves ongoing research to understand the long-term effects of vaccines and to identify any rare or unexpected side effects. This research may involve large-scale epidemiological studies and ongoing monitoring of vaccine safety through various databases and healthcare systems [56]. Additionally, international collaboration and data sharing have become increasingly important in vaccine safety monitoring. Organizations like the World Health Organization (WHO) and the Global Vaccine Safety Initiative (GVSI) facilitate global efforts to monitor and ensure the safety of vaccines. These initiatives enable the rapid sharing of information about vaccine safety, allowing for a coordinated response to potential safety concerns on a global scale. Vaccine safety monitoring is an iterative and continuous process, as safety data are continually reviewed and assessed. If a safety concern arises, regulatory agencies may issue safety alerts, update vaccine recommendations, or even withdraw a vaccine from the market if the risk of adverse events outweighs the benefits [21]. This process highlights the commitment to transparency and accountability in vaccine safety monitoring. In conclusion, vaccine safety monitoring is an integral part of vaccine development and implementation. It encompasses a comprehensive approach that begins in the early stages of vaccine development, continues through clinical trials, and extends into post-marketing surveillance. The goal is to ensure that vaccines are not only effective but also safe for all individuals [57]. Collaboration between regulatory agencies, healthcare professionals, vaccine manufacturers, and the global community is essential to maintain public trust in vaccines and to swiftly address any safety concerns that may arise. As we witness the development of new vaccines, vaccine safety monitoring remains a cornerstone of public health, safeguarding the health and well-being of populations worldwide. Continuous monitoring of vaccine safety, facilitated by advanced surveillance systems, ensures that vaccines meet rigorous safety standards. Real-time data analysis helps identify and address potential concerns promptly [58].

Next-Generation Vaccines

Next-generation vaccines represent the cutting-edge of vaccine innovation, opening new frontiers in addressing both infectious diseases and non-communicable conditions like cancer. This ongoing research reflects the ever-evolving nature of vaccine development and its crucial role in public health [59].

Emerging infectious diseases pose a continuous threat to global well-being, and the quest for rapid, effective, and adaptable vaccines to combat these threats is unceasing. Similarly, therapeutic vaccines for diseases like cancer mark a paradigm shift in treatment approaches, harnessing the immune system's power to target and eliminate specific cellular anomalies. These endeavours underscore the dynamic and interdisciplinary nature of vaccine innovation, which draws upon a spectrum of scientific disciplines to meet contemporary public health challenges head-on. As science advances, the world of vaccines expands, offering hope for a healthier, disease-resistant future [60].

IPR and Vaccine Innovation

Intellectual Property Rights (IPR) constitute a fundamental component in the landscape of vaccine innovation, serving as a legal framework that safeguards the rights of inventors and entities engaged in the development of vaccines [61]. The intricate relationship between IPR and vaccine innovation unfolds through several key dimensions:

Encouraging Innovation: IPR, with patents being a pivotal element, serves as a powerful catalyst for vaccine developers. It does so by conferring exclusive rights upon inventors and companies for a designated period. This exclusivity stands as a significant incentive, motivating extensive investments in research and development within the vaccine industry. As inventors realize that their groundbreaking discoveries will be shielded from unauthorized use or reproduction, they are more inclined to embark on ambitious research projects, explore uncharted territories, and pioneer innovative vaccine solutions [62].

Securing Investments: The development of vaccines, especially in the context of emerging diseases and complex pathogens, demands substantial financial investments. IPR protection acts as a shield for pharmaceutical companies, which often allocate substantial resources to the intricate and resource-intensive process of vaccine research. By safeguarding their investments, IPR ensures that these companies can engage in long-term, high-stakes research and development activities without the constant threat of their discoveries being exploited without consent [63]. This security in investment is pivotal in maintaining a vibrant and forward-moving vaccine industry that continually seeks solutions to complex global health challenges.

Market Competition and Accessibility: IPR, while granting exclusive rights, does not do so indefinitely. A core principle of the intellectual property system is to balance the need for innovation with the broader societal goal of accessibility. Patents have a limited lifespan, after which they expire, rendering the protected technology part of the public domain [64]. This crucial aspect of IPR ensures that once a vaccine's patent protection ceases, other entities can enter the market with generic versions of the vaccine. This creates a competitive environment, potentially driving down vaccine costs and expanding accessibility. The goal is to strike a delicate balance, fostering innovation while ensuring that the fruits of this innovation are ultimately available to the public, especially in the context of essential healthcare products like vaccines [65].

The intersection of Intellectual Property Rights and vaccine innovation is complex and multifaceted. While IPR offers exclusive rights to vaccine developers, thus promoting innovation and protecting their investments, it also ensures that these innovations eventually become part of the public domain, promoting competition and accessibility. Striking the right balance between incentivizing innovation and ensuring broad access to essential vaccines remains a central challenge in the field, with IPR serving as a critical tool in achieving this equilibrium [66]. As the global landscape of vaccine development continues to evolve, IPR will play an ongoing role in shaping the path of vaccine innovation and accessibility.

Technology Transfer and Collaboration

Technology transfer and collaboration facilitated by Intellectual Property Rights (IPR) have emerged as pivotal drivers of progress in vaccine development. Within this intricate web of innovation, licensing agreements take the centre stage, enabling the exchange of intellectual property between various entities. This exchange is not merely a transaction but a catalyst for potent partnerships, igniting a synergy that accelerates every stage of vaccine development, from inception to distribution. At the heart of technology transfer and collaboration is the concept of sharing knowledge, expertise, and resources. In the realm of vaccines, this manifests as pharmaceutical companies, research institutions, and other stakeholders coming together to leverage their respective strengths [67]. For instance, a research institution with cutting-edge scientific expertise may possess a potential vaccine candidate, while a pharmaceutical company excels in the clinical development, manufacturing, and distribution of vaccines. Through licensing agreements, these entities can pool their resources and knowledge, creating a dynamic synergy. This collaborative spirit enables expedited research and development, more efficient clinical trials, enhanced manufacturing capabilities, and broader distribution networks. Furthermore, the sharing of intellectual property enhances the collective understanding of vaccine development. Research findings, proprietary technologies, and innovations become accessible to a broader community, allowing for peer review, scrutiny, and further improvement. This democratization of knowledge fosters an environment of continuous improvement, where each contributor can learn from the successes and challenges of others. Consequently, the entire vaccine development benefits from shared insights, leading to the refinement of existing vaccines and the development of new and more effective ones. The impact of technology transfer and collaboration extends to the global accessibility of vaccines. In the pursuit of equitable vaccine distribution, licensing agreements serve as the bridge connecting vaccine developers with manufacturers worldwide. This connectivity is especially crucial in addressing pressing global health challenges, such as pandemics, where swift and widespread distribution is paramount [65]. By granting manufacturers the rights to produce a vaccine, licensing agreements ensure that the vaccine can be manufactured in multiple locations, often in diverse regions of the world. This global manufacturing network enhances the resilience of vaccine supply chains, reducing the risks associated with localized disruptions and enabling vaccines to reach those in need, regardless of geographic boundaries. In recent years, technology transfer and collaboration have played a prominent role in responding to emerging infectious diseases [68]. For example, during the COVID-19 pandemic, licensing agreements and technology transfer initiatives have been instrumental in expediting the development and distribution of vaccines. Collaborative efforts between vaccine developers, manufacturers, and global health organizations have resulted in the rapid scaling up of vaccine production. Moreover, partnerships with low- and middle-income countries have enabled the transfer of vaccine manufacturing technology, empowering these nations to produce vaccines locally and contribute to global vaccination efforts. In conclusion, technology transfer and collaboration, enabled by IPR through licensing agreements, have become linchpins of vaccine development and distribution. These partnerships amplify the impact of collective knowledge and resources, expediting vaccine research, development, and global distribution. Moreover, they promote equitable access to vaccines, particularly in the face of global health crises. As the landscape of vaccine development continues to evolve, the role of technology transfer and collaboration will remain pivotal in shaping the future of public health, ensuring that vaccines are not just innovations but accessible solutions to the world's health challenges [69].

Balancing Access and Affordability

Balancing access and affordability in the realm of vaccines represents a complex and ethically charged challenge. At its core, this challenge encompasses two paramount objectives: the protection of intellectual property and the imperative of providing global access to life-saving vaccines. Intellectual Property Rights (IPR), particularly patents, serve as a legal shield that grants inventors and pharmaceutical companies exclusive rights to their innovations. This exclusivity, while serving as a powerful incentive for research and development, often results in higher vaccine costs that can impede access, particularly in low-income countries. To address this issue, innovative initiatives like the Medicines Patent Pool have emerged as proactive solutions [21]. The Medicines Patent Pool operates by negotiating licenses with patent holders, typically pharmaceutical companies, to facilitate the production of affordable generic versions of patented medicines, including vaccines. By opening the doors to generic production, this initiative significantly broadens the accessibility of vaccines in low-income countries, where the burden of vaccine-preventable diseases is often most acute. The importance of this balancing act becomes glaringly evident during public health crises, such as the COVID-19 pandemic, which has underscored the need for rapid global vaccine access. While patent protections have traditionally shielded vaccine innovations, initiatives like COVAX aim to ensure equitable access to COVID-19 vaccines, especially for lower-income nations. Through a cooperative framework, COVAX pools resources, negotiates vaccine procurement agreements and allocates doses to participating countries based on population size and need [70]. This international partnership exemplifies the commitment to worldwide vaccine accessibility, even amid the formidable challenges posed by the pandemic response. Critics argue that the tension between IPR and vaccine access is an ethical quandary that requires a broader reassessment. They contend that during a global health emergency, IPR should be temporarily set aside to prioritize human life and mitigate the severity of the crisis. However, proponents of IPR emphasize its indispensable role in incentivizing innovation and long-term investments, underscoring that relinquishing patents might deter future research and development efforts. In the quest for a harmonious resolution, an array of options is explored [71]. For instance, compulsory licensing, as permitted under the World Trade Organization's Trade-Related Aspects of Intellectual Property Rights (TRIPS) Agreement, allows governments to grant licenses to produce generic versions of patented vaccines during public health emergencies or when negotiations for voluntary licenses fail. While this approach could expedite vaccine production, it raises questions about the fair compensation of patent holders, which could affect future incentives for innovation. Moreover, increased funding for research and development, including investments in innovative vaccine technologies, can help mitigate the need for steep vaccine prices. Governments, philanthropic organizations, and global health institutions are actively exploring ways to bolster research efforts while keeping vaccines affordable [72]. In conclusion, the pursuit of a delicate equilibrium between protecting intellectual property and ensuring global vaccine accessibility is an ongoing challenge, marked by ethical complexities and real-world consequences. Initiatives like the Medicines Patent Pool and COVAX strive to bridge the gap, recognizing that equitable vaccine access is not just a humanitarian imperative but a global necessity. While the landscape of intellectual property and vaccine accessibility continues to evolve, it remains vital to approach this issue with an unwavering commitment to fostering innovation and safeguarding the health and well-being of populations worldwide [73]. Ultimately, this delicate balance will shape the future of vaccine development and the path to global health security.

Global Health Challenges

Global health challenges have brought to the forefront the complexities of intellectual property rights (IPR) in the context of public health emergencies. The COVID-19 pandemic, in particular, has raised pertinent questions about equitable access to life-saving vaccines. Calls for temporary waivers on specific intellectual property rights during emergencies have gained traction as a means to accelerate vaccine production and distribution, with a particular focus on addressing the needs of low-income regions. Proponents of these waivers argue that, in times of crisis, such as the current pandemic, ensuring swift and widespread access to vaccines is paramount, transcending individual profit motives [74]. The global nature of the COVID-19 threat underscores the need for a collaborative and cooperative approach to overcome the crisis, and temporary IPR waivers can facilitate the transfer of technology and knowledge needed to expand vaccine manufacturing capacity, thus serving as a powerful tool in the fight against the virus. However, IPR issues remain intricate, encompassing complex legal, economic, and ethical considerations, as well as the need to strike a balance between incentivizing innovation and safeguarding public health. As the world confronts ongoing and future global health challenges, the debate surrounding IPR, vaccine access, and global cooperation will continue to shape the future of public health and vaccine development [75].

Biopiracy Concerns

Biopiracy concerns are an integral part of the intricate relationship between intellectual property rights (IPR) and ethical considerations in the field of vaccine innovation. Biopiracy, at its core, refers to the exploitation of traditional knowledge or genetic resources from indigenous communities without providing fair compensation or recognition. In the context of vaccine development, this issue is particularly pertinent when vaccines are derived from natural products or traditional remedies that have been used for generations by indigenous peoples [76]. The challenge lies in finding a harmonious balance between incentivizing innovation, protecting intellectual property, and respecting the rights of indigenous communities. The exploitation of traditional knowledge and genetic resources without due recognition and compensation raises ethical concerns that necessitate an ongoing dialogue and concerted efforts to ensure that the benefits of vaccine innovation are shared equitably among all stakeholders, including the guardians of this invaluable knowledge.

Incentivizing Research in Neglected Diseases

Incentivizing research and development for vaccines targeting neglected tropical diseases (NTDs) represents a critical and morally compelling endeavor in the realm of global health. Intellectual property rights (IPR) play an instrumental role in this context by providing mechanisms that encourage vaccine manufacturers and pharmaceutical companies to invest in the creation of vaccines for NTDs [77]. Neglected diseases, often afflicting the world's most impoverished and marginalized populations, may not offer the same financial incentives for vaccine development as more common, financially lucrative diseases. However, specialized mechanisms like the Orphan Drug Act have been established to fill this gap. These mechanisms grant companies incentives, such as extended patent protection and marketing exclusivity, for investing in the research and development of vaccines for NTDs. These incentives have proved effective in stimulating research and innovation in this often-neglected field, ultimately leading to the creation of vaccines that offer hope to the millions of people suffering from NTDs. By striking a balance between profit and the greater good, IPR-driven incentives have become indispensable tools in addressing the unique challenges posed by NTDs and advancing global health equity [78].

Regulatory Exclusivity

Regulatory exclusivity, extending beyond the realm of patents, offers a supplementary layer of protection for pharmaceutical and vaccine developers by postponing the approval of generic versions. This practice serves as a safeguard that guarantees companies a designated timeframe during which they can recover their substantial investments before being exposed to market competition. While patents grant inventors exclusive rights to their creations, regulatory exclusivity operates within the framework of governmental health agencies, such as the U.S. Food and Drug Administration (FDA) in the United States [79]. This mechanism, often termed data exclusivity or market exclusivity, provides companies with a secure window to navigate the complex regulatory processes and clinical trials required for drug and vaccine approval. During this period, generic manufacturers are restricted from obtaining approval for their versions, ensuring that the original developers can maximize their returns on investment. The primary goal of regulatory exclusivity is to strike a balance between stimulating innovation, rewarding pharmaceutical innovation, and facilitating fair competition in the healthcare market. This balance supports continued research and development, fosters medical breakthroughs, and ultimately benefits public health [80].

Challenges of Monopolies

The challenges associated with monopolies, often arising from the excessive protection of intellectual property rights (IPR), have ignited considerable debate and scrutiny. Detractors contend that robust IPR protection if taken to the extreme, has the potential to culminate in monopolistic practices. These monopolies, in the context of vaccines and pharmaceuticals, can exert undue control over the market, stifling competition and subsequently propelling vaccine prices to unaffordable heights. This economic scenario raises profound ethical and practical dilemmas, as it has the potential to restrict access to life-saving vaccines and healthcare innovations for large segments of the population, particularly those in resource-constrained regions [74]. The challenge, therefore, lies in navigating the intricate balance between safeguarding the incentives that drive innovation while concurrently fostering a climate of equitable and affordable vaccine access. It is this very equilibrium that necessitates ongoing contemplation, policymaking, and collaborative efforts to shape a future where groundbreaking vaccines are both economically sustainable and accessible to all in need.

CONCLUSION

Myths about IP's function impede a comprehensive evaluation of what IP can and cannot do, postponing or obstructing the kind of policy experimentation that promises to provide the world with more precise vaccinations and medications more swiftly, such as open-science drug research. This chapter's objectives are to provide a succinct overview of the process by which vaccine inventors may be granted patent rights, as well as to elucidate the possible danger of violating third-party patent rights and its possible repercussions. Following a discussion of the benefits and downsides of patent protection, a summary of patent infringement is provided, along with a list of potential legal safe havens for certain research endeavors, global health challenges, regulatory exclusivity, and monopolies. A quick overview of the vaccine innovation, international patent systems, and the patent application procedure was discussed in this chapter.

REFERENCES

[1] Plotkin SA. Vaccines: past, present and future. Nat Med 2005; 11(S4) (Suppl.): S5-S11. [http://dx.doi.org/10.1038/nm1209] [PMID: 15812490]

[2] Dubé E, Laberge C, Guay M, Bramadat P, Roy R, Bettinger JA. Vaccine hesitancy. Hum Vaccin Immunother 2013; 9(8): 1763-73. [http://dx.doi.org/10.4161/hv.24657] [PMID: 23584253]

[3] Lahariya C. Vaccine epidemiology: A review. J Family Med Prim Care 2016; 5(1): 7-15. [http://dx.doi.org/10.4103/2249-4863.184616] [PMID: 27453836]

[4] Strugnell R, Zepp F, Cunningham A, Tantawichien T. Vaccine antigens. PerspectVaccinol 2011; 1(1): 61-88.

[5] Sunita SA, Sajid A, Singh Y, Shukla P. Computational tools for modern vaccine development. Hum Vaccin Immunother 2020; 16(3): 723-35.
[http://dx.doi.org/10.1080/21645515.2019.1670035] [PMID: 31545127]

[6] Schlake T, Thess A, Fotin-Mleczek M, Kallen KJ. Developing mRNA-vaccine technologies. RNA Biol 2012; 9(11): 1319-30.
[http://dx.doi.org/10.4161/rna.22269] [PMID: 23064118]

[7] Rosa SS, Prazeres DMF, Azevedo AM, Marques MPC. mRNA vaccines manufacturing: Challenges and bottlenecks. Vaccine 2021; 39(16): 2190-200.
[http://dx.doi.org/10.1016/j.vaccine.2021.03.038] [PMID: 33771389]

[8] Jackson NA, Kester KE, Casimiro D, Gurunathan S, DeRosa F. The promise of mRNA vaccines: a biotech and industrial perspective. npj. Vaccines (Basel) 2020; 5(1): 11.
[PMID: 33375677]

[9] Wang Y, Zhang Z, Luo J, Han X, Wei Y, Wei X. mRNA vaccine: a potential therapeutic strategy. Mol Cancer 2021; 20(1): 33.
[http://dx.doi.org/10.1186/s12943-021-01311-z] [PMID: 33593376]

[10] Liniger M, Zuniga A, Naim HY. Use of viral vectors for the development of vaccines. Expert Rev Vaccines 2007; 6(2): 255-66.
[http://dx.doi.org/10.1586/14760584.6.2.255] [PMID: 17408374]

[11] Lundstrom K. Application of viral vectors for vaccine development with a special emphasis on COVID-19. Viruses 2020; 12(11): 1324.
[http://dx.doi.org/10.3390/v12111324] [PMID: 33218001]

[12] Choi Y, Chang J. Viral vectors for vaccine applications. Clin Exp Vaccine Res 2013; 2(2): 97-105.
[http://dx.doi.org/10.7774/cevr.2013.2.2.97] [PMID: 23858400]

[13] Ewer KJ, Lambe T, Rollier CS, Spencer AJ, Hill AVS, Dorrell L. Viral vectors as vaccine platforms: from immunogenicity to impact. Curr Opin Immunol 2016; 41: 47-54.
[http://dx.doi.org/10.1016/j.coi.2016.05.014] [PMID: 27286566]

[14] Lundstrom K. Viral vectors for COVID-19 vaccine development. Viruses 2021; 13(2): 317.
[http://dx.doi.org/10.3390/v13020317] [PMID: 33669550]

[15] Moyle PM, Toth I. Modern subunit vaccines: development, components, and research opportunities. ChemMedChem 2013; 8(3): 360-76.
[http://dx.doi.org/10.1002/cmdc.201200487] [PMID: 23316023]

[16] Hansson M, Nygren PA˚, Sta˚hl S. Design and production of recombinant subunit vaccines. Biotechnol Appl Biochem 2000; 32(2): 95-107.
[http://dx.doi.org/10.1042/BA20000034] [PMID: 11001870]

[17] Foged C. Subunit vaccines of the future: the need for safe, customized and optimized particulate delivery systems. Ther Deliv 2011; 2(8): 1057-77.
[http://dx.doi.org/10.4155/tde.11.68] [PMID: 22826868]

[18] Tan M, Jiang X. Recent advancements in combination subunit vaccine development. Hum Vaccin Immunother 2017; 13(1): 180-5.
[http://dx.doi.org/10.1080/21645515.2016.1229719] [PMID: 27649319]

[19] Wang N, Shang J, Jiang S, Du L. Subunit vaccines against emerging pathogenic human coronaviruses. Front Microbiol 2020; 11: 298.
[http://dx.doi.org/10.3389/fmicb.2020.00298] [PMID: 32265848]

[20] Pagliusi S, Dennehy M, Kim H. Vaccines, inspiring innovation in health. Vaccine 2018; 36(48): 7430-7.
[http://dx.doi.org/10.1016/j.vaccine.2018.05.035] [PMID: 29789241]

[21] Stevens H, Debackere K, Goldman M, Mahoney RT, Stevens P, Huys I. Vaccines: accelerating

innovation and access. Global Challenges Report, World Intellectual Property Organization (WIPO). 2017 Nov 7.

[22] Thompson KM, Duintjer Tebbens RJ. National choices related to inactivated poliovirus vaccine, innovation and the endgame of global polio eradication. Expert Rev Vaccines 2014; 13(2): 221-34. [http://dx.doi.org/10.1586/14760584.2014.864563] [PMID: 24308581]

[23] Alshrari AS, Hudu SA, Imran M, Asdaq SMB, Ali AM, Rabbani SI. Innovations and development of COVID-19 vaccines: A patent review. J Infect Public Health 2022; 15(1): 123-31. [http://dx.doi.org/10.1016/j.jiph.2021.10.021] [PMID: 34742639]

[24] Sanders B, Koldijk M, Schuitemaker H. Inactivated viral vaccines. Vaccine analysis: strategies, principles, and control. 2015:45-80. [http://dx.doi.org/10.1007/978-3-662-45024-6_2]

[25] Kaurav M, Madan J, Sudheesh MS, Pandey RS. Combined adjuvant-delivery system for new generation vaccine antigens: alliance has its own advantage. Artificial Cells, Nanomedicine, and Biotechnology. 2018 Nov 12;46(sup3):818-31. [http://dx.doi.org/10.1080/21691401.2018.1513941]

[26] Cordeiro AS, Alonso MJ. Recent advances in vaccine delivery. Pharm Pat Anal 2016; 5(1): 49-73. [http://dx.doi.org/10.4155/ppa.15.38] [PMID: 26667309]

[27] Riese P, Schulze K, Ebensen T, Prochnow B, Guzmán C. Vaccine adjuvants: key tools for innovative vaccine design. Curr Top Med Chem 2013; 13(20): 2562-80. [http://dx.doi.org/10.2174/15680266113136660183] [PMID: 24066891]

[28] Donnelly RF. Vaccine delivery systems. Hum Vaccin Immunother 2017; 13(1): 17-8. [http://dx.doi.org/10.1080/21645515.2016.1259043] [PMID: 28125375]

[29] Tsakiri M, Naziris N, Demetzos C. Innovative vaccine platforms against infectious diseases: Under the scope of the COVID-19 pandemic. Int J Pharm 2021; 610: 121212. [http://dx.doi.org/10.1016/j.ijpharm.2021.121212] [PMID: 34687816]

[30] Petkar KC, Patil SM, Chavhan SS, *et al.* An overview of nanocarrier-based adjuvants for vaccine delivery. Pharmaceutics 2021; 13(4): 455. [http://dx.doi.org/10.3390/pharmaceutics13040455] [PMID: 33801614]

[31] Poland GA, Ovsyannikova IG, Kennedy RB. Personalized vaccinology: A review. Vaccine 2018; 36(36): 5350-7. [http://dx.doi.org/10.1016/j.vaccine.2017.07.062] [PMID: 28774561]

[32] Castiblanco J, Anaya JM. Genetics and vaccines in the era of personalized medicine. Curr Genomics 2015; 16(1): 47-59. [http://dx.doi.org/10.2174/1389202916666141223220551] [PMID: 25937813]

[33] Shemesh CS, Hsu JC, Hosseini I, *et al.* Personalized cancer vaccines: clinical landscape, challenges, and opportunities. Mol Ther 2021; 29(2): 555-70. [http://dx.doi.org/10.1016/j.ymthe.2020.09.038] [PMID: 33038322]

[34] Poland GA, Kennedy RB, Ovsyannikova IG. Vaccinomics and personalized vaccinology: is science leading us toward a new path of directed vaccine development and discovery? PLoS Pathog 2011; 7(12): e1002344. [http://dx.doi.org/10.1371/journal.ppat.1002344] [PMID: 22241978]

[35] Poland GA, Ovsyannikova IG, Jacobson RM. Vaccinomics and personalized vaccinology. US Department of Health and Human Services 2012; pp. 3-18.

[36] Kumar R, Srivastava V, Baindara P, Ahmad A. Thermostable vaccines: an innovative concept in vaccine development. Expert Rev Vaccines 2022; 21(6): 811-24. [http://dx.doi.org/10.1080/14760584.2022.2053678] [PMID: 35285366]

[37] Mvundura M, Frivold C, Janik Osborne A, *et al.* Vaccine innovation prioritisation strategy: Findings

from three country-stakeholder consultations on vaccine product innovations. Vaccine 2021; 39(49): 7195-207.
[http://dx.doi.org/10.1016/j.vaccine.2021.08.024] [PMID: 34412922]

[38] Hayman B, Bowles A, Evans B, Eyermann E, Nepomnyashchiy L, Pagliusi S. Advancing innovation for vaccine manufacturers from developing countries: Prioritization, barriers, opportunities. Vaccine 2021; 39(8): 1190-4.
[http://dx.doi.org/10.1016/j.vaccine.2020.12.085] [PMID: 33487466]

[39] Badizadegan K, Goodson JL, Rota PA, Thompson KM. The potential role of using vaccine patches to induce immunity: platform and pathways to innovation and commercialization. Expert Rev Vaccines 2020; 19(2): 175-94.
[http://dx.doi.org/10.1080/14760584.2020.1732215] [PMID: 32182145]

[40] Qi Y, Fox CB. Development of thermostable vaccine adjuvants. Expert Rev Vaccines 2021; 20(5): 497-517.
[http://dx.doi.org/10.1080/14760584.2021.1902314] [PMID: 33724133]

[41] Chen D, Kristensen D. Opportunities and challenges of developing thermostable vaccines. Expert Rev Vaccines 2009; 8(5): 547-57.
[http://dx.doi.org/10.1586/erv.09.20] [PMID: 19397412]

[42] Kristensen D, Chen D, Cummings R. Vaccine stabilization: Research, commercialization, and potential impact. Vaccine 2011; 29(41): 7122-4.
[http://dx.doi.org/10.1016/j.vaccine.2011.05.070] [PMID: 21651941]

[43] Donati C, Rappuoli R. Reverse vaccinology in the 21st century: improvements over the original design. Ann N Y Acad Sci 2013; 1285(1): 115-32.
[http://dx.doi.org/10.1111/nyas.12046] [PMID: 23527566]

[44] Mitra A. Reverse Vaccinology Approaches for Rapid Vaccine Design Against Emerging Infectious Diseases. Frontiers in Anti-Infective Agents: Volume 6. 2021 Nov 17;6:1.
[http://dx.doi.org/10.2174/9789814998420121060003]

[45] Bruno L, Cortese M, Rappuoli R, Merola M. Lessons from Reverse Vaccinology for viral vaccine design. Curr Opin Virol 2015; 11: 89-97.
[http://dx.doi.org/10.1016/j.coviro.2015.03.001] [PMID: 25829256]

[46] Capecchi B, Serruto D, Adu-Bobie J, Rappuoli R, Pizza M. The genome revolution in vaccine research. Curr Issues Mol Biol 2004; 6(1): 17-27.
[PMID: 14632256]

[47] Moxon R, Reche PA, Rappuoli R. Editorial: Reverse Vaccinology. Front Immunol 2019; 10: 2776.
[http://dx.doi.org/10.3389/fimmu.2019.02776] [PMID: 31849959]

[48] Chatterjee R, Ghosh M, Sahoo S, *et al.* Next-generation bioinformatics approaches and resources for coronavirus vaccine discovery and development—A perspective review. Vaccines (Basel) 2021; 9(8): 812.
[http://dx.doi.org/10.3390/vaccines9080812] [PMID: 34451937]

[49] Kanekiyo M, Ellis D, King NP. New vaccine design and delivery technologies. J Infect Dis 2019; 219 (Suppl. 1): S88-96.
[http://dx.doi.org/10.1093/infdis/jiy745] [PMID: 30715361]

[50] Elbe S, Buckland-Merrett G. Data, disease and diplomacy: GISAID's innovative contribution to global health. Glob Chall 2017; 1(1): 33-46.
[http://dx.doi.org/10.1002/gch2.1018] [PMID: 31565258]

[51] Ilin I, Levina A, Frolov K. Innovative ecosystem model of vaccine lifecycle management. J Open Innov 2022; 8(1): 5.
[http://dx.doi.org/10.3390/joitmc8010005]

[52] Goodson JL. Recent setbacks in measles elimination: the importance of investing in innovations for

immunizations. The Pan African Medical Journal. 2020; 35(Suppl 1). [http://dx.doi.org/10.11604/pamj.supp.2020.35.1.21740]

[53] Healer J, Cowman AF, Kaslow DC, Birkett AJ. Vaccines to accelerate malaria elimination and eventual eradication. Cold Spring Harb Perspect Med 2017; 7(9): a025627. [http://dx.doi.org/10.1101/cshperspect.a025627] [PMID: 28490535]

[54] McNeil MM, Gee J, Weintraub ES, *et al.* The Vaccine Safety Datalink: successes and challenges monitoring vaccine safety. Vaccine 2014; 32(42): 5390-8. [http://dx.doi.org/10.1016/j.vaccine.2014.07.073] [PMID: 25108215]

[55] Baggs J, Gee J, Lewis E, *et al.* The Vaccine Safety Datalink: a model for monitoring immunization safety. Pediatrics 2011; 127 (Suppl. 1): S45-53. [http://dx.doi.org/10.1542/peds.2010-1722H] [PMID: 21502240]

[56] Waldman EA, Luhm KR, Monteiro SA, Freitas FR. Surveillance of adverse effects following vaccination and safety of immunization programs. Rev Saude Publica 2011; 45(1): 173-84. [http://dx.doi.org/10.1590/S0034-89102011000100020] [PMID: 21181055]

[57] Excler JL, Privor-Dumm L, Hotez P, Gilbert DS, Thompson D, Karim SA, Swaminathan S, Kim JH. A new era for vaccine innovation.

[58] Di Pasquale A, Bonanni P, Garçon N, Stanberry LR, El-Hodhod M, Tavares Da Silva F. Vaccine safety evaluation: Practical aspects in assessing benefits and risks. Vaccine 2016; 34(52): 6672-80. [http://dx.doi.org/10.1016/j.vaccine.2016.10.039] [PMID: 27836435]

[59] Koff WC, Burton DR, Johnson PR, *et al.* Accelerating next-generation vaccine development for global disease prevention. Science 2013; 340(6136): 1232910. [http://dx.doi.org/10.1126/science.1232910] [PMID: 23723240]

[60] Sautto GA, Kirchenbaum GA, Diotti RA, Criscuolo E, Ferrara F. Next generation vaccines for infectious diseases. Journal of Immunology Research 2019. [http://dx.doi.org/10.1155/2019/5890962]

[61] Stevens H, Debackere K, Goldman M, Mahoney RT, Stevens P, Huys I. Vaccines: accelerating innovation and access. Global Challenges Report, World Intellectual Property Organization (WIPO). 2017 Nov 7.

[62] Watal J. Innovation. Intellectual Property, and Global Health. Handbook of Global Health 2020; pp. 1-34.

[63] Crager SE. Improving global access to new vaccines: intellectual property, technology transfer, and regulatory pathways. Am J Public Health 2018; 108(S6): S414-20. [http://dx.doi.org/10.2105/AJPH.2014.302236r] [PMID: 25211753]

[64] Yaqub O, Nightingale P. Vaccine innovation, translational research and the management of knowledge accumulation. Soc Sci Med 2012; 75(12): 2143-50. [http://dx.doi.org/10.1016/j.socscimed.2012.07.023] [PMID: 22963923]

[65] Possas C, Martins RM, Homma A. Vaccine innovation and global sustainability. Science Technology and Innovation for Sustainable Development Goals: Insights from Agriculture, Health. Environment and Energy 2020; 1: 219-42.

[66] Aars OK, Clark M, Schwalbe N. Increasing efficiency in vaccine Production: A primer for change. Vaccine X 2021; 8: 100104. [http://dx.doi.org/10.1016/j.jvacx.2021.100104] [PMID: 34151248]

[67] Price WN II, Rai AK, Minssen T. Knowledge transfer for large-scale vaccine manufacturing. Science 2020; 369(6506): 912-4. [http://dx.doi.org/10.1126/science.abc9588] [PMID: 32792464]

[68] Kovac I, Maslac V, Horvatinovic T. CHallenges of technology transfer in the vaccine development process. Economic and Social Development: Book of Proceedings. 2022 Apr 1:424-34.

[69] Mahoney RT. Product Development Partnerships: Case studies of a new mechanism for health technology innovation. Health Res Policy Syst 2011; 9(1): 33. [http://dx.doi.org/10.1186/1478-4505-9-33] [PMID: 21871103]

[70] Stevens H, Huys I. Innovative approaches to increase access to medicines in developing countries. Front Med (Lausanne) 2017; 4: 218. [http://dx.doi.org/10.3389/fmed.2017.00218] [PMID: 29270407]

[71] Smith J, Lipsitch M, Almond JW. Vaccine production, distribution, access, and uptake. Lancet 2011; 378(9789): 428-38. [http://dx.doi.org/10.1016/S0140-6736(11)60478-9] [PMID: 21664680]

[72] Pagliusi S, Ting CC, Lobos F, *et al.* Vaccines: Shaping global health. Vaccine 2017; 35(12): 1579-85. [http://dx.doi.org/10.1016/j.vaccine.2017.02.017] [PMID: 28237501]

[73] Privor-Dumm L, Excler JL, Gilbert S, *et al.* Vaccine access, equity and justice: COVID-19 vaccines and vaccination. BMJ Glob Health 2023; 8(6): e011881. [http://dx.doi.org/10.1136/bmjgh-2023-011881] [PMID: 37290896]

[74] Stevens H, Debackere K, Goldman M, Mahoney RT, Stevens P, Huys I. Vaccines: accelerating innovation and access. Global Challenges Report, World Intellectual Property Organization (WIPO). 2017 Nov 7.

[75] Greenwood B, Salisbury D, Hill AVS. Vaccines and global health. Philos Trans R Soc Lond B Biol Sci 2011; 366(1579): 2733-42. [http://dx.doi.org/10.1098/rstb.2011.0076] [PMID: 21893534]

[76] Mgbeoji I. Global biopiracy: patents, plants, and indigenous knowledge. ubc Press; 2007.

[77] Weng HB, Chen HX, Wang MW. Innovation in neglected tropical disease drug discovery and development. Infect Dis Poverty 2018; 7(1): 67. [http://dx.doi.org/10.1186/s40249-018-0444-1] [PMID: 29950174]

[78] Watal J. Innovation. Intellectual Property, and Global Health. Handbook of Global Health 2020; pp. 1-34.

[79] Xue QC, Ouellette LL. Innovation policy and the market for vaccines. J Law Biosci 2020; 7(1): lsaa026. [http://dx.doi.org/10.1093/jlb/lsaa026] [PMID: 32733687]

[80] Grabowski HG, DiMasi JA, Long G. The roles of patents and research and development incentives in biopharmaceutical innovation. Health Aff (Millwood) 2015; 34(2): 302-10. [http://dx.doi.org/10.1377/hlthaff.2014.1047] [PMID: 25646111]

CHAPTER 4

The Debate on Patent Protection for Vaccines

Nitin G. Dumore[1] and **Manasi M. Choudhari**[2,*]

[1] *Dadasaheb Balpande College of Pharmacy, Besa, Nagpur, India*

[2] *Dadasaheb Balpande College of Diploma in Pharmacy, Besa, Nagpur, India*

Abstract: In recent years, there has been a strengthening and harmonization of global standards for patent protection. Patents are important for development, as evidenced by the discussion surrounding the Trade-Related Aspects of Intellectual Property Rights (TRIPs) Agreement of the World Trade Organization. However, research on the geography of knowledge transfer indicates that knowledge is spatially sticky, indicating that patent impact may be overstated. Amidst the fervent discourse, a few key issues frequently dominate the discourse in the academic, regulatory, and policy domains: is the number of patents excessive? Do patents create impassable "thickets" that hinder the path of new innovators and implementers? Do the cumulative royalties from multiple patents covering a single product amount to excessive royalty rates? How should reasonable licensing terms and damages for patents be defined? However, there is scant or no empirical support for a number of these claims. In order to find holes in the arguments made thus far and areas where more research could help the debate, this chapter provides an overview of the literature on the current patent policy debate. These days, the public is highly aware of patents; debates and questions concerning the patent system's fairness, the legitimacy of a large number of patents, and the rights of those who "have" versus those who "have not" are common.

Keywords: COVID-19, IPR, Patent, Pandemic, Patent debate, TRIPS, TRIPS waiver, Technology transfer, Vaccines.

INTRODUCTION

An invention discovered by an applicant is granted a patent, which is a legal document granted by the government for a specific amount of time regarding the discovery or development of something new. It gives protection, of such discovery, to the petitioner. A patent is granted for a finite amount of time—up to 20 years. A patent defence indicates that the innovation cannot be applied, widely distributed, or sold to third parties without the patent holder's consent. For the

* **Corresponding author Manasi M. Choudhari:** Dadasaheb Balpande College of Diploma in Pharmacy, Besa, Nagpur, India; E-mail: manasipatilp663@gmail.com

Sachin Kumar Jain, Ravikant Gupta, Sudha Vengurlekar, Nidhi Bais & Gajendra P. Choudhary (Eds.)

period that the invention is protected, the patent holder is free to decide who may or may not utilize the patented invention [1]. Even though the notion of intellectual property rights (IPR) is relatively new to the globe, the pharmaceutical business is a successful technology sector that has grown consistently over the past few decades [2]. India's permission from the World Trade Organization and its vow to execute the Trade-Related Aspects of Intellectual Property Rights (TRIPS) concession have witnessed a variance in the Indian pharmaceutical business. In every industry, the manufacturing sector is required to obtain the product's patent; however, many industries are unable to handle patents [3].

The legal exclusive rights granted to an inventor for revealing a novel process, item, or idea that is beneficial, non-obvious, and not naturally occurring are known as patent protection. It is the sole method available for limiting an invention's production, licensing, manufacturing, and sales. Anyone can produce a product that is the same or comparable without facing legal ramifications if there is no patent in place. A specific amount of time is allotted for patent protection.

A method, product, or innovation that offers a novel technical solution is eligible for patent protection. A patent must be granted for an invention that is novel, practical, inventive, and helpful; in other words, the solution for which the patent is sought need not be a simple one. Innovation in product design, technology, and composition typically results in the granting of patent protection. An improvement on previously known patented inventions is the subject of the vast majority of patent applications. Following the patent award, the patent holder is the only one with the authority to stop others from using the patented invention for profit [4].

The number of patents connected to vaccines that have been granted has steadily increased annually for the last 20 years. Therefore, it is critical that individuals working on vaccination research understand the potential hazards as well as the benefits that come with patents. In addition to outlining the possible risk of infringing on the patent rights of other parties and its possible repercussions, this chapter seeks to provide a concise overview of how and when vaccine developers may be granted access to patent rights.

SIGNIFICANCE OF VACCINES IN PUBLIC HEALTH

It is difficult to overstate the influence that vaccinations have had on global health. No other technique has had such a significant impact on population growth and mortality reduction as safe water [5]. One of the most significant scientific developments of the twenty-first century has been the creation of safe and effective vaccinations against diseases that significantly increase morbidity and mortality. Vaccination is unquestionably one of the public health measures that have improved health outcomes worldwide, along with sanitation and good drinking water. An estimated 6 million deaths from vaccine-preventable diseases have been avoided each year as a result of vaccinations [6].

By 2055, the earth's population is estimated to reach almost 10 billion, a feat that in part is due to effective vaccines that prevent disease and prolong life expectancy across all continents. There is still much to be done to ensure the financing, provision, distribution, and administration of vaccines to all populations, in particular those which are difficult to reach, including those sceptical about their protective value and those living in civil disruption. Agencies including the World Health Organization (WHO), United Nations Children's Fund (UNICEF), Gavi, the Vaccine Alliance, The Bill & Melinda Gates Foundation, and the Coalition for Epidemic Preparedness Initiative (CEPI), with their multiple funding streams, have been instrumental in expanding vaccine benefits to all. The importance of these organizations in global co-operation and participation was essential in the setting of the 2019 global pandemic of SARS-CoV-2, in light of the health and economic impact of COVID-19 on societies in high-, middle- and low-income countries.

BRIEF HISTORY OF VACCINE DEVELOPMENT

Human usage of preparations to prevent certain infections has been reported since 1500 AD, beginning in China where smallpox was prevented by variolation, which is the transfer of material from scabs into the skin. In the United Kingdom, Edward Jenner noted in 1796 that milkmaids who had previously contracted cowpox naturally were immune to smallpox [7, 8]. He discovered that vulnerable hosts might become immune to smallpox by receiving little doses of pus from cowpox lesions, which most likely included a vaccinia-related virus. In 1798, a smallpox vaccination was created. It took nearly a century of research to reach the next stage of scientific advancements, which involved manipulating infectious agents to extract appropriate vaccination antigens. At the turn of the 20th century, vaccinations against live-attenuated rabies, inactivated anthrax, and chicken cholera were made possible by Louis Pasteur's work with attenuation by heat or oxygen [9]. Alternative methods of attenuation involving serial passage of *Mycobacterium bovis* led to the live Bacille Calmette-Guerin (BCG) vaccine, still in use today for the prevention of tuberculosis. The creation of yellow fever vaccinations, which are produced in the embryonic tissues of chickens, also took advantage of serial passage [10, 11]. As techniques for treating and killing bacteria with heat or chemicals were developed, whole-cell bacterial vaccines were created, leading to the development of whole-cell typhoid, cholera, and pertussis vaccinations by the end of the 19th century. The diphtheria and tetanus toxoid vaccines were created in 1923 thanks to techniques developed by Alexander Glenny and Barbara Hopkins to use formaldehyde to inactivate bacterial toxins [12]. Advances in virus culture *in vitro* allowed viral pathogens to be studied in greater detail and attenuation methods due to cultivation in artificial conditions led to the live oral polio, measles, rubella, mumps, and varicella virus vaccines. Vaccines against meningococci and later pneumococci were created at the Walter Reed Army Institute of Research in the 1960s utilizing capsular polysaccharides, which are encapsulated organisms [13, 14]. Polyvalent vaccinations were created to provide protection against many serotype variants of polysaccharide capsules. These vaccines were then conjugated to carrier proteins to increase their effectiveness, especially in babies, by enlisting T-cells that help to induce memory B-cells [15]. With the exception of toxoid vaccinations, protein-only vaccines were uncommon. However, the acellular pertussis vaccine, which contains five protein antigens, was created to lessen the side effects of the whole-cell vaccine [16]. Molecular biology underwent a revolution at the close of the 20th century, and discoveries in immunology and microbiology contributed to a better knowledge of pathogen epitopes and host reactions to vaccination. The development of vaccinations against RNA viruses with many epitope variants has been made possible by advances in molecular genetics and genome sequencing. Examples of these vaccines are the live and inactivated influenza and live rotavirus vaccines [17]. The human papillomavirus (HPV) vaccine has improved immunogenicity because the L1 antigen of each virus in the vaccination forms virus-like particles; DNA manipulation and excision made surface antigen for hepatitis B viral vectors possible [18]. In-depth investigation of meningococcal antigens has been made possible by bacterial genome sequencing, which has helped to uncover putative proteins for meningococcal B vaccinations [19]. 2020 saw the testing of vaccine research when SARS-CoV-2, a novel coronavirus, surfaced from China and caused a devastating acute respiratory infection that spread throughout the world. Almost no country survived the pandemic, and 5,697,334 cases had been identified within 5 months of the virus's discovery on January 7, 2020, and person-to-person transmission. Orders of magnitude were probably not measured in this time frame [20, 21]. Pre-clinical research on 73 vaccine candidates was underway by April 8, 2020, thanks to prior advancements in the field of vaccination. By May 28, 2020, one of them was in Phase 2/3 trials and the other six were in Phase 1 or 1/2 trials. This response's speed showed that it was possible to make use of already-available technology, such as adjuvants, recombinant vector vaccines, DNA and RNA vaccine platforms, and vaccinations [22]. Given the urgency of global public health, the regulation, production, and distribution of these vaccines will need to move quickly—from years to months. These vaccines' effectiveness and potential effects on health have not yet been determined, but if they prove to be beneficial, immunizations should be made accessible to all SARS-CoV-2-affected regions of the world. In the global context of national social and economic lockdown and massive government borrowing, financing this endeavour will prove difficult. However, the provision's numerous benefits to society—including the need for healthy citizens to rebuild economies in the decades following COVID-19—will serve as justification.

Without discussing the public health initiative that resulted in the vaccinations becoming routinely administered to children worldwide, the history of vaccination would be incomplete. WHO established the Expanded Program of Immunization (EPI) in 1974 with the goal of vaccinating every child on a regular basis by 1990 [23]. In 1977, global regulations for immunization against diphtheria, pertussis, tetanus, measles, polio, and tuberculosis were established. In many places, the EPI covers pneumococcal, hepatitis B, and Hib vaccinations. As of 2017, 85% of children worldwide (12–23 months of age) had received vaccinations against measles, tetanus, diphtheria, and pertussis [24].

HEALTH BENEFITS OF VACCINATION

- Reduction in Infectious Diseases Morbidity and Mortality
- Eradication of Infectious Diseases
- Herd Immunity
- Reduction in Secondary Infections That Complicate Vaccine-Preventable Diseases
- Prevention of Cancer
- Preventing Antibiotic Resistance

ECONOMIC BENEFITS

- Cost saving
- Productivity Gains
- Minimizing the impact on family
- Cost effective preparedness for outbreaks
- Establishing programs for vaccine development

SOCIAL BENEFITS

- Equity of healthcare
- Strengthening health and social care infrastructure
- Impact of life expectancy and opportunity
- Empowerment of women [25]

OVERVIEW OF THE PATENT SYSTEM FOR PHARMACEUTICAL

Intellectual property law governs intellectual property rights (IPR). Industrial property rights and copyrights are the two categories of intellectual property rights. Patents, trademarks, designs, integrated circuits, geographic indications, plant variety protection, trade secrets, traditional knowledge, and biodiversity are all examples of industrial property rights. Author rights, artistic rights, film rights, broadcasting rights, performers rights, and so on are all included in copyrights. Trade secret protection (such as data exclusivity) does not exist in India.

TERM OF INTELLECTUAL PROPERTY RIGHTS

For industrial property rights, a patent has a 20-year duration from the date of first filing; for other properties, the duration varies between 10 and 15 years, with the possibility of extension for specific properties. The lifespan of the author plus an additional 60 years is the protection period for copyrights, particularly those pertaining to authors. In a number of other instances, particularly with regard to copyright in works produced by governments, public enterprises, international organizations, *etc.*, the duration is 60 years [26].

OBJECTIVE AND ROLE OF INTERNATIONAL AND NATIONAL GOVERNING BODIES

The World Trade Organization (WTO) replaced the General Agreement on Tariffs and Trade (GATT) and added protection for individual rights, such as intellectual property rights. The major goal was to oversee and resolve international conflicts while maintaining a system of stable and predictable international trade. With the establishment of the World Trade Organization (WTO), Trade-Related Components of Intellectual Property Rights (TRIPS) were created. India became a signatory in 1995, upgrading The Patents Act of 1970 infrastructure within the allotted transition period.

The World Intellectual Property Organization (WIPO) is an international organization that fosters global cooperation in the development, sharing, utilization, and protection of intellectual works for the benefit of humankind's collective economic, social, and cultural advancement. The Department of Commerce, Pharmaceutical, and Industrial Policy and Promotion (DIPP) of India are vital to the country's application of intellectual property rights, particularly those pertaining to patents. The Indian Patent Office (IPO) in Mumbai, Kolkata, Chennai, and New Delhi is responsible for receiving and approving patent applications.

WHAT IS A PATENT?

A patent is a document issued by the government to the inventor granting him exclusive rights to sell, make, use, and import the invention for a stipulated period upon disclosure of the invention.

CRITERIA FOR PATENTABILITY

If an innovation is new, non-obvious, practical (with an industrial application), and enabled, it is considered patentable. The invention's subject matter must satisfy every requirement for patentability.

Term of Patent: A term of a patent is 20 years from the date of filing.

TYPES OF PATENT APPLICATIONS

Applications for patents are categorized as divisional, complete, additional, and provisional. An inventor may include a brief, incomplete description of their invention in a provisional application. In the event that the innovation is complete, the inventor must include all necessary details. When an inventor pursues further development of an already-patented invention, they file for an additional patent. When a patent contains multiple inventions, a divisional application is filed. It is required that the inventions be filed *via* the official application forms.

INVENTIONS NOT PATENTABLE

Topics pertaining to nature law, frivolousness, economic exploitation, transgressions of public morals or order, grave harm to human, animal, or plant life, health, or the environment, abstract theory, scientific discovery, new form of known substance discovered, admixture, simple arrangement, re-arrangement, or duplication of known devices, agricultural method, the procedure for medical, surgical, curative, prophylactic, or treatment of humans or animals, the entire plant, entire animal, computer program, literary, dramatic, musical, artistic, cinematography, television productions, simple plans, mental processes, game mechanics, information displays, integrated circuit topography, and conventional wisdom pertaining to atomic energy are not patentable.

CONTENT OF A PATENT

A patent document contains a title, bibliography, abstract, prior art, summary, description of the invention with best mode, tables, figures, and claims comprising independent and dependent claims. It is necessary to understand that scientists, and academicians involved in research are used to drafting research articles for journal publications and it is necessary to understand that persons skilled in the research activity can draft their own provisional/complete specifications.

PROCEDURE FOR FILING A PATENT APPLICATION

The inventor files a preliminary specification in which he describes the results of his extraordinary research activities. Either a provisional specification or a complete specification can be submitted immediately. Put differently, a provisional application summarizes the inventor's research, whereas a complete specification provides all the information needed to fully describe the invention and obtain a patent. The specification must be submitted with the necessary forms. Many industries have the option to apply directly to a nation of interest and then choose *via* PCT.

If biological resources are used in the invention, the National Biodiversity Authority (NBA) license details must be submitted together with the innovation's source information and geographic origin. In case the invention involves biological material that cannot be adequately described or made available to the public, the application must be fulfilled by depositing the material to an International Depository Authority (IDA) within a designated timeframe. This will ensure that the specification mentions the reference numbers of the deposits made.

Applications for patents through PCT and applications for patents granted within India are both accepted by the Indian Patent Office. The controller general of patents must grant prior authorization to the patentee in cases where an application must be filed directly in a foreign patent office.

PROCEDURE INVOLVED AT THE PATENT OFFICE

Depending on a number of factors, as per Fig. (**1**), the grant application submission process can require simple or extremely complex conditions. A well-planned application could result in a patent being awarded as soon as feasible, depending on the state of technology at the time and the specific therapeutic product in question. In relation to the previous work, patent mapping aids in locating the white space that can result in the patentability of topics of current interest. The process of creating bulk drug development and identifying pharmaceuticals that are in the pipeline to be released as generics is aided by patent mapping [27].

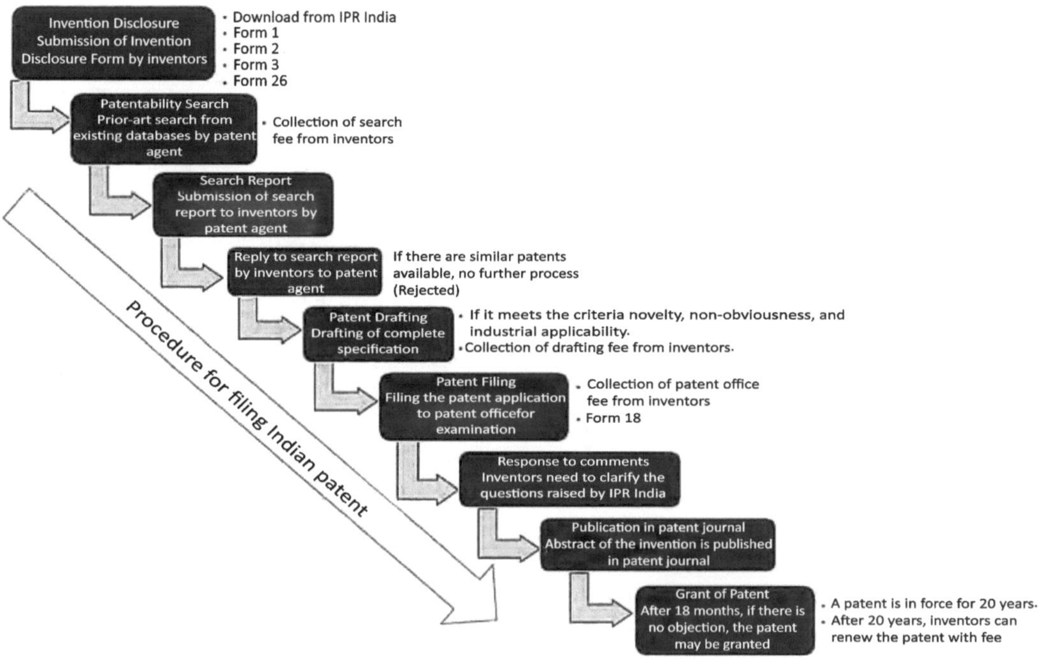

Fig. (1). Indian patent filing [28].

The procedure for filing an Indian patent begins with the Invention Disclosure phase, where inventors submit the Invention Disclosure Form by downloading it from IPR India and filling out Forms 1, 2, 3, and 26. Following this, a Patentability Search is conducted by a patent agent to check for prior art in existing databases, and the search fee is collected from the inventors. Once the search is completed, a Search Report is prepared and submitted to the inventors by the patent agent. The inventors then reply to the search report and provide clarifications to the patent agent. If the search reveals similar patents, the process stops, and the application is rejected. However, if the invention meets the criteria of novelty, non-obviousness, and industrial applicability, the process proceeds, and the drafting fee is collected.

The next step is Patent Drafting, where the complete specification is drafted. This is followed by Patent Filing, in which the patent application is filed at the patent office for examination. At this stage, the patent office fee is collected from the inventors, and Form 18 is submitted.

During the examination process, inventors may need to provide responses to comments or questions raised by IPR India. If no significant objections remain, the Publication in the Patent Journal occurs, where an abstract of the invention is published. After 18 months, if there are no objections, the patent may be granted.

A granted patent is in force for 20 years, after which inventors can renew it by paying a renewal fee as mentioned in Fig. (**1**) [28].

HISTORIC CONTEXT

The Role of Patents in Encouraging Innovations

Over the past 20 years, the patent system has undergone significant modifications, the majority of which have strengthened and expanded the protection of inventions. This evolution has been largely driven by the patent community, which includes courts, attorneys, patent authorities, and members of intellectual property business associations [29]. According to what we now know about the economics of patents, are these modifications economically justified? The answer is nuanced and contingent upon determining if the economic literature offers insightful inferences regarding what may be deemed an ideal patent regime. There is still a long way to go, and this study aims at enhancing the communication between economists and the patent community, as economists have only just begun to participate in policy discussions around patents and exchange ideas in public forums [30].

A long-standing debate on patent economics has focused on whether or not innovation benefits from the existence of a patent system. Numerous studies have looked into this issue, and some findings have come out of them. First, there is no question that upgrading or establishing a patent system (extending the patent term, expanding the permissible breadth or subject matter coverage, bolstering enforcement) leads to a rise in patenting as well as the use of patents as a weapon of company strategy.

Secondly, it is not as evident that these modifications lead to a rise in innovative endeavours, but they might divert such endeavors toward patentable items and away from those that can be kept under wraps within the company [31]. A third conclusion drawn from the empirical literature is that, in the event that patents have a positive impact on innovation, it is most likely to be concentrated in the biotechnology, pharmaceutical, and medical instrument sectors, as well as possibly specialty chemicals. This conclusion is based primarily on survey data from a number of nations, which indicates rather conclusively that patents are not among the important ways to appropriately return to innovation, with the exception of such industries [32, 33].

A reasonable explanation for this result could be that chemicals naturally lend themselves to clear codification because of the commonly used system of notation for chemical compounds. This is obviously oversimplified because many patents in these fields do not solely rely on chemical formulas, but generally speaking, this fact does make such patents easier to enforce and clearer about their boundaries [34].

Fourth, the strength of a domestic patent system and domestic innovation activity may have a U-shaped relationship, where domestic innovation first declines as patent rights increase and then rises again for developed economies with high patent rights index levels.

Fifth and lastly, the existence and power of the patent system influence how the industry is organized by facilitating knowledge commerce, which encourages the entry of new businesses that solely own intangible assets and the vertical disintegration of knowledge-based sectors [35]. The claim is that the patent system allows activities that previously had to be kept inside the company due to secrecy and contracting issues to move out into separate entities by establishing a strong property right for the intangible asset. Limited research in this area in the chemical and semiconductor industries supports this conclusion.

Past Instances of Patent Disputes in the Pharmaceutical Industry

Legal disagreements pertaining to patent ownership, validity, and infringement between pharmaceutical corporations are known as patent disputes in the industry. Since they grant the patent holder a legal monopoly over the manufacture, marketing, and distribution of the patented product, patents are essential to the business. A patent may be contested for a number of reasons, including patent validity, patent breadth, and patent infringement by other businesses.

In the pharmaceutical industry, patent disputes are not uncommon. Typically, cases involving patent infringement, patent invalidation, and trademark and trade secret violations are included in these disputes. The Patents Act, of 1970 governs the granting, revocation, and application procedure for patents in India. Guidelines for the kinds of inventions that qualify for patent protection are also provided under the Act.

Since most drugs and medical devices have an active pharmaceutical ingredient that can be protected by a patent, patents are arguably the most important kind of intellectual property accessible to the pharmaceutical and medical device industries. As a result, knowing the Indian patent system is essential to conducting business there [36].

Patent disputes in the pharmaceutical sector can arise for various reasons, reflecting the complex and competitive nature of the industry. Here are some common reasons for patent disputes in the pharmaceutical sector:

Patent Infringement Allegations

- **Generic Competition:** Generic drug manufacturers may challenge the patents held by pharmaceutical companies, claiming that their generic version of a drug does not infringe on the existing patents.
- **Biosimilar Competition:** Similar to generic drugs, biosimilar manufacturers may challenge the patents of biologic drugs, arguing that their products are not infringing or that the patents are invalid.

Patent Validity Challenges

- **Invalidity Claims:** Companies may dispute the validity of a competitor's patent, arguing that the patent is not novel, non-obvious, or lacks sufficient disclosure. This can lead to court cases where the validity of the patent is assessed.

Market Exclusivity

- **Extension Challenges:** Pharmaceutical companies may file for extensions to their existing patents or for additional exclusivity based on new uses or formulations of existing drugs. Competitors may challenge these extensions, questioning their legitimacy.

Regulatory Approval and Market Entry

- **Paragraph IV Challenges:** In the United States, generic manufacturers often file a Paragraph IV certification with the FDA, challenging the patents of the brand-name drug they seek to copy. This can trigger a legal process where the brand-name company can sue for patent infringement.

Technology Transfer and Licensing Disputes

- **Contractual Disputes:** Disagreements may arise between companies involved in technology transfer or licensing agreements related to pharmaceutical patents. This can include disputes over royalty payments, sublicensing rights, and other terms of the agreement [37].

Evergreening and Secondary Patents

- **Evergreening Tactics:** Pharmaceutical companies may attempt to extend their market exclusivity by obtaining additional patents on secondary aspects of a drug, such as new formulations, dosages, or methods of use. Competitors may challenge these secondary patents.

Global Competition

- **International Patent Conflicts:** Pharmaceutical companies operating globally may face patent disputes in multiple jurisdictions. Differences in patent laws and regulations across countries can lead to varying outcomes in legal battles.

Counterclaims and Defensive Litigation

- **Defensive Strategies:** Companies facing the threat of patent infringement lawsuits may file counterclaims, asserting their own patents or challenging the validity of the patents held by the suing party. This can lead to complex legal battles with multiple claims and counterclaims.

Anticompetitive Practices

- **Antitrust Issues:** Allegations of anticompetitive behaviour, such as sham litigation or misuse of the patent system to stifle competition, can lead to legal challenges [38].

Patent disputes in the pharmaceutical sector often involve a combination of legal, scientific, and regulatory considerations. The resolution of these disputes can impact market competition, patient access to medications, and the overall dynamics of the pharmaceutical industry.

Following are some famous past instances of patent disputes in the pharma sector:

- **AbbVie *vs.* Amgen (Humira):** Humira, a blockbuster drug for rheumatoid arthritis, faced patent challenges. Amgen, along with other companies, sought to produce biosimilar versions of Humira, leading to legal battles over patent infringement.
- **Gilead Sciences *vs.* Merck (Hepatitis C drugs):** Gilead's hepatitis C drugs, such as Sovaldi and Harvoni, faced legal challenges from Merck. The dispute involved claims of patent infringement related to the development of direct-acting antiviral drugs for treating hepatitis C.
- **Novartis *vs.* Roche (Rituxan):** Novartis and Roche engaged in a patent dispute over Rituxan, a drug used for treating certain types of cancer and autoimmune diseases. The companies contested the validity of each other's patents related to the drug.
- **Bristol-Myers Squibb *vs.* AstraZeneca (Onglyza):** AstraZeneca and Bristol-Myers Squibb were involved in a patent dispute over Onglyza, a type 2 diabetes medication. The companies filed lawsuits accusing each other of patent infringement.
- **Bayer *vs.* Generic Manufacturers (Nexavar):** Bayer faced challenges from generic drug manufacturers seeking to produce generic versions of Nexavar, a

cancer medication. The legal disputes revolved around patent validity and infringement.

- **Eli Lilly *vs.* Teva (Cialis):** Eli Lilly defended its patent for Cialis, a popular erectile dysfunction drug, against generic competition from Teva. The legal battle involved issues of patent infringement and validity.
- **Pfizer *vs.* Teva (Viagra):** Pfizer, the manufacturer of Viagra, has been involved in patent disputes with generic drug manufacturers, including Teva, over attempts to produce generic versions of the erectile dysfunction medication [39].

Emergence of Global Health Crisis and Needs for Vaccines

Finding a vaccine to stop the extremely contagious disease from spreading further has been one of the world's biggest, if not the most critical, problems since the COVID-19 epidemic was announced in late 2019. While the race to produce a COVID-19 vaccine got underway shortly after, numerous successful and effective efforts were made to do so, and the vaccine's progress was being made every day all over the world, a complicated new set of problems surrounding the COVID-19 vaccines also surfaced. These included preserving fair access to vaccinations, preventing vaccination nationalism, and boosting public faith in vaccines to reduce vaccine reluctance.

A number of national and international efforts were proposed and put into action to try and alleviate some of these issues. One of the most powerful global initiatives put forth by South Africa and India is known as the TRIPS Waiver. It is presently being discussed at the World Trade Organization (WTO) to reduce access issues by easing vaccine patent restrictions, albeit slowly since late 2020. Big Pharma is actively working through the strong nations of the Global North to thwart this endeavour [40].

Another potential program, COVAX, sought to provide unmatched equitable access to the vaccine; however, when the Global North circumvented COVAX and entered into bilateral arrangements with Big Pharma, it too failed. The Pharma-Industrial Complex, a phenomenon where a sizable pharmaceutical business has amassed significant economic and political power, sufficient to influence public policy about life-saving pharmaceuticals, is the reason behind the failure of both of the aforementioned projects. The pharma-industrial complex has been facilitated by the current patent legislation, which is predicated on an illusory patent agreement. This is not surprising, but it is a substantial contributing element.

ROLE OF TECHNOLOGY TRANSFER IN COVID 19

The COVID-19 pandemic has led to an increased focus on the function of firm-t--firm knowledge transfer, as multinational pharmaceutical companies looked to establish global production networks in order to increase the availability of vaccinations. Although the amount of international vaccine technology transfer has received a lot of attention, little is known about how partnerships were formed and function in real-world scenarios. Gaining insight into the obstacles these kinds of projects encounter and how they could be solved is vital. This essay describes the collaboration between Bio-Manguinhos, a public laboratory connected to Brazil's Ministry of Health, and AstraZeneca, a multinational pharmaceutical company based in Sweden and Britain that developed vaccines and engaged in the most technology transfer and global manufacturing network building.

One noteworthy aspect of the COVID-19 pandemic is that vaccinations, which were made accessible very early in the health crisis, have been a central topic of discussion in the wake of innovation initiatives and subsequent talks about technology transfer. Unlike most therapeutics, vaccines are more difficult for non-originators to independently produce because they are biological products rather than synthetic chemical ones that are more difficult to replicate at scale. Additionally, the absence of regulatory pathways for the approval of "generic" vaccines makes independent production of vaccines more challenging.

Indeed, non-originator pharmaceutical companies could create knockoff versions of vaccines if they put in enough work, but only at high costs and on schedules that could make them ineffective during a pandemic. The connection between intellectual property and worldwide production is significantly impacted by these variations. Where production depends on the active engagement of the originator, to help master production methods and satisfy regulatory criteria, the lack or removal of IP is unlikely to expand global supply. Additive technology transfer from the original creator to collaborators is required, not subtractive technology transfer, such as IP removal. In contrast, then, to what was witnessed with AIDS, where generic producers (public and private) could make abundant and affordable treatments available, efforts to expand the global supply of vaccines during the COVID-19 pandemic have depended on originator firms transferring technology and know-how to manufacturing partners [41].

THE CURRENT DEBATE

Arguments in Favour of Patent Protection

Patent protection is a legal mechanism that provides inventors with exclusive rights to their inventions for a limited period of time. The following are some arguments in favour of patent protection:

Encouraging Research and Development

Patent protection plays a crucial role in the field of research and development (R&D) by providing inventors and innovators with exclusive rights to their inventions. This protection encourages investment in R&D, fosters innovation, and helps bring new technologies and products to the market.

Incentive for Innovation

Patent protection serves as a reward for inventors, offering exclusive rights to their inventions for a limited period. This incentive encourages researchers and companies to invest time and resources in developing new and innovative technologies.

Securing Funding for R&D

Patents can be valuable assets that enhance the ability of inventors to attract funding for their R&D projects. Investors are more likely to support projects with the potential for exclusive rights and market advantage.

Technology Transfer and Collaboration

Patents facilitate the transfer of technology by providing a clear framework for licensing and collaboration. Universities and research institutions can use patents to transfer knowledge to industry partners, promoting the commercialization of inventions.

Protection of R&D Investments

Patents protect R&D investments by granting inventors the exclusive right to exploit their inventions. This exclusivity allows companies to recoup their investments and gain a competitive advantage in the marketplace.

Encouraging Disclosure of Knowledge

The patent system encourages the disclosure of knowledge by requiring inventors to provide detailed information about their inventions in exchange for protection.

This disclosure contributes to the pool of public knowledge and promotes further innovation [42].

Providing Incentives for Innovation

Providing incentives for invention is the main goal of patent grants. The incentive is the commercialization of the innovation in order to prevent the inventor from keeping it a trade secret and to allow him to profit from it, accounting for the significant expenses invested. This encourages the innovator to invest money in a new line of business or develop novel manufacturing techniques, and it also makes it more difficult for rivals to steal the ideas and produce goods that perform identically. Thus, the foundation of the notion of patent protection is the idea of an "incentive for innovation."

Furthermore, since discoveries that comply with forbidden subject matter are not patentable, the tremendous significance of technological advancement in the public interest cannot be overstated.

Because of the "ever greening of patents" phenomena, which has been observed in the fields of medical sciences, drug development, and life-saving medications, patents encourage innovation but are also scrutinized in these areas. Generally speaking, ever greening refers to gaining additional patents covering various inventive elements of a core drug invention, so extending the monopoly beyond the life of the original patent. The many patents covering different creative aspects may occasionally result in an extension of the patent period. In an effort to prevent ever greening, Section 3(d) of the Indian Patents Act states that changes made to medications that are already well-known cannot be copyrighted unless such changes considerably increase the treatments' efficacy. Put another way, unless a product demonstrates increased efficacy, incremental innovations based on a single substrate are not eligible for patent protection.

After having its patent for its treatment "Glivec" (beta crystalline polymorph of imatinib mesylate), which treats chronic myeloid leukemia, refused, Novartis A. G. filed a challenge to the constitutional validity of S. 3 (d) before the Madras High Court, claiming that it violates TRIPs. It was determined that it did not satisfy the standards of Patent Act of 1970, Section 3 (d), as revised by Patent (Amendment) Act of 2005. Although Novartis did not create Glivec until 1995, the company did file a new patent for Imatinib mesylate, the active ingredient in Glivec, in its crystalline form.

It is difficult to overstate the significance of this case, but Novartis AG, a major player in the Swiss pharmaceutical industry, argues that incremental innovation fosters invention and that obstacles to an invention's patentability beyond the requirements of basic patentability will deter inventors. This argument is sure to stir up controversy in the Indian intellectual property protection space [43].

Protecting Intellectual Property Rights

Intellectual Property Rights (IPR) can be protected through various means, and one of the most common ways is by obtaining a patent. A patent is a legal document granted by a government that gives the patent holder exclusive rights to their invention for a specified period, generally 20 years from the filing date.

A patent grants the inventor exclusive rights to make, use, sell, and import the patented invention. This exclusivity provides a competitive advantage and allows the inventor to control the use of their invention in the market. If someone else tries to make, use, sell, or import the patented invention without the patent holder's permission, the patent holder has the legal right to take legal action against them. This can include seeking injunctions to stop the infringing activities and claiming damages. The existence of a patent serves as a deterrent to potential infringers, as they are aware of the legal consequences associated with unauthorized use of the patented invention. This can help protect the inventor's market share and investment in research and development. Patent holders have the option to license their patented technology to others. Through licensing agreements, the patent holder can allow others to use the invention in exchange for licensing fees or royalties. This can be a source of revenue for the patent holder. Patents can facilitate the commercialization of inventions. Knowing that an invention is protected by a patent can make it more attractive to investors, partners, and collaborators, encouraging the development and marketing of the invention. In exchange for the exclusive rights granted by a patent, the inventor is required to disclose the details of the invention in the patent application. This information becomes part of the public domain, contributing to the body of knowledge and promoting further innovation.

It is important to note that patents are specific to inventions and are granted for a limited period. Once the patent expires, the invention enters the public domain, allowing others to use it freely. Additionally, obtaining a patent requires meeting certain criteria, including novelty, non-obviousness, and industrial applicability. Consulting with a patent attorney or agent is advisable for a comprehensive understanding of the patenting process and to ensure that the invention meets the necessary requirements [44].

ARGUMENTS AGAINST PATENT PROTECTION

Access to Medicine in Low-income Countries

Arguments against strong patent protection, especially in the context of access to medicines in low-income countries, often revolve around concerns related to public health, affordability, and the ethical imperative of ensuring access to essential medications. Here are several points often raised by critics:

Affordability and Accessibility

High Drug Prices: Patent protection grants pharmaceutical companies a monopoly on the production of a specific drug, allowing them to set high prices. This can make essential medicines unaffordable for individuals and healthcare systems in low income countries. Barriers to Generic.

Competition: Patents create barriers to the entry of generic versions of medicines, which are typically more affordable. This lack of competition can perpetuate high prices and limit access to life-saving treatments.

Public Health Impact

Disease Burden: In low-income countries, there is often a higher burden of diseases such as HIV/AIDS, malaria, and tuberculosis. Strict patent protection can impede the availability of affordable drugs needed to address these public health challenges.

Pandemic Response: During global health crises, like a pandemic, quick and affordable access to medicines becomes crucial. Critics argue that patent protection may hinder timely access to treatments and vaccines in times of urgent need.

Intellectual Property Barriers

Knowledge Monopoly: Critics argue that patents create a knowledge monopoly, limiting the dissemination of scientific knowledge and hindering further research and development by other scientists and institutions.

Obstacles to Innovation: Some argue that the current patent system can stifle innovation by discouraging collaboration and knowledge-sharing among researchers and institutions, as they may be incentivized to protect their intellectual property rather than advancing scientific progress.

Compulsory Licensing and Flexibilities

Flexibilities under TRIPS: While the Trade-Related Aspects of Intellectual Property Rights (TRIPS) agreement allows for certain flexibilities to address public health concerns, critics argue that these provisions are not always effectively utilized, and more needs to be done to enable countries to make use of compulsory licensing.

Legal Challenges: Countries that attempt to use compulsory licensing or other flexibilities may face legal challenges from pharmaceutical companies, creating a deterrent for governments seeking to improve access to medicines.

Ethical Considerations

Right to Health: Access to healthcare, including essential medicines, is considered a fundamental human right. Critics argue that the current patent system may violate this right, particularly when it leads to preventable suffering and loss of life due to lack of access to affordable medications.

Social Justice: There are concerns about the ethical implications of a system that allows pharmaceutical companies to prioritize profits over public health, especially when it comes to diseases that predominantly affect marginalized and vulnerable populations [45].

ACCELERATING VACCINE DISTRIBUTION DURING PANDEMIC

Low-income nations should take into account the negative features implied by the waiver of intellectual property protections for COVID-19 vaccines.

First, future research should carefully assess the resources that are materially required to make vaccinations. The need for new vaccines may rise in the years to come, even though the current vaccinations are not based on the multiplication of the SARS-CoV2 live virus strain but rather on synthetic mRNA or genetic recombinant adenovirus vectors. Unfortunately, only a small number of pharmaceutical businesses now control the tools and technologies needed for this purpose. Furthermore, not every nation would have pharmaceutical firms located there that could ensure sufficient safety precautions for both the workers who work directly in the labs and the general public in the neighbourhoods that surround them.

It is obvious that manipulating viral strains poses a risk to human safety (*e.g.*, inadvertent release of pandemic viruses could set off future worldwide outbreaks). As a result, strict safety standards for the biological risk involved are necessary.

Second, there is a chance that requirements for health surveillance are not met globally right now. It ought to cover the identification, evaluation, comprehension, and mitigation of unfavourable vaccination reactions. This is crucial because the first COVID-19 vaccination wave in the West has brought to light the potential for a few uncommon side effects that were not previously documented during phases 1, 2, and 3 of clinical research. One such effect is vaccine-induced thrombocytopenia/thrombosis, which is linked to the use of viral vector vaccines. Regretfully, it is possible that national health surveillance protocols are not standardized, and local laboratory and clinical capacities will determine how well they work.

Notably, underdeveloped health systems in low-income nations are probably going to lack the infrastructure, governance, human resources, and trained personnel necessary to promptly avert potential negative outcomes.

Third, possible issues relate to the finished product (vaccine), which will eventually be created in these locations (South America or Africa, for example). Therefore, production under non-GMP (good manufacturing practices) and with inadequate biological quality control may be a sign of unfavourable reactions.

Fourth, the deregulation of vaccinations may deter pharmaceutical companies from making future investments in the development of new vaccines or their upgrades. As the epidemic is still in its early stages, further vaccinations will probably be required in the upcoming years.

Furthermore, some pharmaceutical corporations may choose to use their production lines for vaccinations at the expense of the development and production of experimental molecules due to the success of vaccine sales and the miscalculation of the value of various medicinal therapies.

In general, any kind of vaccine may be linked to any of these issues. Furthermore, as pandemics strike and vaccine manufacture becomes more accessible, these issues may become more severe [46].

MORAL AND ETHICAL CONSIDERATIONS

Protecting and defending IP rights frequently presents difficult moral conundrums. This article explores the moral issues surrounding intellectual property conflicts, highlighting the necessity of striking a balance between rights and obligations.

Beyond simple legal arguments, intellectual property disputes are rife with profound ethical issues. It takes a thorough grasp of each party's rights and obligations to navigate these situations. Here, we look at a few of the most prevalent moral dilemmas that arise in Intellectual Property (IP) disputes.

Copyright violations and plagiarism rank among the most important moral conundrums involving intellectual property. The rights of the creators are violated and their creative efforts are compromised when people or organizations exploit another person's work without giving due credit or authorization. Given how simple it is to copy, spread, and repurpose content in the digital era, this problem is especially acute.

Here, it is evident what the moral need is: authors must receive credit for their work and, if required, financial compensation. Intellectual property is respected, and those who consume and distribute content uphold these values.

Because they provide creators the only right to their inventions, patents encourage innovation. But when these patents are obtained not for invention but rather for legal exploitation, an ethical conundrum arises. Let the patent trolls begin. These organizations gather patents, frequently of questionable quality, in order to pursue businesses for infringement. Such acts have the potential to result in drawn-out and expensive legal disputes, taking funds away from worthwhile projects. The misuse of patent rights is a legitimate ethical concern raised by this conduct. It is the ethical duty of patent holders to make sure that their inventions are truly novel and to use their rights sparingly, emphasizing innovation promotion over limiting rivalry [47].

IP holders have a great deal of control over their works, regardless of whether they are protected by patents, copyrights, or trademarks. But with this authority also comes moral obligations. Intellectual property owners need to use their rights wisely. When IP holders use aggressive litigation strategies to target smaller firms or impede competition, it presents one of the most obvious ethical quandaries. The abuse of intellectual property rights can give rise to justifiable ethical concerns when such activities are taken.

A moral approach to intellectual property ownership is upholding one's rights and encouraging appropriate usage. Mechanisms such as license options and fair use provisions can accomplish this. Intellectual property holders promote ethical innovation and information transmission by granting limited usage rights to others. Intellectual property owners who uphold ethics are aware that the effects of their works can be profound, and they strike a balance between their rights and their dedication to the greater good. Ethics codes and legal frameworks are crucial in determining how people and organizations that deal with intellectual property behave. The legal basis for IP rights protection is provided by both national and international treaties. The parameters that determine rights and obligations are set by these legal systems. They act as the cornerstone around which moral behaviour is constructed. Intellectual property rights are protected and moral behaviour is encouraged in a peaceful atmosphere that is produced by the interaction of legal requirements and ethical concerns. By following these guidelines, people and organizations interested in intellectual property can ethically and clearly negotiate the complicated landscape of rights and obligations [48].

IMPACT ON GLOBAL ACCESS TO VACCINES

High Prices and Limited Access in Developing Countries

The high prices and limited access to vaccines in developing countries pose significant challenges to global health equity. Several factors contribute to this issue like Economic disparities, Global chain supply issues, lack of infrastructure, Global vaccine distribution inequities, vaccine nationalism. The problems of distribution, cost, accessibility, and acceptability at the national and individual levels are among the obstacles to the uptake of the COVID-19 vaccination.

To achieve broad immunity, vaccinations must be developed and distributed, and part of this involves making sure that safe and effective vaccines are made consistently and sent to every nation. There has never before been a need for as many COVID-19 vaccination doses as there is now. It would take about 11 billion COVID-19 doses to fully vaccinate 70% of the world's population. The global supply chains were severely strained as a result of the production turnaround having to operate at full capacity to satisfy the demand, which came as a complete surprise to them due to the epidemic.

It was extremely difficult to develop the COVID-19 vaccine in a short amount of time because it had to be both safe and effective but also reasonably priced. To hasten the development of vaccines, the US established the Operation Warp Speed program. Since high-income nations invested billions of dollars in the development and procurement of vaccines, low-income nations (LICs) were unfairly denied access to these treatments. The World Health Organization (WHO) set a target of vaccinating 70% of the global population by September 2021. However, less than 1% of people in lower-income countries and 10% of people in lower-middle-income countries have received vaccinations against more than 50% of people in high-income countries.

The United Nations (UN) reported on March 28, 2022, that while vaccination distribution has increased globally, inequality has also increased. Just 1% of the 10 billion pills that were given out globally ended up in low-income nations, meaning that about 2.8 billion individuals are still awaiting their first treatment. Not even COVID-19 vaccinations Global Access (COVAX) was able to obtain and distribute vaccinations for nations with lower incomes. AstraZeneca and Serum Institute of India worked together to develop and supply vaccinations for low- and middle-income countries in an effort to partially avoid this. To develop and obtain vaccines, a number of task teams and funds were established, including the African Vaccine Acquisition Task Team of the African Union in Africa and the PM Cares Fund in India.

The most impoverished nations can combat this pandemic with immediate access to funding and vaccines; the World Health Organization and other international organizations, such as the Global Dashboard for Vaccine Equity, can assist these nations in formulating the best plans of action for their people [49].

Role of Intellectual Property Right in Vaccine Distribution

The last year has seen a remarkable advancement in innovation with the quick creation of new COVID-19 vaccinations and treatments. During the following 18 months, billions of doses of vaccines should be produced and given to all people worldwide. However, some governments and health non-governmental organizations (NGOs) contend that granting developing nations speedier access to vaccines would result from suspending Intellectual Property (IP) rights to allow unrestricted vaccine manufacture.

A temporary worldwide waiver of IP rights linked to COVID-19 has been presented to the World Trade Organization (WTO) by India and South Africa. Tedros Adhanom Ghebreyesus, the director of the World Health Organization, offered implicit support this week by announcing that unequal access to Covid vaccinations would result in a "catastrophic moral failure."

Though incorrect, such calls are morally alluring. IP has been essential to the development, production, and dissemination of vaccines at every stage. As of January 2020, our knowledge about COVID-19 was limited. One year later, there are over 1,000 active clinical trials (219 of which are for vaccinations), and three safe and efficacious vaccines have been created and approved for use in a recorded amount of time .Contrary to what some opponents said at the beginning of the pandemic, intellectual property rights have proven essential for the dozens of partnerships and research consortia that have been formed to combat the virus.

Because they are aware that intellectual property is legally protected from misuse, potential competitors are able to cooperate and exchange valuable proprietary knowledge. Robust intellectual property rights were essential for the Pfizer/BioNtech collaboration that resulted in the first vaccination approved in the United States. Others were concerned that intellectual property rights might result in excessively costly Covid vaccinations; Médecins Sans Frontières, a health

NGO, called for "no profiteering or patents." IP was not the main source of support for the development of medications and vaccines during the epidemic. Myths about IP's function impede a comprehensive evaluation of what IP can and cannot accomplish, postponing or obstructing the kind of policy experimentation that promises to provide the world with more precise vaccinations and medications more swiftly, such as open-science drug research [50].

Calls for Waiving Patents Rights During Public Health Emergencies

Following over twenty years of dispute over the cost-effectiveness of treatments for the HIV/AIDS pandemic, especially in developing nations, the COVID-19 outbreak has created a new global health emergency that requires an urgent supply of pharmaceuticals and medical supplies. As a corollary of the right to life, the COVID-19 pandemic has brought attention to the issue of how to strike a balance between patent protection and the requirement to guarantee affordable and accessible medical care in the event of a public health emergency. India and South Africa applied for a temporary waiver of intellectual property protection for pharmaceutical and medical products to the WTO TRIPS Council in October 2020.

The goal of this application is to ease the importation of medicinal products, by poor countries desiring to do so, in response to the pandemic. This waiver application takes into consideration the significant challenges that poor and least developed nations encounter when attempting to import pharmaceutical items for the pandemic under the mandatory licensing system. Because the COVID-19 pandemic has brought "nationalism" back into international trade regulation, it has put "multilateralism" and its institutions under threat.

Since the production of vaccines requires a significant investment of time, money, resources, people, and human brain, patent waivers may deter pharmaceutical companies from developing new vaccines. For the patent owner whose intellectual property is at risk, financial loss is the largest drawback of patent waiver. The basic foundation of the pharmaceutical industry's business model—the patents that safeguard its breakthroughs and grant businesses a monopoly over the sale of drugs based on the technology for a number of years—may be threatened by the proposal to waive the COVID-19 vaccine patents.

Patents with IP waivers give rivals a cheap way to purchase pricey technology. Additionally, companies argue that because building capacity from scratch can take years and ingredients are scarce, IP relief will not speed up the production of vaccines.

The technology know-how must be transferred or the IP rights cannot be waived, which will make it impossible to increase production. Similar skills are needed to prepare biosimilars as they are original vaccinations. Furthermore, setting up the facilities and hiring the necessary personnel would take about a year due to India's tight restrictions around biosimilars. Strict oversight will also be necessary to ensure the biosimilar's safety and effectiveness [51].

ALTERNATIVES TO TRADITIONAL PATENT MODELS

Open-source Approaches to Vaccine Development

Drug discovery using open-source models is a relatively recent technique. They depend on cooperation and information exchanged between various academic institutions, organizations, and companies. All academic levels are welcome to participate in the open conversation and ideas. The Open-Source Drug Discovery (OSDD) initiative of the Council for Scientific and Industrial Research and The Synaptic Leap's Schistosomiasis (TSLS) project demonstrate how this strategy has been successful in the past in fostering the development of novel drugs for tropical diseases. The collaboration initially released findings in 2009 that described the TB genome map. Since then, 7,500 registered researchers from all around the world have started 110 projects. Re-mapping the M. tuberculosis genome and creating eleven models with anti-tuberculosis effectiveness are the organization's two greatest achievements to date.

These strategies are thought to be effective because data is readily available, participants can be flexible, communication is open, and community efforts are used, in which parties from various institutions collaborate rather than compete to achieve related goals. Projects that want to be accessible to all users must have certain criteria, according to Results for Development, a non-profit organization:

- The data must be open access and uncharged.
- A forum for collaboration should be opened.
- The project must follow a set of rules that comply with 'openness'

To be the first to produce a successful therapy, research organizations, and pharmaceutical corporations are naturally choosing to use "closed-door" tactics in addition to joint efforts. Drug targets have been found, and the next step is to fund clinical trials to evaluate the drug's safety and effectiveness. Remdesivir is a prodrug that inhibits viral RNA polymerases and is a nucleotide analog, and Gilead Sciences is funding clinical trials for this drug. In one trial, 68% of patients showed clinical improvement, and the trial's clinical safety profile seemed to be good. It will be necessary to carry out continuous experiments in order to precisely quantify efficacy. Gimsilumab is a monoclonal antibody that targets granulocyte-macrophage colony-stimulating factor (GM-CSF). It is being developed by Roivant Sciences and is now being tested in phase II clinical studies for patients suffering from acute respiratory distress syndrome (ARDS). Based on the gathered data, an appreciable safety and tolerability profile has been shown thus far. Vaccines based on messenger RNA (mRNA) have shown remarkable progress. The development of a vaccine based on messenger RNA designated mRNA-1273, is being undertaken by Moderna. Due to the mRNA's capacity to elicit an anti-SARS-CoV-2 immune response, the vaccine has demonstrated a neutralizing effect in every subject after its initial phase I trials involving 45 healthy individuals. Phase III clinical studies for immunization are presently underway, and the National Institute of Health and the Biomedical Advanced Research and Development Authority have both endorsed it. Using adenovirus vectors, AstraZeneca hopes to boost the production of an immune response to the S proteins, thereby lowering their quantity and blocking the SARS-CoV-2 virus's ability to enter cells [52].

In a phase I/II experiment, vaccinations with the ChAdOx1 virus produced T cell responses that peaked at 14 days, while IgG antibody responses peaked at 28 days, both of which were specific to the S protein. Additionally, Inovio Pharmaceuticals has been employing the deoxyribonucleic acid (DNA) plasmid pGX9501 to target the spike glycoprotein of SARS-CoV-2 in an effort to elicit an immunological response to the protein. Phase I trials for the INO-4800 vaccine have just started, and the results are awaited.

Public-private Partnerships & Collaborations

PPP can be defined as a sustained level of cooperation between certain public and private actors in which they work together to develop infrastructure, goods, and services (including knowledge and information dissemination) and share costs, resources, and risks (financial and/or prestige-related), all of which are used in the process of development and delivery.

PPPs can be profitable for private sector organizations, particularly in LMICs where there is a large untapped market for a pharmaceutical company's product line. Attractive concepts for private sector partners include enhanced brand awareness, greater market penetration, access to new markets, maintaining the current client base, acquiring new customers, and achieving advantageous status for the introduction of new products. The lowering of entry obstacles into the market (such as taxes and tariffs) and the availability of raw LMIC data would encourage the commercial sector to collaborate with the public sector.

For problems relating to pharmaceuticals and vaccines, such as supply chain management, data collection and analysis, quality assurance, and inventory optimization, the public sector can be encouraged to formally establish a PPP. PPPs would help expedite the scaling necessary to produce enough COVID-19 vaccines and medications, and LMICs would be better equipped to fend off pandemics in the future.

The bulk of LMICs lack the capacity needed to conduct domestic vaccine production; patent exemptions would not address this. Developable cold chain infrastructure, data and logistics systems, stable supply chains (with availability to raw materials for vaccine/medication manufacture and illness testing), storage, and administration are all necessary. In order to permanently address the ongoing issues of the present pandemic and any future pandemic, as well as to increase capacity and jobs in the biomedical industries, there is a critical need to train and retain a qualified workforce.

Expanding access to COVID-19 vaccines and treatments in low and middle-income countries (LMICs) is most likely to be achieved by implementing a PPP funded by impact bonds that completely develops, manages, and maintains a vaccine and critical drug supply/cold chain. It is a lofty objective that calls for collaboration between organizations with different goals, yet the existing solutions are ineffective. The patent waiver argument may pay off if TRIPS' mandatory licensing procedure is streamlined or if nations with the ability to produce generics at a cheaper cost are granted waivers. Without utilizing the knowledge and resources of the private sector and gaining access to capital markets, the primary long-term issue facing the majority of LMICs will persist. PPPs are the most effective means by which these nations will be able to build up their supply chains, infrastructure, and technical know-how adequately and permanently to be able to respond to pandemics in a way that is both equitable and necessary for the security of world health [53].

Voluntary Licensing Agreement

A remedy offered by Indian patent laws is both compulsory and voluntary licensing. The problem of patented drug prices that are too expensive gave rise to voluntary licensing or VL. Through the process of reverse engineering, a voluntary license (VL) assists the license holder in creating, manufacturing, and marketing a generic medication that may be purchased by patients at a reasonable cost. Since this license access is achieved by a mutually agreed-upon contractual arrangement, no legal provisions under the Patent Act are applicable.

The agreement between the patent owners and any third party from any country to provide reasonably priced medications in their respective nations, often with discounts, is known as voluntary licensing. A patent holder may provide a third party a license that grants them the ability to manufacture, import, and distribute pharmaceutical products, among other things, either exclusively or nonexclusively. The patent licensee will represent the business as its agent.

A voluntary license's terms could include other clauses like the holder's royalty from the sales distribution, or they could just define a range of prices. At the holder's discretion, voluntary licensing agreements are typically negotiated for strategic purposes rather than as token gestures related to price, and they may not even involve a price decrease [54].

Implementation of Voluntary License Over Compulsory License

The patenting of pharmaceutical products during the TRIPS (Trade-Related Aspects of Intellectual Property Rights) discussions led to an evolution of the agreement between the countries and caused numerous problems for India because patented medications are expensive. The Indian Patent Act was amended in 2005, and Section 84 of the Act established the process for compulsory licensing. This section lays out three requirements, and if any of them are broken, the government will grant the applicant a compulsory license without the third party's consent.

- That the reasonable requirements of the public with respect to the invention have not been satisfied.
- That the patented product is not available at a reasonably affordable price.
- That the patented invention is not worked in the territory of India [55].

Although the TRIPS agreement permitted compulsory licensing, the global legal process makes its implementation exceedingly challenging. The applicant may submit an application for a compulsory license to the Controller General, who will make the final decision, provided that the necessary waiting period of three years has passed. The three-year interval may have a significant impact on patients' life because of the scarcity or excessive cost of medications. In fact, the mere knowledge that laws requiring licenses exist may be sufficient to promote volunteer licenses. The reciprocal contractual agreement between the patent holder and the third party, a generic manufacturer, is the basis of the voluntary licenses. A voluntary license is preferable since it can save many patient deaths and save both parties money and time in court.

RECENT DEVELOPMENT

International Efforts to Address Vaccine Inequity

Given that the number of COVID-19 cases worldwide has increased dramatically, vaccine development has to speed up by the end of 2020. This is because the

WHO COVAX Facility (WCF) has chosen the motto "No one is safe unless everyone is safe," emphasizing the importance of immunization and equitable distribution. This is an important component of the article, especially when it comes to how vaccination equity is used. As a result, the questions and variable analysis in this part are related to vaccine inequities. The list of variables included vaccination cost, distribution, accessibility, affordability, and production capabilities of industrialized and poor nations. There is a GHD issue if these variables are not practical. The effectiveness of GHD's pursuit of healthcare facility equity, especially with regard to vaccination distribution, will determine the outcome.

Why does vaccine disparity still exist in developing nations while there are so many multinational institutions for global health that have existed for decades? Poverty, a lack of resources, the advancement of science and technology, *etc.*, are some clear causes in developing nations. However, multilateralism has failed them badly in addressing and resolving the crisis for some reasons. Given the disillusionment with globalization, the absence of global leadership, the geopolitical tug-of-war between the major powers that can provide global leadership, the lack of support for multilateralism, the inadequacy of current multilateral rules to meet new challenges, the decision-making capacity for vaccine distribution, *etc.*, the multilateral forums have remained reactive and less proactive.

One of the other major factors affecting vaccine equity is intellectual property rights. Apart from this, other factors that contribute to vaccination disparities, especially in developing nations, are manufacturing and purchasing power. The most significant elements causing the acute vaccine shortages include bilateral agreements, export prohibitions, vaccine diplomacy, and production and supply chain bottlenecks. Furthermore, considering the resources, economics, multifaceted and sophisticated scientific advances, *etc.*, the world is unfair and uneven. On the other hand, some contend that there is no way for the rich and the poor in the world to expect vaccination disparities. 2.3–2.6 billion of the 7.8 billion people on the planet reside in LMIC nations. Approximately 333 million people in the upper middle class reside in nations with high middle incomes. On the other hand, high-income countries are home to around 972 million individuals. However, it is ironic that just 20% of the world's wealth, productive potential, *etc.* is accessible to the 80% of the impoverished. "Vaccine equity is the problem of our time," stated Tedros Adhanom Ghebreyesus, the General Director of WHO, in his opening remarks. "We're not doing as well."

To examine the vaccine inequity, one has to delve into the deployment of the COVID19 vaccines. As of 20 July 2021, about 3.73 billion COVID-19 doses had been administered across the globe. The world's population is at 7.8 billion, meaning that about half of the people get only one dose to date.

When we compare developed and underdeveloped countries, the disparity in vaccine access becomes more evident. While the developing world is in dire straits, the European Union (EU), the United Kingdom (68.3%), Spain (63.5%), and Canada (70%) are among the nations and regions with the highest vaccination rates. Preorders for vaccines comprised more than 53% of the total doses, with 16 wealthy nations accounting for just 14% of the global population. Only 1% of COVID-19 cases worldwide are found in nations like Australia, Canada, and Japan, according to one more study. However, the same has reserved about a billion doses of vaccines. Parallel to this, worries have been expressed that wealthy nations will be able to fulfil their vaccination obligations by 2020-2021, while developing nations might not be able to do so until 2023-2024 [56].

Proposals for Patent Waivers and Technology Transfer

The C-TAP program originated with Costa Rica's March 2020 request for a voluntary pool of intellectual property, data, and expertise, among other things. In response, the WHO and the Costa Rican government established C-TAP in May 2020 as a globally coordinated framework for the voluntary exchange of intellectual property, data, and expertise, among other things, in the fight against COVID-19. As indicated above, the WHO's C-TAP plan has not, to now, been backed by industry (and there are also concerns about a lack of support for a similar vehicle, the mRNA Vaccine Transfer Hub facility). In the meanwhile, COVAX is far from meeting the needs of LMICs.

India and South Africa proposed the TRIPS waiver in October 2020 due to concerns about the impact intellectual property rights were having on the world's equitable access to health technologies for COVID-19 and the anticipated inequality of vaccine access that was expected to develop once vaccines were approved for use.

In order to prevent intellectual property rights—such as patents, industrial designs, copyright, and the protection of confidential information—from impeding timely access to reasonably priced medical products, such as vaccines and medications, or from preventing the scaling-up of research, development, manufacturing, and supply of medical products necessary to combat COVID-19, India and South Africa proposed that members of the World Trade Organization (WTO) "work together. "India and South Africa requested a waiver that would "continue until widespread vaccination is in place globally, and the majority of the world's population has developed immunity," citing "exceptional circumstances" to support their proposal. This request has not been answered at subsequent WTO sessions, but it recently gained momentum in May 2021 when the US supported a more limited IP waiver that only applied to COVID-19 vaccinations. Despite being colloquially called a "patent waiver," the India/South Africa proposal, in both its first and updated versions, is actually a comprehensive package that covers vaccinations, treatments, and diagnostics. Presently, 62 WTO members—including South Africa and India—co-sponsor it. The waiver would cover not only the temporary waiver of patents (and, where relevant, copyrights) internationally, but also, and this is vital, the sharing of intellectual property under the purview of "undisclosed information," which includes trade secrets and know-how. The waiver would apply "in relation to prevention, containment or treatment of COVID-19."

Technology transfer (TT) is a cooperative procedure that enables the public and private sectors to access scientific discoveries, knowledge, and intellectual property that has been created by creators like universities and research facilities. Its objective is to create new, beneficial goods and services from scientific discoveries and technologies. Knowledge transfer and technology transfer are closely related. Universities and research facilities must function within a strong innovation ecosystem, which is a network of industry, government, and academic institutions as well as supportive elements (like human capital, sophisticated business and market environments, and technology transfer frameworks) for technology transfer to be successful. Within this kind of ecosystem, the participants pool their resources and knowledge to jointly create innovation for the benefit of economic and regional development.WIPO has created an adaptable platform for technology transfer and innovation support. Concerning the COVID-19 outbreak. The platform includes institutional frameworks and policies, evidence-based analysis, capacity building, and relevant information and knowledge resources.

The platform's components include links to resources about:

- Successful technology licensing;
- IP valuation;
- Database of IP Policies from Universities and Research Institutions containing National IP Policy Models and specific university and R&D institution policies;
- Capacity building programs forTechnology and Innovation Support Centres(TISCs) and stechnology transfer structures [57].

Industry Response and Adaptation

The Indian pharmaceutical business, which ranks thirteenth in terms of value and third in terms of volume, is expanding. Twenty percent of the value of worldwide exports is made up of generics from India. Yet, branded generics control 70–80%

of the pharmaceutical market, making them the dominant player. Innovation has a significant effect on the pharmaceutical sector. Innovation carries a high risk of failure, which might endanger a company's ability to survive. The pharmaceutical industry must stay up to date with innovations that have a substantial influence on millions of lives as well as a company's bottom line. Businesses are leveraging innovation to drive expansion and produce measurable outcomes. In the pharmaceutical sector, managing innovation enables businesses to find new drugs and increase return on investment.

Industry estimates state that the big pharmaceutical corporations are currently paying USD 5 billion for authorized compounds. Conversely, smaller businesses typically spend less. Research and development come at an astronomical cost; a new medicine typically costs USD $1.3 billion. The average period from research to medicine launch is 12–15 years (clinical trials can take up to 8 years).These discoveries result in the development of novel medications that save lives, and they must be safeguarded by Intellectual Property Rights (IPRs). For a 20-year period, patents grant pharmaceutical corporations the only authority to commercialize their products and bar anyone from producing, distributing, or manufacturing them. Pharma firms need intellectual property rights (IPR) in order to identify, plan, commercialize, and defend their inventions. It is also a crucial instrument for safeguarding capital, labour, and time, and it fosters healthy competition, all of which support the advancement of industry and economic expansion. Pharma businesses are also encouraged to spend in research and development by IPRs.

IPR protection functions in a variety of ways:

- Offers equitable and efficient motivation for creativity (Innovation)
- Shields pharmaceutical businesses from potential infringers
- Gives robust enforcement tools to protect patents that are being violated [58]. Also, to help creative and motivated start-ups secure their patents, trademarks, and designs, the Start-Ups Intellectual Property Protection Scheme (SIPP) has been introduced. The program's goal is to increase start-ups' understanding and use of intellectual property rights. It also tends to support and guide them in developing novel technologies and helps them secure and market them by giving them access to top-notch IP services and resources. Since the patent regulations were amended, there is no cost associated with an applicant's withdrawal of an application. To expedite business transactions, the CGPDTM office has enabled the automatic issuing of electronic patent certificates. These are some positive initiatives that are taken by the government to strengthen innovation and creativity through start-ups & pharmaceutical industries.

VFUTURE IMPLICATIONS

Potential Changes in Patent Policies for Pharmaceuticals

- **Global Efforts for Access to Medicines:** There has been a growing global conversation about improving access to essential medicines, especially in low-income countries. Some international organizations and advocates have been pushing for changes in patent policies to ensure broader availability of affordable generic drugs.
- **TRIPS Flexibilities:** The Agreement on Trade-Related Aspects of Intellectual Property Rights (TRIPS) provides certain flexibilities that allow countries to take measures to protect public health. Countries might explore and utilize these flexibilities to address health emergencies or ensure access to medicines.
- **COVID-19 Pandemic Impact:** The COVID-19 pandemic highlighted the importance of global cooperation in addressing health crises. Some countries and organizations have advocated for temporary waivers on certain intellectual property rights related to COVID-19 vaccines and treatments to facilitate broader access.
- **Gene and Cell Therapies**: Advancements in gene and cell therapies may lead to discussions about adapting patent policies to accommodate new and innovative forms of pharmaceuticals. Balancing the need for innovation with ensuring patient access may influence policy changes.
- **Data Exclusivity and Regulatory Pathways**: Besides patents, regulatory data exclusivity is a significant factor in the pharmaceutical industry. Changes in policies related to data exclusivity can impact market competition and the availability of generic drugs.
- **Antimicrobial Resistance (AMR):** Concerns about antimicrobial resistance have led to discussions about incentivizing the development of new antibiotics. Policymakers may consider changes in patent policies to encourage research and development in this area.
- **Collaborative Initiatives:** Collaborative efforts between public and private sectors, such as public-private partnerships, could influence patent policies. These initiatives aim to address health challenges while ensuring fair returns on investments for pharmaceutical companies.
- **Patient and Advocacy Group Involvement**: Increased involvement of patient groups and advocates in policymaking may shape patent policies to consider not only the economic interests of pharmaceutical companies but also the needs and rights of patients [59].

Lessons Learned from the COVID-19 Pandemic

The importance of effective IP systems that take into account the needs of a wide range of stakeholders, including research and development organizations, start-ups, investors, and most importantly, the general public who ultimately benefits from the innovation, has been further highlighted by the IP challenges faced during the Covid19 pandemic. Nevertheless, it is by no means simple to put such a regime into place. This would necessitate considerable changes to the domestic intellectual property laws, including the application of the TRIPS Agreement's flexible provisions for public health purposes and their application under national law. The intellectual property regime allows for specific patent rights and exceptions to facilitate national access to innovations and medical technology. Another option is to add a research exception to domestic IP laws where none exists at the moment. Patent infringement does not apply to research and development on the patented COVID-19 technology in nations where domestic laws allow for such an exception.

Additionally, a regulatory review exception allows information to be developed to obtain regulatory marketing approval while using patented technology without the patent holder's consent. Government-use licenses and mandatory licenses are two more options that work well in this context [60].

CONCLUSION

The above chapter concludes that the debate on patent protection is multifaceted, encompassing various perspectives and considerations. While patent protection encourages innovation by providing inventors with exclusive rights and incentives, it also raises concerns about limiting access to knowledge and hindering further progress. Striking the right balance between rewarding inventors and promoting the greater good of society is essential. Proponents argue that strong patent protection stimulates research and development, fostering economic growth and technological advancement. It incentivizes inventors to invest time and resources into creating new products and technologies, ultimately benefiting society as a whole. Moreover, patent protection helps attract investment and encourages the dissemination of knowledge through the publication of patent documents. On the other hand, critics contend that the current patent system can stifle competition, leading to monopolies that limit access to essential technologies and medicines. They argue that some patents, particularly in industries like pharmaceuticals, can result in high prices and restricted access to life-saving treatments. Additionally, concerns have been raised about the increasing number of low-quality or overly broad patents that may hinder innovation rather than promote it. Finding a middle ground may involve reforming the patent system to strike a better balance between rewarding inventors and ensuring the public interest. This could include measures such as more rigorous examination of patent applications, shorter patent terms, and clearer guidelines on patentability. Additionally, fostering collaboration and open innovation models could help address some of the drawbacks associated with strict patent protection.

In conclusion, the debate on patent protection requires ongoing dialogue and careful consideration of the trade-offs involved. Striking the right balance is crucial to ensure that innovation is incentivized, while also promoting accessibility, affordability, and the greater benefit to society.

REFERENCES

[1] Bagade OM, Pujari RR, Vanave MD, Shete AM, Kharat PP, Nemlekar NA. Evolving pace of patent in india and its corollary in past, present and future. Am J Adv Drug Deliv 2014; 2: 503-21.

[2] Nandini V. Patents for pharmaceutical sector & people's right to access to health in India - issues and challenges. Indian J Integrated Research In Law 2000; 342: 1902-4.

[3] Savale SK, Savale VK. Intellectual property rights (IPR). World J Pharm Pharm Sci 2016; 5: 2559-92.

[4] Anetta Caplanova, 5 - Intellectual property, Editor(s): Pacheco-Torgal F, Rasmussen E, Granqvist CG, et al. Impact of Vaccines; Health, Economic and Social Perspectives, Frontiers in Microbiology 2020; 11.

[5] Ehreth J. The global value of vaccination. Vaccine 2003; 21(7-8): 596-600. [http://dx.doi.org/10.1016/S0264-410X(02)00623-0] [PMID: 12531324]

[6] Needham J. Biology and Biological Technology. Science and Civilisation in China Cambridge. Cambridge University Press 2000; 6.

[7] Jenner E. An Inquiry Into The Causes And Effects Of The VariolæVaccinæ, A DiseaseDiscovered. Some Of The Western Counties Of England, Particularly Gloucestershire, And Known By The Name Of The Cow Pox. London: Sampson Low 1798.

[8] Pasteur L. Mèthode pour prévenir la rage apresmorsure. ComptesRendus De l'Acad. Sci 1885; 101: 765-72.

[9] Theiler M, Smith HH. The effect of prolonged cultivation in vitro upon the pathogenicity of yellow fever virus. J Exp Med 1937; 65(6): 767-86. a [http://dx.doi.org/10.1084/jem.65.6.767] [PMID: 19870633]

[10] Theiler M, Smith HH. The use of yellow fever virus modified by in vitro cultivation for human immunization. J Exp Med 1937; 65(6): 787-800. b [http://dx.doi.org/10.1084/jem.65.6.787] [PMID: 19870634]

[11] Glenny AT, Hopkins BE. Diphtheria toxoid as an immunising agent. Br J Exp Pathol 1923; 4: 283-8.

[12] Gold R, Artenstein MS. Meningococcal infections. 2. Field trial of group C meningococcal polysaccharide vaccine in 1969-70. Bull World Health Organ 1971; 45(3): 279-82. [PMID: 5316907]

[13] Artenstein MS. Control of meningococcal meningitis with meningococcal vaccines. Yale J Biol Med 1975; 48(3): 197-200. [PMID: 808913]

[14] Schneerson R, Barrera O, Sutton A, Robbins JB. Preparation, characterization, and immunogenicity of Haemophilus influenzae type b polysaccharide-protein conjugates. J Exp Med 1980; 152(2): 361-76.

[http://dx.doi.org/10.1084/jem.152.2.361] [PMID: 6967514]

[15] Sato Y, Sato H. Development of acellular pertussis vaccines. Biologicals 1999; 27(2): 61-9. [http://dx.doi.org/10.1006/biol.1999.0181] [PMID: 10600185]

[16] Clark HF, Offit PA, Plotkin SA, Heaton PM. The new pentavalent rotavirus vaccine composed of bovine (strain WC3) -human rotavirus reassortants. Pediatr Infect Dis J 2006; 25(7): 577-83. [http://dx.doi.org/10.1097/01.inf.0000220283.58039.b6] [PMID: 16804425]

[17] Kirnbauer R, Booy F, Cheng N, Lowy DR, Schiller JT. Papillomavirus L1 major capsid protein self-assembles into virus-like particles that are highly immunogenic. Proc Natl Acad Sci USA 1992; 89(24): 12180-4. [http://dx.doi.org/10.1073/pnas.89.24.12180] [PMID: 1334560]

[18] Serruto D, Bottomley MJ, Ram S, Giuliani MM, Rappuoli R. The new multicomponent vaccine against meningococcal serogroup B, 4CMenB: Immunological, functional and structural characterization of the antigens. Vaccine 2012; 30(0 2) (Suppl. 2): B87-97. [http://dx.doi.org/10.1016/j.vaccine.2012.01.033] [PMID: 22607904]

[19] Zhu N, Zhang D, Wang W, *et al.* A novel coronavirus from patients with pneumonia in China, 2019. N Engl J Med 2020; 382(8): 727-33. [http://dx.doi.org/10.1056/NEJMoa2001017] [PMID: 31978945]

[20] Chan JFW, Yuan S, Kok KH, *et al.* A familial cluster of pneumonia associated with the 2019 novel coronavirus indicating person-to-person transmission: a study of a family cluster. Lancet 2020; 395(10223): 514-23. [http://dx.doi.org/10.1016/S0140-6736(20)30154-9] [PMID: 31986261]

[21] World Health Assembly (27th: 1974). The expanded programme on immunization: the 1974 resolution by the world health assembly. Assignment Child 1985; 69-72: 87-8. [PMID: 12280461]

[22] St. John, Tonya Y. Lowery. Use of Immunization Registries for Achieving Child Immunizations Goals in Healthy People 2000 (1995). UCHC Graduate School Masters Theses 2003 – 2010. 106.

[23] Janssens W. Externalities in program evaluation: the impact of a Women's empowerment program on immunization. J Eur Econ Assoc 2011; 9(6): 1082-113. [http://dx.doi.org/10.1111/j.1542-4774.2011.01041.x]

[24] Dash DK, Vaiswade R, Gupta G. A Review on the Indian Patent System and Its Implication on the Pharmaceutical Industry. Journal of Health Science and Medical Research, 2023.

[25] India – A Comparative Review of The New Manual of Patent Office Practice and Procedure – Key Changes, 2019.

[26] Kang, Simran. A Study of Patent System in India: Patentability, Registration and Objection to the Grant of Patent, 2021.

[27] Hall BH. Patents, innovation, and development. Int Rev Appl Econ 2022.

[28] Encaoua D, Guellec D, Martínez C. Patent systems for encouraging innovation: Lessons from economic analysis, Research Policy, 2006; 35:(9) 1423-1440. ISSN 0048-7333

[29] Moser P. How Do Patent Laws Influence Innovation? Evidence from Nineteenth-Century World's Fairs. Am Econ Rev 2005; 95(4): 1214-36. [http://dx.doi.org/10.1257/000282805482550l]

[30] Mansfield E. Patents and Innovation: An Empirical Study. Manage Sci 1986; 32(2): 173-81. [http://dx.doi.org/10.1287/mnsc.32.2.173]

[31] Arora A, Fosfuri A, Gambardella A. Markets for Technology: TheEconomics of Innovation and Corporate Strategy 2002; 27(4): 624-626. [http://dx.doi.org/10.2307/4134409]

[32] Adelman MJ. The New World of Patents Created by the Court of Appeals for the Federal Circuit. Journal of Law Reform 1987; 20(4): 979-1007.

[33] Arora A. Licensing Tacit Knowledge: Intellectual Property Rights And The Market For Know-How. Econ Innov New Technol 1995; 4(1): 41-60.
[http://dx.doi.org/10.1080/10438599500000013]

[34] Antony K, Kurup RR, Siddique N. Arbitration and intellectual property disputes: the global perspective, 2021.

[35] Raju KD. The Intellectual Property Rights and Competition Law- A comparative analysis. 1st ed., Eastern Law House 2014.

[36] Dash DK, Vaiswade R, Gupta G. A Review on the Indian Patent System and Its Implication on the Pharmaceutical Industry. Journal of Health Science and Medical Research, 2023; 2023926.
[http://dx.doi.org/10.31584/jhsmr.2023926]

[37] The Economist There has been 7m-13m excess deaths worldwide during the pandemic, 2021. Available from: https://www.economist.com/briefing/2021/05/15/there-have-been-7m-13m-e-cess-deathsworldwide-during-the-pandemic

[38] Saher R, Anjum M. Role of technology in COVID-19 pandemic. Researches and Applications of Artificial Intelligence to Mitigate Pandemics 2021; pp. 109-38.

[39] Arrow, K. Economic Welfare and the Allocation of Resources for Invention. In The Rate and Direction of Inventive Activity: Economic and Social Factors, Princeton University Press. 1962; pp. 609-626.
[http://dx.doi.org/10.1515/9781400879762-024]

[40] Jong JPJ, Kemp RGM, Meijaard J. Incentives to innovate. EIM Business and Policy Research, Scales Research Reports, 2002.

[41] Manso G. Creating Incentives for Innovation. Calif Manage Rev 2017; 60(1): 18-32.
[http://dx.doi.org/10.1177/0008125617725287]

[42] Ozawa S, Shankar R, Leopold C, Orubu S. Access to medicines through health systems in low- and middle-income countries, Health Policy and Planning, 2019; 34(3), iii1–iii3.

[43] Kumar VM, Pandi-Perumal SR, Trakht I, Thyagarajan SP. Strategy for COVID-19 vaccination in India: the country with the second highest population and number of cases. NPJ Vaccines 2021; 6(1): 60.
[http://dx.doi.org/10.1038/s41541-021-00327-2] [PMID: 33883557]

[44] Gold ER. What the COVID-19 pandemic revealed about intellectual property. Nat Biotechnol 2022; 40(10): 1428-30.
[http://dx.doi.org/10.1038/s41587-022-01485-x] [PMID: 36207587]

[45] Chamsi-Pasha H, Chamsi-Pasha M, Albar MA. Ethical dilemmas in the era of COVID-19. Avicenna J Med 2020; 10(3): 102-5.
[http://dx.doi.org/10.4103/AJM.AJM_119_20] [PMID: 32832425]

[46] Wouters OJ, Shadlen KC, Salcher-Konrad M, *et al.* Challenges in ensuring global access to COVID-19 vaccines: production, affordability, allocation, and deployment. Lancet 2021; 397(10278): 1023-34.
[http://dx.doi.org/10.1016/S0140-6736(21)00306-8] [PMID: 33587887]

[47] Gilbert P, Fawcett R, Coles J, Hillson W. Intellectual Property Rights and Vaccines. Methods Mol Biol 2022; 2412: 505-18.
[http://dx.doi.org/10.1007/978-1-0716-1892-9_28] [PMID: 34918265]

[48] Agejoh PA. Temporary Waiver of Patent Rights in Public Health Emergencies: Inadequacy of Provisions during the COVID-19 Crisis. Afr Rev 2022; 50(3): 300-29.
[http://dx.doi.org/10.1163/1821889x-bja10032]

[49] Gebre MS, Brito LA, Tostanoski LH, Edwards DK, Carfi A, Barouch DH. Novel approaches for vaccine development. Cell 2021; 184(6): 1589-603. [http://dx.doi.org/10.1016/j.cell.2021.02.030] [PMID: 33740454]

[50] Akomea-Frimpong I, Robert OK, Xiaohua J, Tumpa RJ. A critical review of public-private partnerships in the COVID-19 pandemic: key themes and future research agenda. Smart and Sustainable Built Environment, 2022. [http://dx.doi.org/10.1108/SASBE-01-2022-0009]

[51] Raju K. D., Compulsory v Voluntary Licensing: A Legitimate way to Enhance Access to Essential Medicines in Developing Countries, Journal of Intellectual Property Rights, 2017; 22, pp. 23-31. [http://dx.doi.org/10.1108/SASBE-01-2022-0009]

[52] Gupta A, Raza A. Patent Law and Compulsory Licensing: Indian Perspective. Journal of Intellectual Property Rights 2024; 29(1): 5-17. [http://dx.doi.org/10.56042/jipr.v29i1.602]

[53] Ning C, Wang H, Wu J, Chen Q, Pei H, Gao H. The COVID-19 Vaccination and Vaccine Inequity Worldwide: An Empirical Study Based on Global Data. Int J Environ Res Public Health 2022; 19(9): 5267. [http://dx.doi.org/10.3390/ijerph19095267] [PMID: 35564661]

[54] T. Sivaramjani. The TRIPS Intellectual Property Waiver Proposal: Creating the Right Incentives in Patent Law and Politics to end the COVID-19 Pandemic 2021. [http://dx.doi.org/10.2139/ssrn.3851737]

[55] West NEJ, Cheong WF, Boone E, Moat NE. Impact of the COVID-19 pandemic: a perspective from industry. Eur Heart J Suppl. 2020 Dec 23;22(Suppl Pt t):P56-P59. [http://dx.doi.org/10.1093/eurheartj/suaa187] [PMID: 33390873] [PMCID: PMC7757706]

[56] Dash DK, Vaiswade R, Gupta G. A Review on the Indian Patent System and Its Implication on the Pharmaceutical Industry. Journal of Health Science and Medical Research, 2023. [http://dx.doi.org/10.31584/jhsmr.2023926]

[57] Khoo EJ, Lantos JD. Lessons learned from the COVID-19 pandemic. Acta Paediatr 2020; 109(7): 1323-5. [http://dx.doi.org/10.1111/apa.15307] [PMID: 32289175]

[58] Chaudhari A, Gokhale S. Intellectual property rights: An overview and implications in pharmaceutical industry. J Adv Pharm Technol Res. 2012; 3(2):88-93.

[59] Tu SS, Nagar S, Kesselheim AS. Recent patent reform bills and their implications for prescription drugs. JAMA. 2023;329(6):459-460. [http://dx.doi.org/10.1001/jama.2022.24983]

[60] Ahmed SK. The impact of COVID-19 on nursing practice: lessons learned and future trends. Cureus. 2023 Dec 7;15(12):e50098. [http://dx.doi.org/10.7759/cureus.50098]

CHAPTER 5

Access to Vaccines and Intellectual Property

Aarti K. Thakre[1,*], **Nitin G. Dumore**[1] and **Monali N. Dumore**[1]

[1] *Dadasaheb Balpande College of Pharmacy, Besa, Nagpur, India*

Abstract: Intellectual property and patents have become one of the most controversial issues relating to access to medications since the World Trade Organization (WTO) was established and the Agreement on Trade-Related Aspects of Intellectual Property Rights (TRIPS Agreement) was put into effect. While patents are not the only obstacles to obtaining life-saving medications, they can be very important or even decisive. Due to the patent holder's ability to set prices during the period of protection in the absence of competition, the majority of people living in developing countries might not be able to afford the treatment. Many nations within the Global South confront significant barriers to vaccine access, owing in part to restrictive intellectual property law. With reference to the TRIPS agreement, the World Trade Organization (WTO), and the World Intellectual Property Organization (WIPO), this chapter attempts to resolve the issues of intellectual property and vaccination availability.

Our aim is a global legislative framework for human rights and health that is based on universal cooperation and collaboration, with a focus on long-term goals and unfettered access to pharmaceuticals without any regard for intellectual property.

The trade-related portions of intellectual property rights that regulate the creation, manufacturing, and distribution of medications and medical technologies are a relatively recent area of pharmaceutical policy.

Keywords: Intellectual Property(IP), Trade-Related Aspects of Intellectual Property Rights(TRIPS), Worldwide health legislation, World Trade Organisation (WTO), World Intellectual Property Organization (WIPO).

INTRODUCTION

The establishment of the World Trade Organization (WTO) and the implementation of the agreement on Trade-Related Aspects of Intellectual Property Rights (TRIPS Agreement), intellectual property, and patents have emerged as one of the most contentious topics pertaining to access to medications

* **Corresponding author Aarti K. Thakre:** Dadasaheb Balpande College of Pharmacy, Besa, Nagpur, India; E-mail: thakreaarti27@gmail.com

Sachin Kumar Jain, Ravikant Gupta, Sudha Vengurlekar, Nidhi Bais & Gajendra P. Choudhary (Eds.)

[1, 2]. While patents are not the only obstacles to obtaining life-saving medications, they can be very important or even decisive. Given the patent owner's ability to set prices during the treatment's duration of protection in the absence of competition, the majority of people in developing countries might not be able to afford it. Many nations in the Global South confront significant barriers to vaccine access, owing in part to restrictive intellectual property law [3 - 5]. This chapter aims to introduce important topics related to intellectual property and vaccine access on the basis of COVID-19, Malaria, and SARS vaccines. We envision a human rights and global health legislation framework built on solidarity and international cooperation, with funding focused on long-term goals and access to medicines free of intellectual property constraints. This paper provides a prompt case-by-case evaluation of the initial patent landscape that scans and develop side for accelerating development and access through patent pools and other forms of intellectual property management [6 - 8].

One of the biggest health catastrophes of the past century worldwide is the COVID-19 pandemic. Although a number of COVID-19 vaccines have been developed swiftly, giving millions of people hope, many nations find it extremely difficult to obtain access to them, partly because of stringent intellectual property (IP) rules. This is due to the fact that vaccination patents, a particular kind of intellectual property right, establish production monopolies, which raise costs and restrict access. Because of the stark differences in vaccination availability that it causes between the Global North and the Global South, as well as between nations among rulers and others, this injustice has been nicknamed "vaccine apartheid" [6, 7].

Effect of Technology Transfer on Access to Vaccines

In the context of pharmaceutical technology transfer, it can be challenging to present concrete proof that the transfer affects local product accessibility. When it comes to immunizations, this is considerably simpler to prove. There are several instances of technology transfer to developing nations improving immunization access, which in turn improves population health. The technology for several fundamental vaccines was transmitted to many developing nations in the early to mid-20th century to support national supplies [9]. Due to this technological transfer, producers from developing nations today produce 64% of the basic (Essential Programme of Immunization) EPI vaccines (Fig. **1**) [10, 11].

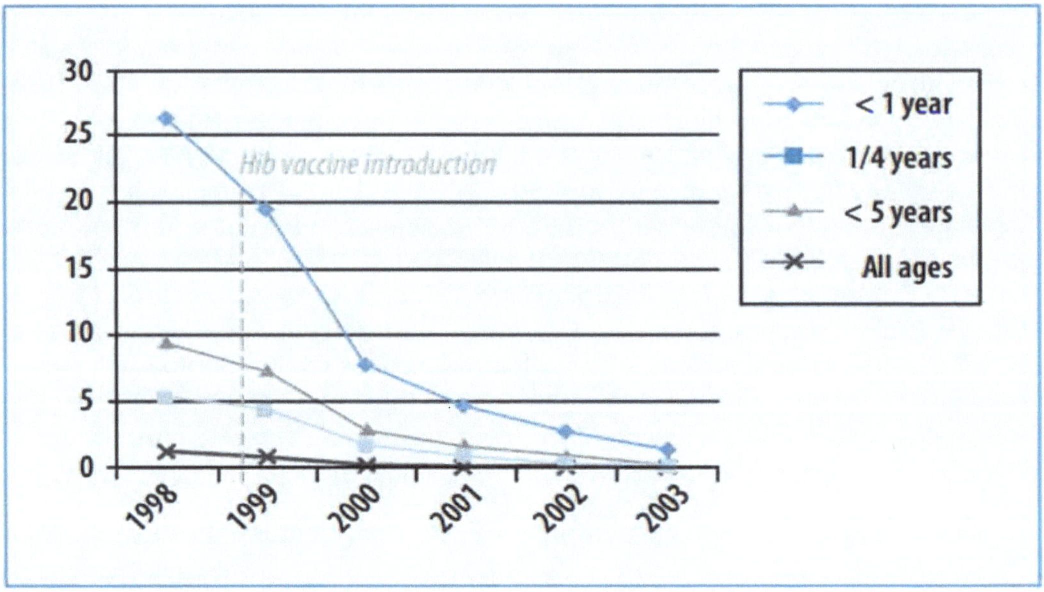

Fig. (1). Example of Haemophilus influenzae type b(Hib)Vaccines.

Source: MS/SVS/COVER

These technology transfer initiatives led to a significant drop in vaccination costs and an increase in vaccine capacity. Eight prequalified producers are currently offering vaccinations containing Hib.

This enhanced ability was reinforced by WHO epidemiological research that showed the condition was widespread in numerous nations.

The Functions of Patent

The overwhelming majority of participants (81.2%) agreed that patents are meant to promote innovation.

Merely 5% of the participants expressed disagreement with this viewpoint, while the remaining 13.6% responded neutrally.

Knowledge of the role of the patent indicates that the participants were familiar with the objectives of the patent [6, 12, 13] (Fig. **2**).

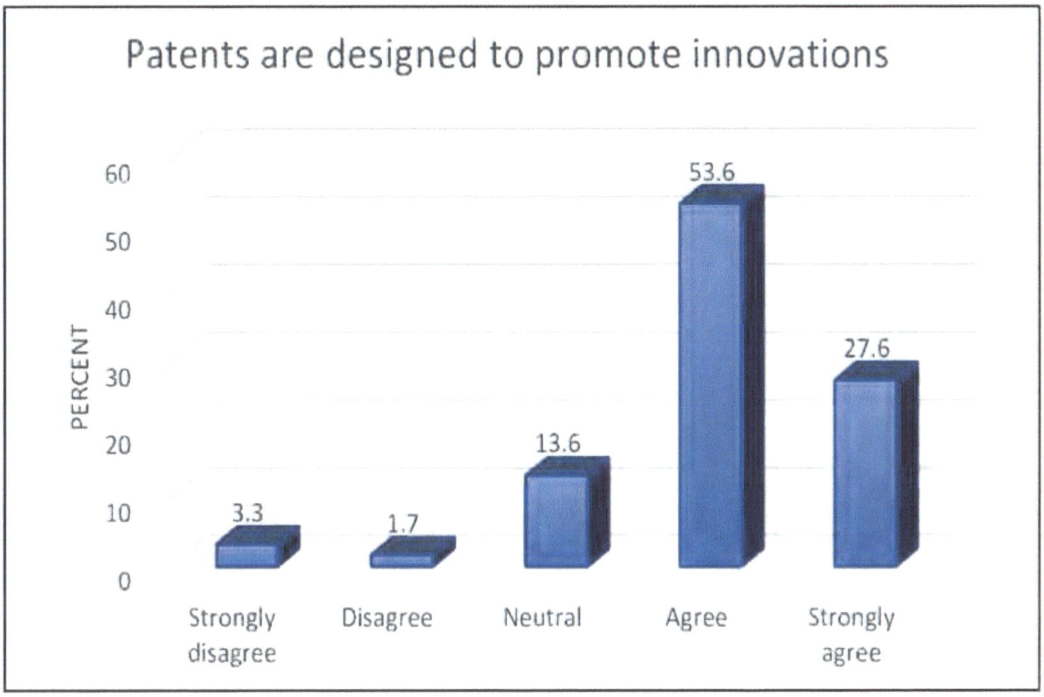

Fig. (2). Knowledge of the role of patent.

The World Trade Organisation (WTO) (TRIPS) Agreement

With 164 member nations as of right now, the World Trade Organization (WTO) is an international organization that deals with trade legislation and offers its members an institutional framework for conducting business. When members join the WTO, they agree to many accords, the Agreement on Trade-Related Aspects of Intellectual Property Rights (TRIPS) being the most significant of them.

The TRIPS Agreement defines baseline requirements for the protection and enforcement of a set of intellectual property rights, which WTO members must apply through national legislation. The TRIPS Agreement was adopted and entered into force in 1995; nevertheless, depending on their level of economic growth and the level of intellectual property protection they had previously provided. Before the TRIPS Agreement, each nation handled patent matters differently and had its process for protecting patents and other forms of intellectual property to suit its particular circumstances [14, 15].

Patent

A title is a patent awarded by the government that grants a brief exclusive right to make use of an innovation. It gives the patent holder a negative right, which is the ability to prevent third parties from creating, importing, selling, utilizing, or marketing the patented invention while the patent is still in effect [16, 17].

International Patent

Territoriality is an essential term in patent rights. This indicates that a patented innovation's rights are restricted to a certain area. Patents are frequently given by national patent offices under the authority of the nation's patent laws. Within such circumstances, the patent right has a national territorial reach, meaning that until a similar patent has been granted in Country B, the holder of a patent issued by the patent office of country A will not enjoy patent rights in Country B. In some circumstances, there might be a regional patent office; under that scenario, subject to specific standards and procedures, a patent awarded by the regional patent office may be acknowledged in the countries that are parties to the regional patent agreement. An EPO patent, for instance, is recognized by all signatories to the European Patent Convention and may be granted by the European Patent Office. A patent is identified in this case as a 'bundle of nationally enforceable' rights, meaning that each member country must independently enforce the patent's rights. The Organization for African Intellectual Property (OAPI).

The 16 OAPI Member States (Benin, Burkina Faso, Cameroon, Central African Republic, Chad, Congo, Côte d'Ivoire, Equatorial Guinea, Gabon, Guinea, Guinea Bissau, Mali, Mauritania, Niger, Senegal, and Togo) are served by this regional patent organization as their shared patent authority. OAPI agreement is revised with Intellectual Property Rights: Trade-Related Aspects of the World Trade Organization (WTO) (TRIPS). Every OAPI Member State immediately acknowledges a patent awarded by OAPI, which sets the OAPI patent regime apart. As a result, OAPI accepts applications and grants patents in its capacity as the national patent office for each of its member states. While a Member State's relevant national administration may receive an application, the patent is granted by OAPI. Once awarded, according to the provisions of the Bangui Agreement, patents are independent of national rights, but they are also governed by national laws of the Member States, if applicable. In contrast, a single patent application may be filed at the African Regional Intellectual Property Organization (ARIPO), any contracting state's Industrial Patent Office, or directly with ARIPO, indicating the nations that are being sought protection for. However, ARIPO's national impact is not always felt in its member states. Within six months of receiving the notification, Patents granted by ARIPO may be rejected by any of the 16 member states (Botswana, Gambia, Ghana, Kenya, Lesotho, Malawi, Mozambique, Namibia, Sierra Leone, Somalia, Sudan, Swaziland, Tanzania, Uganda, Zambia, and Zimbabwe), on the grounds that they violate national laws or the Harare Protocol's rules for trademarks, patents, models, and designs [18 - 20].

Intellectual Property and Development in WIPO

Adopted in 1970, The World Intellectual Property Organization (WIPO) is responsible for overseeing the Patent Cooperation Treaty (PCT), which comprises over 150 agreements with signatory governments with just one "international" patent application submitted rather than multiple distinct regional or national patent applications. PCT enables the simultaneous filing of patent protection requests for an innovation in numerous jurisdictions. In what is known as the national or regional patent, or the "national phase," offices continue to have authority over the awarding of patents [21, 22].

Following the filing of an 'international patent application in the International Bureau of WIPO or the Patent Office of a PCT member state, the application is searched and examined by a patent office certified as a PCT International Search and Examination Authority within a PCT member state. Any state participant in the Paris Agreement may file the related patent application first, and then the "international" application within the following twelve months. Without comparing the adoption of national legal rules concerning the patentability requirements thresholds. The application is then transmitted to the International Search Authority, which performs a prior art search using publicly available records. Based on the prior art search, the International Search Authority issues a written opinion and an international search report indicating whether or not the application generally satisfies the requirements for patentability.

Within eighteen months of the application being filed for the first time in any nation, the search report, written opinion, and application are all released. The applicant then has the choice to ask for an additional search that an international search authority will carry out -a recognized patent office. Additionally, the candidate may request to take a second international exam, typically depending on a revised version of the software, to assess the patentability of the submission. The time frame for making these requests is 22 months from the date of the initial application. Either the International Preliminary Report on Patentability or the Supplementary International Search Report will be available in 22 months. After that, during a 30-month window from the original application, the applicant may choose to request the national stage of the patent application's prosecution through the appropriate national offices [23, 24].

Although they may use it as a guide for their search and examination, it is not necessary for national patent offices to adhere to the worldwide search and examination report. This does, however, also give patent offices the ability to have an impact on the country's evaluation of that application in a developing nation when they generate the worldwide.

As a global Search Authority (ISA), they have prepared a search and examination report. Note 2 Indeed, one benefit of the PCT system is that "patent offices' search and examination work can be significantly reduced or eliminated," as stated by the WIPO Secretariat.

Bilateral and regional free trade agreements are frequently promoted by the European Union (EU) and the United States that impose requirements on developing nations to enlist in the PCT. Despite the fact that many developing nations have acceded to the PCT, applicants from a small number of nations mostly use the system [22, 24]. Despite the reality that the quantity of applications for patents filed in these developing nations via the PCT method has significantly increased, many of them lack the capacity to perform meaningful examinations.

Validity of Patent

A patent office's granting of it is not implied by a patent that this is the final word on the subject. An issued patent may occasionally be declared void in whole or in part for a variety of reasons. It might be possible to challenge the patent's validity, for instance, if it turns out that, upon closer examination, it does not meet one or more of the National Patent Office's standards for patentability legislation). Certain types of inventions may also be excluded by stipulations in patent laws; surgical or therapeutic procedures are common examples. Inventions that are forbidden from being commercialized because they would violate public order or morals may also not be eligible for patent protection under some patent rules. Moreover, patents issued in the banned sectors would be void. The patent holder still needs to pay the necessary maintenance fees to the Patent Office in order to maintain the validity of their patent, even in cases when they have been duly issued. Failure to pay the fees will cause the patent to expire and lose its validity [3, 25].

Minimum Standards of Patent Protection

- All WTO members must provide patent protection for "inventions" across all technological fields. Any invention relating to a pharmaceutical product or method must be patented by WTO members [25].
- The criteria for patentability include industrial application, inventive step (non-obviousness), and originality. Utility will be applied by WTO members. It is

within the purview of individual nations to decide how these criteria are actually defined and used. Since there is no definition of innovation, creative step, or industrial applicability in the TRIPS Agreement, it gives nations a great deal of leeway. As a result, the requirements for patentability constitute the primary and greatest degree of flexibility allowed by the agreement to protect public health and medicine access [26]. 'Legislators and politicians have a great deal of discretion in implementing those flexibilities legally [1, 27].
- Additionally, a minimum 20-year duration of defence as of the date of application filing is mandated by the TRIPS Agreement for patent rights. As a result, WTO members are no longer permitted to have patent protection for less time than the requisite 20 years.

Nevertheless, uniform legal requirements or a uniform international law were not imposed by the TRIPS Agreement. It has clauses that give nations some leeway and flexibility to modify Patents obtained by WTO members for any invention involving a pharmaceutical good or process. In light of this, WTO Members retain the authority to decide how specific elements to advance the social and economic welfare of their respective countries, national patent protection policies should be enacted or administered (Table **1**).

Table 1. Examples of drugs with multiple patents granted [3].

Sr. No.	Product	Company	Condition treated	No. of patents granted	Years of protection
1	Humira	ABBVIE	Arthritis	132	39
2	Rituxan	BIOGEN	Cancer	94	47
3	Revlimid	CELGENE	M. Myeloma	96	40
4	Enbrel	AMGEN	Arthritis	41	39
5	Herceptin	ROCHE	Cancer	108	4

Source:-I-MAK 'Overpatent, Overpriced', Nov. 2018 [28].

Protecting intellectual property rights and promoting technical innovation for the good of society and the economy are the objectives of the TRIPS Agreement. The WTO also increases public interest in technological advancement and social-economic welfare. These two clauses, as well as the Preamble of the TRIPS Agreement, both reflect the fundamental idea that intellectual property rights protection should be seen as a public policy tool that the protection of such rights should be balanced against other public interests to achieve public policy goals.

Patent Protection Strategies

Today's pharmaceutical businesses must contend with rising costs associated with drug development and discovery as well as fierce competition from generic medicine manufacturers (Table **2**).

Table 2. Revenue losses following patent expiration and generic drugs entry [29].

Brand Name	Manufacture	US sale prepatent expiration (in US $ million)	US sale post-patent expiration (in US $ million)	Year Expired
Claritin	Schering-plough	>3	370	2002
Prozac	Eli Lily	>2.9	480	2001
Pepcid	Merck	755	110	2000

Pharmaceutical businesses are prepared to enter a market once a patent expires, despite the skyrocketing expenses of research (Table **3**).

Table 3. Patent expiry of bestselling drugs 2023 [29, 30].

Drug Name	Route	Patents	Expiration Date
Sacubitril, Valsartan	Oral (Tablet)	US8404744	July 14, 2023
		US8796331	July 14, 2023
		US7468390	November 27, 2023
		US8101659	January 15, 2025
Inotersen Sodium	Subcutaneous	US7015315	March 21, 2023
		US7101993	September 05, 2023

For successful products, prolonging the duration of the product and preventing generic competition can be achieved by optimizing the patent term. New inventions are given exclusive control and ownership by their patent holders. For the duration of the patent, this gives the inventor the ability to stop others from using their concepts or innovations for profit without their consent (Judge David M. Gersten). The ideal way to safeguard an inventor's rights requires a careful balance of practical, legal, and scientific factors. Pharmaceutical scientists and attorneys must work closely together to create, defend, and challenge pharmaceutical patents. It also calls for a solid grasp of the foundational ideas in each other's fields of study. Thus, it is imperative that scientists and lawyers work together [17, 30].

A number of pharmaceutical firms have been successful in obtaining patent protection for novel applications. For example, Under the brand name Proscar, Merck initially created, patented, and sold finasteride as a treatment for benign prostatic enlargement. When male pattern baldness was discovered to be a new use for finasteride, requests for FDA permission and extra patent protection were made. Propecia is the brand name used to sell Finasteride as a hair loss treatment. Similar to this, Lilly first patented the substance Atomoxetine in the early 1980s after it was shown to be effective in treating depression. Atomoxetine has a novel potential application with regard to treating attention deficit hyperactivity disorder as a result of ongoing research and development. Lilly has received FDA permission and patent protection for this new usage and marketing [16, 30].

Quantity of patents that are issued to safeguard pharmaceutical goods. A large many applications for patents are made in order to safeguard pharmaceutical goods, even though the number of novel chemical entities granted each year is quite low. For instance, since the mid-1990s, the US Department of Agriculture and Food approved a significantly smaller number of novel molecular entities (NMEs) from 53 in 1996 to 22 in 2016 [14, 30]. Pharmaceutical patent applications are filed using criteria other than the most recent chemical molecule or compound. A growing number of patents have been applied for and frequently granted for variations of pharmaceutical products, including salts and other molecular derivatives as well as the particular medication formulation or dosage form. Certain nations have allowed patent protection for even supposedly "incremental" changes to already-existing products, such as minor adjustments or insignificant changes to form color, or inactive substances. Combinations of well-known medications have also resulted in the granting of patents. Because of the awarding of several different patents, a specific pharmaceutical product may remain protected for a long time even after the chemical compound it employs is no longer covered by a patent. The criteria used to evaluate and approve pharmaceutical patents are crucial in these circumstances not only for patent and industrial policy but also for public health policies. Both patent examiners and public health policymakers should be aware that judgments about whether to award a patent can have a direct and unwarranted impact on people's lives and health.

Patent and Access to Essential Medicines in Africa

The World Trade Organization (WTO) has reignited long-standing debates regarding the impact of the intellectual property (IP) system on accessibility for the general public necessary medications through the TRIPS agreement covering trade-related aspects of intellectual property rights. In this context, important medications are those required for the purpose of treating diseases like HIV, malaria, TB, and sleeping sickness in areas such as sub-Saharan Africa, as well as for symptom management and palliative care. Some contend that patents will make it even harder for African people to obtain these medications. On the other hand, some contend the reverse. The latter argue that the TRIPS agreement's patent protection can help the pharmaceutical sector expand in regions like sub-Saharan Africa. Additionally, they claim that pharmaceutical patents are not the cause of sub-Saharan Africa's lack of access to essential medications. Rather, they attribute the access issue to non-patent variables including the dearth of infrastructure, bad governance, and poverty [18, 31]. HIV/AIDS in sub-Saharan Africa did not come to the attention of the world until the 1990s when it was thought to pose a threat to U.S. national security. However, when anxieties subsided in the United States and other Western nations, so did media coverage. Insufficient global media attention may hinder or postpone the mobilization of the necessary resources to guarantee a prompt and consistent supply of medications to ailing individuals in sub-Saharan Africa [31]. The issue of access to essential medicines in sub-Saharan Africa is exacerbated by a number of factors, including ineffective infrastructure and healthcare delivery systems [32], the "brain drain" of qualified medical personnel from sub-Saharan Africa to foreign countries [19], and high import tariffs (Médecins Sans Frontières and Health Action International, 2000). In certain cases, these tariffs may reach 30% (International Intellectual Property Institute, 2000).

Impact of Waiver of Intellectual Property Rights on the Pharmaceutical Industry

The results presented in Fig. (**3**) demonstrate that a majority of the participants (56.0%) believed that the capacity of the pharmaceutical industry to innovate could be hindered by the waiver of intellectual property rights, while 31.3% expressed no opinion at all. Furthermore, over 50% of the participants mentioned that the industry's R&D efforts may decrease if intellectual property rights are waived [6, 33].

Public health, the Doha Declaration, and TRIPS

In an attempt to address this issue politically, the World Trade Organization's ministerial conference in Doha on November 14th adopted a declaration on the TRIPS agreement and public health. This declaration reminded member nations of certain so-called flexibilities that have been incorporated into the Agreement since its adoption. It is doubtful that these supposedly beneficial flexibilities would be effectively implemented by developing and least-developed nations [34, 35].

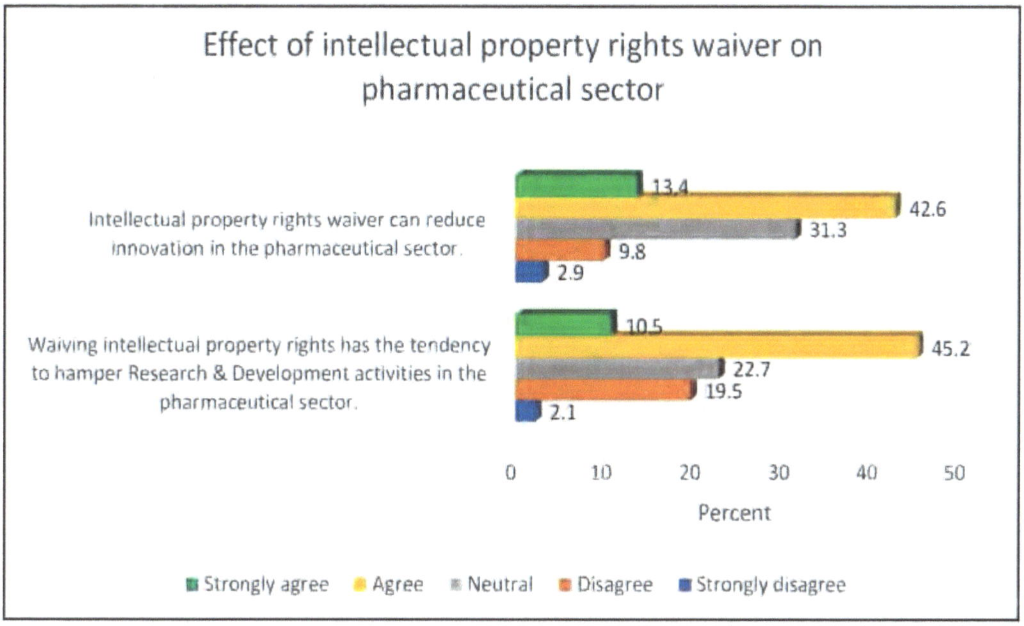

Fig. (3). There have been worries that the pharmaceutical industry's R&D efforts may be impacted by patent waivers, which may also reduce innovation. To find associations between variables and demographic data, and to conduct inferential statistical analysis, the chi-square test was employed in addition to the descriptive statistical analysis . The results showed that while a higher percentage of individuals holding doctoral degrees (83.6%) and master's degrees (86.7%) concurred that patents are meant to encourage inventions, a higher percentage of respondents who hold first degrees and diplomats expressed no opinion on the matter. There was statistical significance ($p<0.001$) in these results. Furthermore, the majority of participants (54.5%) who held doctorates disagreed that intellectual property rights waivers are likely to impede research and development efforts. Additionally, this outcome was $p<0.001$, statistically significant (Table **4**) [6].

Table 4. Cross tabulation of the level of education with intellectual property. https://doi.org/10.1371/journal.pgph.0000683.t002

Statement	Educational Level	Strongly Disagree n(%)	Disagree n(%)	Neutral n(%)	Agree n(%)	Strongly Agree n (%)	X^2	P-value
Patents are designed to promote innovations	ND/NCE	2 (2.8)	1 (1.4)	14 (19.7)	50 (70.4)	4 (5.6)	63.175	<0.001
	First degree/ HND	8 (2.8)	2 (0.7)	46 (16.3)	154 (54.6)	72 (25.5)		
	Master's	1 (0.9)	3 (2.8)	10 (9.4)	54 (50.9)	38 (35.8)		
	PhD	6 (10.9)	3 (5.5)	-	19 (34.5)	27 (49.1)		

(Table 4) cont.....

Statement	Educational Level	Strongly Disagree n(%)	Disagree n(%)	Neutral n(%)	Agree n(%)	Strongly Agree n (%)	X^2	P-value
Waiving intellectual property rights has the tendency to hamper Research & Development activities in the pharmaceutical sector	ND/NCE	1 (1.4)	7 (9.7)	29 (40.3)	31 (43.1)	4 (5.6)	79.796	<0.001
	First degree/HND	7 (2.5)	38 (13.4)	56 (19.8)	153 (54.1)	29 (10.2)		
	Master's	3 (2.8)	26 (24.5)	23 (21.7)	41 (38.7)	13 (12.3)		
	PhD	-	30 (54.5)	7 (12.7)	9 (16.4)	9 (16.4)		

doi: 10.1371/journal.pgph.0000683

The proliferation of free trade agreements (FTAs), the majority of which contain intellectual property clauses that restrict access to medications and may make it more difficult to treat HIV and related illnesses sustainably. Clarifying WTO Member States' ability to use TRIPS flexibilities linked to public health to expand access to medications was made possible by the Doha Declaration [36, 37].

A multilateral framework for the protection of intellectual property rights has been established under the TRIPS Agreement, which imposes minimum binding standards. However, the Agreement's provisions still allow for flexibility, allowing nations to decide how to construe and implement intellectual property regulations in a way that best serves their national public interests and priorities. However, several countries have voiced doubts about how this flexibility would be interpreted and how much their rights to use it would be respected [4, 37].

Even while TRIPS gives national governments some latitude in interpreting and carrying out their duties, developing nations have encountered challenges when attempting to employ policies to support access to reasonably priced medications. For instance, 39 pharmaceutical businesses and the South African Pharmaceutical Manufacturers' Association (PMA) disputed the 1997 amendment to the Medicines and Related Substances Act of South Africa, which permitted parallel importation before to country's Supreme Court. In the end, the pharmaceutical corporations decided not to pursue their lawsuit due to strong opposition from civil society and international organizations, most notably WHO. In a different instance, the US contested the validity of a Brazilian law that permits the granting of mandatory licenses in cases where the owner of the patent has not "worked" their creation locally, meaning they have not produced the copyrighted good within the nation. In the WTO dispute settlement process, the US government filed a lawsuit against Brazil, although it was later withdrawn in 2001 [38, 39].

In Thailand, for example, Abbott Laboratories delayed the introduction of multiple new medications when the latter country requested a mandatory license to manufacture Wong-Anan (2008), which is an HIV/AIDS medication that was covered by an Abbott patent.

The High-Level Panel of the United Nations Secretary-General (UN SG) on access to medicines report mentions further instances, like the 2006 decision made by Thailand to import generic forms of the antiviral drug efavirenz from India under a license that was required (UNHLP, 2016). The US government and the manufacturer, Merck, expressed their disapproval of this decision, questioning the legitimacy of the mandatory license and pressuring Thailand to reverse its decision. Retaliatory actions also followed Later, in 2007, Thailand decided to give two further mandatory licenses for lopinavir/ritonavir and clopidogrel. Abbott pulled all of its medications that were pending Thai regulatory approval from sale. In a letter to the Thai government, the European Trade Commissioner criticized the country's use of compulsory licenses, calling them " harmful" to medical advancement and cautioning that such actions would cut off Thailand from the global biotechnology investment scene.

Developments in Colombia were brought to light by a letter to the co-chairs of the High-Level Panel from the Permanent Mission of Colombia to the UN and letters from civil society organizations. The Ministry of Health of Columbia enacted resolution 2475 at the beginning of 2016, indicating that it was in the "public interest" to have access to imatinib, a medicine that is on the WHO Essential Medicines List, for the treatment of leukemia. The resolution made it possible for the necessary license to be issued. "TRIPS "can and should be interpreted and implemented," including the sovereign determination of the circumstances in which a compulsory license may be granted, as the Doha Declaration highlights [13, 40].

TRIPS Flexibilities

WTO Members maintained significant flexibilities in public health that may be utilized to adjust intellectual property laws, policies, and practices to satisfy human rights and public health goals [41]. A new era of obligations for the defence and enforcement of intellectual property was ushered in by the TRIPS Agreement. These include the authority to establish standards for patentability, grant licenses under duress, permit parallel imports, apply for broad exemptions, and apply competition laws to stop and deal with intellectual property rights violations in national laws, competition legislation, mandatory licenses, and patentability standards [42].

The 1994 Agreement establishing on Trade-Related Aspects of Intellectual Property Rights (TRIPS), a component of the World Trade Organization (WTO), established fundamental standards for intellectual property (IP) protection that all WTO Members were required to uphold States. Numerous analysts have documented the lengthy and intricate nature of the TRIPS negotiations. The World Bank identified many nations with low and intermediate levels of income as having argued against the inclusion of an intellectual property regime in the WTO framework because they believed it would hinder their ability to achieve development objectives and get key items like pharmaceuticals. In the end, nevertheless, they had to concede that the "TRIPS package" was an integral part of the WTO framework. Bilateral and regional trade agreements have been established since TRIPS went into effect [43].

Criteria of Patentability

Apart from stating that an invention needs to be novel, involve a creative or novel step, and be helpful or applicable in industry, Patentability standards are not specifically defined in the TRIPS Agreement. This gives countries a great deal of latitude to determine what constitutes a patentable invention. On one extreme across the spectrum, some national agencies either don't carry out meaningful patent reviews or apply a broad interpretation of the criteria, resulting in the issuance of secondary patents that essentially prolong the original patent based on different forms, dosages, and methods of use of the component substances. Conversely, national authorities possess legislation that forbids patenting the simple act of discovering a novel chemical compound if it does not improve its effectiveness. Similar to the usage of flexibilities in general, nations that have applied a patentability criteria interpretation based on public health have encountered opposition to doing so under their national laws.

Secondary patents are sometimes awarded for small but significant modifications made to an already-existing product. However, secondary patents have the ability to extend exclusivity (a practice known as "evergreening"). This will restrict patient access to health technology by preventing the entry of generic or rival products and keeping costs high. Moreover, secondary patents have the potential to cast legal doubt on a health technology's patent status, discouraging organizations from obtaining generic copies of goods out of concern for patent infringement [44, 45]. However, in certain cases, modifications to currently available medications may provide significant therapeutic benefits by, for example, improving drug tolerance in patients. Consequently, this can encourage rivalry using the prescribed drug. Furthermore, secondary patents may be essential for the development of less hazardous and safe to healthy drugs [46, 47].

More sophisticated patenting techniques are being used as a result of the growing perception of patents as a potential funding source for medical researchers considering the TRIPS Agreement went into effect. Known as "patent thickets," conflicting patent rights that could be difficult to work out are the result of inventors and patent rights holders filing multiple applications for the same innovation. These procedures have the effect of requiring approval from several patentees for a party wishing to commercialize new technology. According to a 2011 review of the patent landscape, the antiviral drug, for instance, ritonavir was protected by 805 patent families held by the producer and additional research-based businesses.

Researchers in the biomedical field reported that they were having trouble obtaining patented innovations, leading to half of them changing their plans for research, and 28% giving up on them completely, according to a study with these researchers. The commercial decisions made by potential makers and sellers are likewise influenced by patent thickets and distributors of pharmaceuticals and medical equipment. Lawmakers have the power to enact restrictions on excessive patenting, which hinders the development and availability of health technologies. A key policy instrument to increase access to health technology may be the implementation of standards for public health in national patent offices [48].

Compulsory Licences

The owner of the patent is available for free to use an innovation that is covered by the patent or give permission to another party to use it. However, the government could allow a third party to make use of the innovation under an obligatory license without the patent owner's consent when it deems necessary to address anticompetitive behaviours or serve the public interest. Thus, the patent holder has a little choice but to put up with the government or a third party using his innovation. In these situations, it is decided that the public interest in guaranteeing is more important than the patent holder's private interest in making full use of his exclusive rights which is a broader access to the copyrighted idea. Therefore, through forced licenses, third parties can make use of an innovation without the patent holder's consent. For instance, in 1995, 27 countries forced licenses for pharmaceuticals to be issued to 108 attempts in which the copyrighted medicine was made available to the people who lived there. Regional pharmacies then produced generic versions of the foreign manufacturers' proprietary medications [3, 48].

Government Laws

Most patent laws allow the government or its authorized agencies to use privately held patents for public, non-commercial applications without the patent holder's consent. National laws frequently provide comprehensive provisions pertaining to the government's use of patents intended for non-commercial and public use, and the procedure is frequently far more straightforward. Putting it another way, it makes it possible for the government to "fast-track" the utilization of patents, which is crucial when immediate access to life-saving medications is needed. The only requirement is to notify the owner of the patent of any intended application of the invention or as soon as possible afterward. For example, government use allows generics to be imported or produced by the public sector and used in public hospitals [48].

Examples of Government Use

As per its patent law's, Malaysia permitted the import of zidovudine, lamivudine, and generic didanosine from India in October 2003 for use in public hospitals. In 2004, Indonesia gave permission for the government to use patents so that lamivudine and nevirapine may be produced locally. Sofosbuvir was licensed for "government use" in Malaysia in September 2017 in order to cure hepatitis C.

Principles of Patent Law

Under the theory of right exhaustion, patented goods that have been lawfully placed on the exporting nation's market may be brought into another country without the patent holder's permission. According to this theory, the moment a pharmaceutical product is initially released onto the market, the right holder's control over it expires. Parallel importation is used to make it easier to import patented products from countries where they are sold for less money., as certain copyrighted goods are offered for sale in various market places.

Indian Principles Law

An innovation needs to be novel.

It needs to involve a creative move.

Able can be applied in industries or industrial use.

It must not belong to the list of exclusions or non-patentable topics.

The following are the criteria for a patent [49]:

- Novelty,
- Non-obviousness,
- Utility

Novelty

The invention needs to be original and distinct from any other ideas or goods already on the market.

Non-obviousness

Ensures that the invention is unique and that no one with specialized knowledge in that sector knows about it.

It also restated the four obviousness tests. These are the following:

The inventive step in the form of earlier application, art, or knowledge must be recognized by a skilled individual.

He needs to be able to distinguish between the invention and the subject matter.

It is important to take note of the variations.

A certain amount of creativity is required.

Utility

This is yet another crucial standard for patent approval. In addition to being novel and obscure, an innovation ought to be practical and have an industrial use. Innovation must have commercial use, according to the Act's definitions of "invention" and "capable of industrial application " utility in order to be used in the industries, as the Court noted in Cipla Ltd. V.F. Hoffmann-La Roche Ltd. (2015). The Court noted in Indian Vacuum Brake Co. Ltd. v. E.S. Luard (1925) that the Act does not utilize the term "utility" in an abstract sense. An innovation needs to have some use in order to qualify for the patent defence. Being useful alone is insufficient [50].

Governments' assessments of the appropriate balance between the public and private interests vary, therefore, patentability standards have been applied differently over time and in different nations. Although the WTO TRIPS Agreement specifies the patentability requirements, there are no clear guidelines or explanations of how these standards ought to be applied or comprehended at the national level. Therefore, as long as it most effectively advances the interests of the whole public, WTO members are free to create and apply the standards definition and analysis of the three patentability requirements are probably the most flexible provisions in this regard [51].

Limitations to Patent Rights

Exclusive patent rights are seen as a means of encouraging investment in creative endeavours and knowledge creation. Nonetheless, the ultimate objective of the public good, which is the goal of the patent system, might not always be achieved by permitting the enforcement of the entire breadth of exclusive rights in every situation. Therefore, under national patent laws, the extent of enforceable patent rights is regulated by particular exceptions and limitations in order to appropriately balance the interests of the public, third parties, and rights holders. Subject to their obligations under international law, individual nations are free to decide whether to implement or keep such exceptions or limitations under national law [52, 53].

Different Limitations of Patent Rights

- Private and/or non-commercial use;
- Scientific research; experimental use;
- Prior use; impromptu medicine preparation;
- Use of articles on foreign ships, airplanes, and land vehicles;
- Actions to obtain regulatory approval from authorities;
- Patent rights exhaustion;
- Mandatory licensing and/or government use;
- Farmers' and breeders' particular use of patented inventions

TRIPS Agreement

Safeguarding public health and the evidence from clinical tests, WTO members have a great deal of freedom in accordance with the TRIPS Agreement to develop trial data protection guidelines that promote public health. Countries should, if feasible, avoid enforcing the uniqueness of the data and instead utilize the latitude provided by the TRIPS agreement to provide exclusive data protection for particular types of data without granting exclusive rights to the data's original author [52, 53].

CONCLUSION

Notwithstanding the Doha Declaration despite the TRIPS Agreement, there will still be significant obstacles to medication availability in the future. Whether or not the required policy decisions and actions are done, as well as how countries apply intellectual property regulations to maximize the TRIPS flexibilities in their national laws, will determine whether or not they are successful in securing effective access to medicines in poor countries. There are still significant obstacles to drug access in the context of trade agreements and intellectual property rights. The entirety of the TRIPS flexibilities has not yet been incorporated into the national laws of many developing nations. This delay could have a number of causes. In order to create and design patent laws and regulations that may take developing countries' requirements and concerns into consideration, it may first be necessary to have specialized legal competence.

Secondly, governments can face pressure from other governments or the sector to exclude such flexibilities.

REFERENCES

[1] Arias E. Guidelines for the examination of patentability of chemical-pharmaceutical inventions. Argentina: INPI 2014.

[2] Correa CM. Public Health Perspective on Intellectual Property and Access to Medicines: A Compilation of Studies Prepared for WHO. South Centre 2016.

[3] Velásquez, G. Intellectual property and access to medicines and vaccines. In: Vaccines, Medicines and COVID-19: How Can WHO Be Given a Stronger Voice? Springer, Cham 2022; pp. 73-92. [http://dx.doi.org/10.1007/978-3-030-89125-1_5]

[4] Correa CM. Interpreting the Flexibilities under the TRIPS Agreement. Access to Medicines and Vaccines 2022; pp. 1-30. [http://dx.doi.org/10.1007/978-3-030-83114-1_1]

[5] World Health Organization. Increasing access to vaccines through technology transfer and local production: 2011; 1-34.

[6] Adigwe OP, Oturu D. The role of patent waivers and compulsory licensing in facilitating access to COVID-19 vaccines: Findings from a survey among healthcare practitioners in Nigeria. PLOS Global Public Health 2022; 2(7): e0000683. [http://dx.doi.org/10.1371/journal.pgph.0000683] [PMID: 36962435]

[7] Krattiger, A., Kowalski, S.P., *et al.* Intellectual property management strategies to accelerate the development and access of vaccines and diagnostics: case studies on pandemic influenza, malaria and SARS. 2006; 2(2): 67-122.

[8] Boschiero N. COVID-19 vaccines as global common goods: An integrated approach of ethical, economic policy and intellectual property management. Global Jurist 2022; 22(2): 177-230. [http://dx.doi.org/10.1515/gj-2021-0042]

[9] Barton H, Grant M. A health map for the local human habitat. J R Soc Promot Health 2006; 126(6): 252-3. [http://dx.doi.org/10.1177/1466424006070466] [PMID: 17152313]

[10] Kikerkov I. Miceska MS, Pavlovska K, Babulovska A, Sivevski A. Project management in pharmaceutical industry. Knowledge - Int J 2023; 57(1): 23-8.

[11] Abbott FM, Reichman JH. The Doha Round's Public Health Legacy: Strategies for the Production and Diffusion of Patented Medicines under the Amended TRIPS Provisions. J Int Econ Law 2007; 10(4): 921-87. [http://dx.doi.org/10.1093/jiel/jgm040]

[12] Smil V. Creating the twentieth century: Technical innovations of 1867-1914 and their lasting impact. Oxford University Press 2005. [http://dx.doi.org/10.1093/0195168747.001.0001]

[13] Matthews D. Globalising intellectual property rights: the TRIPS Agreement. Routledge 2003. [http://dx.doi.org/10.4324/9780203165683]

[14] Mullard A. 2018 FDA drug approvals. Nat Rev Drug Discov 2019; 18(2): 85-9. [http://dx.doi.org/10.1038/d41573-019-00014-x] [PMID: 30710142]

[15] Pedrique B, Strub-Wourgaft N, Some C, *et al.* The drug and vaccine landscape for neglected diseases (2000–11): a systematic assessment. Lancet Glob Health 2013; 1(6): e371-9. [http://dx.doi.org/10.1016/S2214-109X(13)70078-0] [PMID: 25104602]

[16] Rouhi MA. Chirality At Work. CENEAR 2003; 81(18): 56-61.

[17] Mackenzie M, Keating P, Cambrosio A. Patents and free scientific information in biotechnology: Making monoclonal antibodies proprietary. Sci Technol Human Values 1990; 15(1): 65-83. [http://dx.doi.org/10.1177/016224399001500108]

[18] Shashikant, S. The African Regional Intellectual Property Organization (ARIPO) protocol on patents: Implications for access to medicines (No. 56). Research Paper. 2014.

[19] Lippoldt D. Intellectual property rights, pharmaceuticals and foreign direct investment. Group d'Economie Mondale de Sciences Po 2006; pp. 1-10.

[20] Son KB, Lee TJ. Compulsory licensing of pharmaceuticals reconsidered: Current situation and implications for access to medicines. Glob Public Health 2018; 13(10): 1430-40. [http://dx.doi.org/10.1080/17441692.2017.1407811] [PMID: 29183271]

[21] Eric M. Solovy, *et al.* United Nation Secretary Generals High Level Panel on Access to Medicine. Promoting Innovation and access to health technologies. 2016; 3-68 .

[22] Syam, N. Mainstreaming or dilution? intellectual property and development in WIPO. Intellectual Property and Development in WIPO (July 10, 2019). South Centre Reasearch Paper, (95).

[23] Shavell S, van Ypersele T. Rewards versus intellectual property rights. J Law Econ 2001; 44(2): 525-47. [http://dx.doi.org/10.1086/322811]

[24] Sekalala S, Forman L, Hodgson T, Mulumba M, Namyalo-Ganafa H, Meier BM. Decolonising human rights: how intellectual property laws result in unequal access to the COVID-19 vaccine. BMJ Glob Health 2021; 6(7): e006169. [http://dx.doi.org/10.1136/bmjgh-2021-006169] [PMID: 34253631]

[25] Swanson, A. Big pharmaceutical companies are spending far more on marketing than research. The Washington Post, 11. 2015.

[26] Velásquez, G. Guidelines on patentability and access to medicines (No. 61). Research Paper. 2015.

[27] World Health Organization. Globalization, TRIPS and access to pharmaceuticals (No. WHO/EDM/2001.2). World Health Organization.2001

[28] I-MAK. Overpatented, overpriced: How excessive pharmaceutical patenting is extending monopolies and driving up drug prices, November 2018.

[29] Gupta H, Kumar S, Roy S, Gaud RS. Patent protection strategies. J Pharm Bioallied Sci 2010; 2(1): 2-7. [http://dx.doi.org/10.4103/0975-7406.62694] [PMID: 21814422]

[30] Goyal D, *et al.* Team Lead. Life Science Team, and Madan Ekhande, Research Analyst, Life Science Team 2023.

[31] Velásquez, G. Intellectual property and access to medicines and vaccines. In: Vaccines, Medicines and COVID-19: How Can WHO Be Given a Stronger Voice? Springer, Cham 2022; pp. 73-92. [http://dx.doi.org/10.1007/978-3-030-89125-1_5]

[32] Attaran A, Gillespie-White L. Do patents for antiretroviral drugs constrain access to AIDS treatment in Africa? JAMA 2001; 286(15): 1886-92. [http://dx.doi.org/10.1001/jama.286.15.1886] [PMID: 11597292]

[33] Meijer M, Verschuuren M, Weggen E. COVID-19 vaccines a global public good? Moving past the rhetoric and making work of sharing intellectual property rights, know-how and technology. Eur J Public Health 2021; 31(5): 925-6.
[http://dx.doi.org/10.1093/eurpub/ckab144] [PMID: 34473255]

[34] Mathews DN, Correa C. The Doha Declaration ten years on and its impact on access to medicines and the right to health.2011.

[35] Syam N, Munoz V, Correa CM, Ido V The Doha Ministerial Declaration on TRIPS and Public Health on its Twentieth Anniversary.pp. 2021;1-12.

[36] Velásquez G, Boulet P. Globalization and access to drugs: Perspectives on the WTO TRIPS Agreement, 1997; p. 58.

[37] Stewart, TP. Declaration on Trips Agreement and Public Health WT/MIN (01)/Dec/2 (20 November 2001). In After Doha: The Changing Attitude and Ideas of the New WTO Round. 2002;(pp. 123-126). Brill Nijhoff.

[38] Fink C, Maskus KE, Qian Y. The economic effects of counterfeiting and piracy: A review and implications for developing countries. World Bank Res Obs 2016; 31(1): 1-28.

[39] World Health Organization, *et al.* Public health, innovation and intellectual property rights: report of the Commission on Intellectual Property Rights, Innovation and Public Health. 2006.

[40] Gervais DJ, *et al.* The TRIPS agreement. Eur Intellect Prop Rev 1999; 21: 156-62.

[41] Haugen HM. Does TRIPS (Agreement on Trade-Related Aspects of Intellectual Property Rights) prevent COVID-19 vaccines as a global public good? J World Intellect Prop 2021; 24(3-4): 195-220.
[http://dx.doi.org/10.1111/jwip.12187] [PMID: 34230807]

[42] Correa CM. Intellectual property and competition law. International centre for trade and sustainable development. 2021; (21): 1-44.

[43] Nicol D, Owoeye O. Using TRIPS flexibilities to facilitate access to medicines. Bull World Health Organ 2013; 91(7): 533-9.
[http://dx.doi.org/10.2471/BLT.12.115865] [PMID: 23825881]

[44] Nguyen PT, Gilmour S, Le PM, Onishi K, Kato K, Nguyen HV. Progress toward HIV elimination goals: trends in and projections of annual HIV testing and condom use in Africa. AIDS. 2021;35(8):p 1253-1262.

[45] Secretary-General, U.N., 2020. The United Nations secretary-general's high-level panel on access to medicines report: promoting innovation and access to health technologies. 2016. UNSG-HLP-Repo-t-FINAL-12-Sept-2016. pdf (accessed 21 Aug 2017).

[46] Roemer-Mahler A. Business conflict and global politics: The pharmaceutical industry and the global protection of intellectual property rights. Rev Int Polit Econ 2013; 20(1): 121-52.
[http://dx.doi.org/10.1080/09692290.2011.645848]

[47] Yadav D. Trade-Related Aspects of Intellectual Property Rights. Journal of Legal Studies & Research 2022; 8(5): 110-23.

[48] Gersten JDM. The quest for market exclusivity in biotechnology: Navigating the patent minefield. NeuroRx 2005; 2(4): 572-8.
[http://dx.doi.org/10.1602/neurorx.2.4.572] [PMID: 16489366]

[49] Monesh Mehndiratta. Patentability criteria 2022.

[50] Velásquez G. Intellectual property, public health and access to medicines in international organizations (No. 78). Research Paper. 2017.

[51] Correa CM. Guidelines for the examination of pharmaceutical patents: developing a public health perspective. Châtelaine: ICTSD. 2007.
[http://dx.doi.org/10.7215/IP_WP_20070101]

[52] Hoen ET, *et al.* Protection of clinical test data and public health: A proposal to end the stronghold of data exclusivity. Access to Medicines and Vaccines. Implementing Flexibilities Under Intellectual Property Law 2022; pp. 183-200.
[http://dx.doi.org/10.1007/978-3-030-83114-1_7]

[53] World Health Organization. (2002). Implications of the Doha Declaration on the TRIPS agreement and public health / Carlos M. Correa.

CHAPTER 6

International Agreements and Vaccine IP

Vikas K. Jain[1,*], **Himanshu Vishwakarma**[2], **Khushi Jain**[2] and **Sachin Kumar Jain**[2]

[1] *Department of Pharmacology, Acropolis Institute of Pharmaceutical Education and Research, Indore 453771, MP, India*

[2] *Oriental College of Pharmacy & Research, Oriental University Near Aurobindo Hospital, Sanwer Road, Indore 453555, MP, India*

Abstract: This chapter mainly discusses international agreements and treaties related to vaccines, including their types and functions. International agreements are formal understandings between two or more sovereign states or international organizations that set obligations, standards, and guidelines to ensure stability, collaboration, and resolve conflicts among nations. It has been mentioned that international agreements are formal understandings between sovereign states or international organizations to ensure stability, collaboration, and conflict resolution among nations. Typical types of agreements include bilateral, multilateral, regional, and trade agreements. The World Trade Organization is the only international organization that deals with trade regulations, and Trade-Related Aspects of Intellectual Property Rights and oversees minimum standards for intellectual property regulation, including vaccines and medical products. Additionally, it also includes a regulatory process for vaccines including preclinical and clinical studies, the Biologics License Application, and the marketing authorization application. Specific regulations related to biological products, blood products, and diagnostic materials are also mentioned. These also highlight international agreements and initiatives related to vaccines before the COVID-19 pandemic, such as the Global Alliance for Vaccines and Immunization and the World Health Organization. Overall, international agreements and treaties related to vaccines, the regulatory process for vaccines, and the importance of international cooperation in addressing vaccine-related challenges and promoting public health are discussed in this chapter.

Keywords: Regulatory process, Biologics license application, International agreement, Marketing authorization application, Patent, Public health, Treaties, Vaccine equity, Vaccines, World Health Organization, World trade organization.

* **Corresponding author Vikas K. Jain:** Department of Pharmacology, Acropolis Institute of Pharmaceutical Education and Research, Indore 453771, MP, India; E-mail: vikaspharma2209@gmail.com

Sachin Kumar Jain, Ravikant Gupta, Sudha Vengurlekar, Nidhi Bais & Gajendra P. Choudhary (Eds.)

INTRODUCTION

A formal understanding or arrangement between two or more sovereign states or international organizations is called an international agreement. These agreements may be in the form of pacts, accords, conventions, protocols, or treaties, among other formats. International agreements are used to set obligations, standards, and guidelines that control how the parties interact. To promote stability, resolve conflicts, and encourage collaboration among nations, international accords are essential. They can address a broad spectrum of topics, representing the many interests and worries of the participants. Trade agreements, accords pertaining to human rights, arms control, and environmental norms are a few examples of international agreements [1].

Any legally binding agreement between states is referred to as a "treaty" under international law (countries). A treaty may go by many different names, such as a convention, protocol, pact, accord, etc.; what distinguishes a treaty from other agreements is its contents, not its formal title. A treaty is defined by U.S. law as a legally binding agreement between nations that needs to be ratified and receive the Senate's "advice and consent." Executive Agreements refer to all other agreements, which are international treaties. A group of nations negotiates a treaty, either through an institution created especially for that purpose or through an already-existing entity like the UN Council on Disarmament. Several years may pass during the negotiation process, depending on the nature of the agreement and the number of signatory nations. Following the conclusion of discussions, officials from each of the participating states sign the treaty. Before the treaty is ratified and becomes legally enforceable, the terms may stipulate that it must be signed. A government can ratify a treaty by depositing an instrument of ratification—a document that formally confirms the government's agreement to the conditions of the treaty—at a site designated by the treaty.

Only the language of a treaty is legally binding unless it calls for other agreements or actions. A treaty's amendments are often only legally obligatory on the states that have ratified them. Agreements made at summits, review conferences, or gatherings of the state's parties are enforceable in politics but not in law. The UN Charter is one treaty that does provide provisions for other legally binding agreements. Countries committed to be legally bound by resolutions enacted by UN organizations like the General Assembly and Security Council when they signed and ratified the Charter. As a result, UN resolutions are enforceable against UN Member States without the need for ratification or signature.

An international agreement known as the IHR (2005) was made between the World Health Organization and 194 States Parties to keep an eye on, report, and address any incidents that might endanger public health worldwide. It aims to avoid needless interference with international trade and traffic while preventing, controlling, and responding to the international spread of illness in a way that is appropriate for and limited to public health threats [2].

TREATY PERSUASION

International agreements and treaties come in a variety of forms, each with a distinct function and a broad scope of topics covered. These are a few typical kinds:

Bilateral Treaties

There are two parties involved in these. Bilateral treaties between two countries can address a variety of topics, including trade, security, and cultural interaction.

Multilateral Treaties

Multilateral treaties, as opposed to bilateral ones, involve three or more participants. These agreements frequently deal with complicated problems that call for international cooperation. The Treaty on the Non-Proliferation of Nuclear Weapons and the United Nations Framework Convention on Climate Change are two examples.

Regional Treaties

Aimed at resolving regional issues, these accords encompass nations that are part of a certain geographical area. For instance, the Treaties of Rome and other European Union accords regulate how the EU operates.

Trade Agreements

The purpose of these agreements is to encourage and control international trade. Examples are the Trans-Pacific Partnership (TPP) and the North American Free Trade Agreement (NAFTA), which have been superseded by the United States-Mexico-Canada Agreement (USMCA).

These are but a few instances of the various kinds of treaties and agreements that the international community has, which deal with certain problems or situations [3].

World Trade Organization (WTO)

The only international organization that deals with international trade regulations is the WTO. It was established on 1st Jan 1995 by Uruguay Round negotiations. It is situated in Geneva, Switzerland, and has 164 members representing 98% of world trade. The WTO accords, which were negotiated, signed, and adopted by parliaments of most of the world's trading states, form its foundation. Ensuring that trade moves as easily, reliably, and freely as possible is the aim.

The WTO serves a variety of purposes, including managing a global system of trade regulations, mediating trade disputes amongst its members, and assisting developing nations with their requirements. Opening trade for everyone's benefit is the WTO's main goal.

Trade-Related Aspects of Intellectual Property Rights (TRIPS)

The WTO is responsible for overseeing the international agreement known as TRIPS. It establishes minimal requirements for a variety of IP regulations, such as those pertaining to vaccination and other medical product patents.

TRIPS is an international agreement that sets minimum standards for intellectual property regulation, including patents on vaccines and medical products. It requires member countries to grant patents for inventions in all fields of technology, including pharmaceuticals and vaccines. Proponents argue that patent protection under TRIPS provides an incentive for innovation, while critics argue that it can hinder access to essential medicines, particularly in developing countries. TRIPS also includes flexibilities that allow countries to take measures to protect public health. The COVID-19 pandemic has brought renewed attention to the role of TRIPS in vaccine access, with calls from various quarters to waive certain obligations related to intellectual property rights for vaccines and treatments [4].

REGULATORY APPROVAL FOR VACCINES

Although national vaccination regulations differ, they often adhere to a similar set of guidelines to guarantee vaccine quality, safety, and efficacy. Based on standard procedures used by several regulatory bodies, such as the World Health Organization (WHO), the European Medicines Agency (EMA), and the U.S. Food and Drug Administration (FDA), it is an outline of the standard regulatory process for vaccines included in Fig. (**1**) [5].

Preclinical Development

Preclinical studies, which employ animals to investigate the potential of a therapeutic drug or strategy, are crucial steps prior to clinical trials; however, data has demonstrated that subpar study design and execution has not only hampered clinical translation but also resulted in a substantial waste of precious research funds.

Preclinical research can be broadly divided into two categories: "hypothesis-generating" (exploratory) and "hypothesis testing" (confirmatory) research, based on the goal and purpose of the experiment.

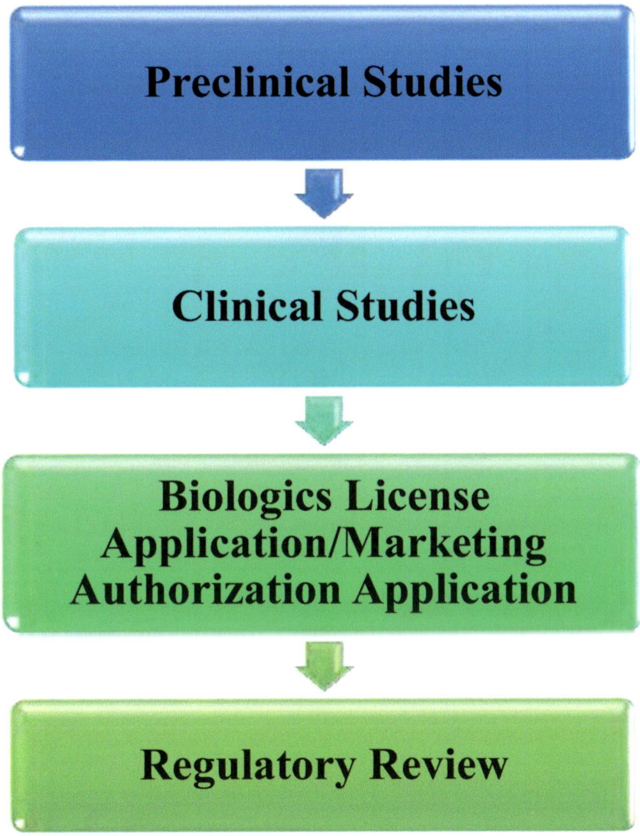

Fig. (1). Regulatory procedure for vaccines.

Studies that create hypotheses are frequently intuitive, and scientifically informed investigations that have the potential to produce testable theories about the pathophysiology of disease and possible therapeutic targets. However, hypothesis testing studies that aim to demonstrate repeatable intervention effects in pertinent animal models must be planned, carried out, analyzed, and reported to the highest possible levels of rigor and transparency to subsequently assess the validity of hypotheses generated in this manner and undoubtedly to justify clinical development of a therapeutic target. Additionally, this will help cut down on "waste" from research [6].

Clinical Development

The alternative language for medical research is "clinical research." Clinical research is conducted on human subjects to assess the effectiveness of a medicinal substance, a surgical or medical operation, or a gadget in the context of patient care and treatment. A clinical trial is a methodical procedure designed to determine if a medication or medical technology is safe and effective in treating, preventing, or diagnosing a disease or other medical conditions. Phase 0 (micro-dosing studies), phase 1, phase 2, phase 3, and phase 4 are among the phases of a clinical trial.

Phase 0

Phase 0 examines medication microdosing, or excessively low (1/100th) concentrations, for shorter periods of time. It determines the dose for phase I investigations by researching pharmacokinetics. This was previously conducted on animals but is currently done on people.

Phase 1

Approximately fifty healthy volunteers are enlisted in phase 1trial. The goal of the phase 1 trial is to determine the maximum dosage for humans and a safe dose range. During this phase, the researcher observed the impact on pharmacokinetics and pharmacodynamics. Single-center investigations are typical. In addition to evaluating the safety and optimal dosage, the appropriate method of drug administration, such as oral, intravenous, or topical is also decided.

Phase 2

Several hundred patients who have the aliment that the new drug is intended to treat are involved in phase 2 trials. The same dosage that was determined to be safe in the preceding phase is often administered to them. To determine the drug's effectiveness and to learn more about any potential side effects for a few months or even years. It determines the course of treatment and interactions between drugs.

Phase 3

This study involves the recruitment of over 300 participants (up to 3000) of both sexes and is a multicentric trial. The drug's safety and effectiveness are assessed during the pre-marketing phase. Typically, phase 3 trials are double-blind, meaning that neither the researcher nor the participant is aware of the medication the participant is taking. This supports eliminating bias when interpreting results.

Adverse occurrences and medication responses are recorded. The NDA procedure is initiated by contacting the FDA or other relevant regulatory bodies.

Phase 4

Phase 4 trials happen after the FDA has approved the drug. This phase considers thousands of patients and can last for a long time. Researchers use this phase to get more information about the drug's long-term safety, and effectiveness and investigate possible drug interactions [7].

Biologics License Application

In the United States, developers file a BLA if clinical trials are successful. The 21 CFR 600–680 regulations govern the BLA. A request for authorization to introduce, or deliver for introduction, a biological product into interstate commerce is made through the Biologics License Application (21 CFR 601.2). In general, genetic therapies, vaccinations, and other allergy-causing pharmaceutical items require the filing of a Biologics License Application (BLA).

The license is issued once it has been determined that the product, the manufacturing procedure, and the manufacturing facilities satisfy all applicable standards for maintaining the product's potency, safety, and purity. Assessments of safety and purity need to consider, among other things, the testing and storage of cell substrates, which are frequently used to make biological substances [8].

CFR Part 600 – 680

Title 21 of the Code of Federal Restrictions (CFR) is referenced in CFR Parts 600–680, with a particular emphasis on food and drug restrictions. Regarding the Food and Drug Administration's (FDA) supervision and control of food, medications, cosmetics, medical devices, and other relevant products, these regulations address a wide range of subjects. A summary of some of the subparts in this range is provided below.

- General biological products under CFR Part 600.
- General biological product standards are found in CFR Part 610.
- Additional requirements for human blood and blood products are found in CFR Part 640.
- Additional guidelines for diagnostic materials used in laboratory testing are included in CFR Part 660.
- Further regulations for various items are outlined in CFR Part 680.

Marketing Authorization Application

In the US, the average review period for MAAs was 201 days, whereas in the EU, it was 337 days. In the European Union, the average evaluation period for new anticancer medications involving MAAs was 136 days longer than in the United States. Small molecules made up almost two-thirds of the products (n = 49), whereas compounds produced from biotechnology made up one-third (n = 27). The product type, such as tiny molecules or biotechnology-derived products, did not significantly affect the review time [9].

Mutual Recognition Procedure

Through the Mutual Recognition procedure, applicants who have already had their medicine approved in the Reference Member state (RMS) may now acquire marketing authorization in the Concerned Member States (CMS).

The applicant presents an identical dossier, complete with all necessary information, to each EU member state where they want marketing authorization. One Member State tells the others as soon as it decides to analyze the medical product (thus designating it as the "RMS"). It rules to more Member States (which subsequently become the "CMS"), to whom additional petitions have been filed.

RMS reports on its results to other states. The primary consumer of this kind of medicine approval process is the generic business.

Nationalized Procedure

Only one member state is permitted for applicants to receive marketing authorization under the Nationalised method. A Member State's competent authority must receive an application to provide a national marketing authorization. Under this approach, new active chemicals that are not required under the Centralised procedure can receive marketing authorization. This process has a 210-day timeline.

INTERNATIONAL AGREEMENT ON VACCINES

Before COVID-19 Pandemic

Numerous international agreements and initiatives addressed vaccine-related concerns, such as vaccine production, distribution, and access, prior to the COVID-19 pandemic. Among the important accords and institutions, GAVI are:

Global Alliance for Vaccines and Immunization

GAVI is an organization that was founded in 1996. The goal of the public-private global health cooperation is to improve immunization access in underdeveloped nations. Supporting immunization programs and giving vaccinations to people in need, it brings together governments, international organizations, the commercial sector, and civil society [10].

World Health Organization

The WHO is essential to the coordination of global vaccination initiatives. It offers recommendations on vaccination distribution, safety, and development. Strategies to increase vaccination rates and stop the spread of diseases that can be prevented by vaccination are included in the WHO's Global Vaccine Action Plan (GVAP) [11].

International Coordinating Group on Vaccine Provision for Epidemic Meningitis Control

The WHO, UNICEF, Médecins Sans Frontières, and the International Federation of Red Cross and Red Crescent Societies are members of the International Coordinating Group on Vaccine Provision for Epidemic Meningitis Control. This group works together to make sure that vaccines are provided in a timely manner during meningitis outbreaks in Africa [12].

Introduction of Rotavirus Vaccine in GAVI-Eligible Countries

To avoid severe diarrhea in children, GAVI has supported the introduction of rotavirus vaccines in GAVI-eligible countries in partnership with organizations like the WHO and UNICEF [13].

Measles and Rubella Initiative

Through vaccination campaigns and regular immunization programs, this international collaboration—which includes the World Health Organization (WHO), UNICEF, the American Red Cross, and the U.S. Centres for Disease Control and Prevention (CDC)—aims to lower the number of measles and rubella deaths globally [14].

After COVID-19 Pandemic

To address the worldwide problems posed by the virus and to guarantee fair and equal access to COVID-19 vaccines, several international agreements and initiatives were developed during the COVID-19 pandemic. Among the important accords and partnerships are:

COVAX Facility

To ensure that everyone has fair access to COVID-19 vaccinations, Gavi, the Vaccine Alliance, the World Health Organization (WHO), and the Coalition for Epidemic Preparedness Innovations (CEPI) together spearheaded the COVAX initiative. COVAX aimed to consolidate resources from member nations to facilitate the creation, manufacturing, and delivery of vaccines to high-income as well as low- and middle-income countries [15].

Advance Purchase Agreements (APAs)

Several nations signed APAs with pharmaceutical firms that were creating COVID-19 vaccines. These agreements enabled nations to obtain vaccination doses ahead of schedule, frequently even before the immunizations [16].

Global Vaccination Supply Chain

To create a global vaccination supply chain, several international organizations worked together, including UNICEF, Gavi, and the WHO. This included organizing the manufacturing, shipping, and distribution of COVID-19 vaccinations to various global locations [17].

Vaccine Multilateralism

Nations took part in international initiatives to resolve issues with vaccine distribution. While some advocated technology transfer and the sharing of intellectual property to increase vaccine production capacity globally, others joined campaigns to donate vaccinations to underprivileged nations [18].

World Trade Organization Waiver

In 2020, South Africa and India put out a proposal at the WTO to temporarily waive some intellectual property rights pertaining to COVID-19 technology, including vaccines. By enabling more nations to develop generic versions, the intention was to enable wider access to vaccinations [19].

Bilateral Agreements and Donations

Countries have bilateral agreements in place for the purchase and donation of COVID-19 vaccinations to boost vaccination campaigns in areas with limited resources; a few high-income nations promised to give vaccinations to low- and middle-income nations [20].

IPR CONFLICT REGARDING VACCINE

IPR disputes have emerged with different vaccinations and in different situations. Among the noteworthy instances are:

COVID-19 Immunizations

Intellectual property rights became controversial during the COVID-19 epidemic, especially in relation to vaccines. AstraZeneca, Moderna, Pfizer-BioNTech, and other pharmaceutical firms created vaccines at a rate never seen before, raising questions about fair access. Due to production capacity constraints and patent restrictions, developing nations had difficulty obtaining vaccines. To facilitate wider access and quicken international immunization campaigns, requests were made to waive several intellectual property rights pertaining to COVID-19 vaccines.

Human Papillomavirus (HPV) Vaccine

There have been intellectual property conflicts surrounding the HPV vaccination, which prevents cervical cancer and other disorders brought on by an infection with the human papillomavirus. HPV Vaccine businesses are patent holders for HPV vaccinations [21].

The patent holders of HPV vaccines have come under fire for charging exorbitant prices that prevent many developing nations—where cervical cancer rates are frequently highest—from accessing the vaccines. Price discussions, agreements for voluntary licensing, and technology transfer programs have all been a part of the endeavors to increase access to HPV vaccines [22].

Pneumococcal Conjugate Vaccine (PCV)

A further focal point for disputes pertaining to intellectual property has been the PCV, which offers protection against pneumococcal illnesses like pneumonia and meningitis. In many low- and middle-income nations, where PCV infections represent a substantial public health burden, access to the drug has been restricted due to high costs and patent hurdles. To overcome these issues, initiatives like the Gavi Alliance's Advance Market Commitment have provided vaccine makers with financial incentives to develop and distribute PCV at competitive costs [23].

Influenza Vaccine

The topic of intellectual property issues has also come up in relation to the influenza vaccine. Although vaccines are widely available worldwide, access to them may still be restricted in some areas due to issues like supply chain constraints and cost. Other factors that have affected access to vaccines in different contexts include competition among vaccine manufacturers, patent disputes, and difficulties in transferring technology [24].

GLOBAL SCENARIO OF VACCINES DEVELOPMENT

Millions of lives are saved annually by vaccination, making it a success story in global health and development. Vaccines lower the likelihood of contracting an illness by enhancing your body's defences against infection. Your immune system is stimulated when you receive a vaccination. With the availability of vaccinations against over 20 deadly illnesses, individuals of all ages can now enjoy longer and healthier lives. As of now, vaccinations can put an end to between 3.5 and 5 million fatalities annually due to illnesses including measles, tetanus, diphtheria, and pertussis. Health systems suffered severe setbacks in 2020 and 2021 because of the COVID-19 pandemic, & related disruptions, amidst all round COVID-19 vaccine efforts. Globally speaking, however, recovery is imminent in 2022; vaccination coverage for diphtheria, pertussis, and tetanus (DTP) has nearly reached 2019 levels, albeit unevenly across nations. Due to its high transmissibility, measles serves as a "canary in the coal mine," rapidly revealing any gaps in the population's immunity. Nonetheless, compared to 19 million in 2019, 22 million children in 2022 did not receive their scheduled first dose of the measles vaccination [25].

The Cervical Cancer

The fourth most frequent malignancy in women is cervical cancer. Around 3,11,000 women globally lost their lives to cervical cancer in 2018, according to estimates of the disease's 5,70,000 new cases. Most occurrences of cervical cancer can be avoided with effective primary (HPV vaccine) and secondary preventive strategies (screening for and treating precancerous lesions). If cervical cancer is identified early and treated appropriately, it is among the most curable types of cancer. Palliative care combined with the right treatment can help control cancers that have been detected in their later stages. Within a generation, cervical cancer as a public health issue can be eradicated with a comprehensive strategy for prevention, screening, and treatment [25].

The Cholera

Acute diarrheal illness known as cholera is caused due to consuming food or water tainted with the Vibrio cholerae bacteria. Cholera is still a global public health concern and a sign of inequality and underdevelopment in society. According to research estimates, there are between 1.3 and 4.0 million cases of cholera worldwide each year, and between 21,000 and 1,43,000 deaths are attributed to the virus. Through widespread campaigns, more than 50 million doses of oral cholera vaccines (OCV) have been effectively administered in a variety of contexts since the establishment of the global stockpile in 2013. OCV is a tool that is utilised in addition to traditional methods of cholera control. It ought to be methodically considered during outbreaks and emergencies, as well as in areas where cholera is endemic [25].

The Malaria

A novel vaccination called R21/Matrix-M has been approved by the World Health Organisation (WHO) to prevent malaria in children. The recommendation was approved by the WHO Director-General after its normal biannual meeting, which took place on September 25–29. It was based on the advice from the WHO's Malaria Policy Advisory Group (MPAG) and Strategic Advisory Group of Experts on Immunisation (SAGE). The RTS, S/AS01 vaccine was recommended by the WHO in 2021; it is the second vaccine against malaria that the WHO has recommended. It has been demonstrated that both vaccinations are safe and effective in preventing childhood malaria, and they should have a significant influence on public health if widely used. There is an enormous demand for malaria vaccinations, but there is a limited supply of RTS,S. It is anticipated that the inclusion of R21 on the WHO's recommended list of malaria vaccines will lead to an adequate supply of vaccines to protect all children residing in places where malaria poses a risk to public health [25].

The Rabies

Human-use rabies vaccines that are licensed rely on pure, inactivated rabies virus that is cultured in tissue culture or in duck or chicken embryos. The use of nerve-tissue-produced vaccines has essentially been halted and is no longer advised by the World Health Organisation (WHO). These vaccines are less expensive but also less immunogenic and, more critically, can have major side effects. Rabies vaccinations can be administered intramuscularly (IM) or intradermally (ID) at a dose ten to fifteen times lower. For usage in humans, several different regimens have been approved. The vaccination for PrEP is normally administered three times, on days 0–7, 21–28, and 28 [26].

The Tuberculosis

Developing an effective vaccine or vaccines that may break the cycle of transmission will be necessary to achieve the WHO's ambitious strategic goal of eliminating the tuberculosis epidemic by 2035. Bacille Calmette-Guérin (BCG), which was originally given orally to a kid in Paris in 1921 by Dr. Benjamin Weill-Halle, is the only vaccine that is officially approved to prevent tuberculosis. Today, most nations still administer BCG to infants (parenterally) as part of the WHO's Expanded Programme on Immunisation. While infant BCG has been shown in several clinical trials to be somewhat helpful in preventing severe extrapulmonary forms of tuberculosis in young children, its effectiveness in preventing tuberculosis in adults and adolescents has been inconsistent, and it has not been able to contain the global epidemic.

To confirm and expand on these findings, BCG revaccination is presently being assessed in a second, larger trial in IGRA-negative South African teenagers (1800 participants assigned 1:1 to either BCG or placebo), with sustained IGRA conversion as the primary objective (NCT04152161). If the current trial is successful in confirming the vaccine's efficacy, BCG revaccination may prove to be a valuable tool for managing Mtb infection in populations at high risk of infection. This is because BCG is an inexpensive, already licensed intervention with a long and solid safety record in immunocompetent individuals [27].

The COVID-19

Although we may need more data on hospitalisations and deaths resulting from the adverse outcomes of COVID-19 in children (SARS-CoV-2 infections rarely cause severe symptoms or death in children), the Pfizer/BioNTech and Moderna vaccines have currently provided some clinical trial data to support the notion that their adaptive application is able to expand to adolescents and children. Long-term human clinical studies and crucial phase II and III clinical trials are also necessary to guarantee long-term human safety. On December 11, 2020, the USA FDA issued an EUA for the Pfizer/BioNTech vaccines, to be used in people who are at least 16 years old. Only the Pfizer/BioNTech vaccine was approved for use in teenagers between the ages of 12 and 17 as of July 30, 2021. On May 10, 2021, the EUA was extended to encompass adolescents between the ages of 12 and 15 years [28].

The Dengue

The Takeda pharmaceutical business is manufacturing TAK-003 (TDV), a live-attenuated tetravalent dengue vaccine that was initially created and assembled by scientists at the US Division of Vector-Borne Diseases of the Centres for Disease

Control and Prevention. The vaccine is based on chimeric viruses made with recombinant DNA technology and an attenuated virus included in Table **1**. The genetic foundation for all four of the vaccine viruses is derived from a live-attenuated DENV-2 virus, which is the basis of TAK-003. In partnership with GlaxoSmithKline (GSK), the Walter Reed Army Institute of Research (WRAIR) created the live-attenuated tetravalent dengue (TDEN) vaccine. The vaccine consists of four strains of DENV: DENV-1 (45AZ5), DENV-2 (S16803), DENV-3 (CH53489), and DENV-4 (341750). Adults who are not vaccinated against flaviviruses are given two doses at a 6-month interval. After being extracted from spontaneous infections in C6/36 cells, all four viruses were serially passaged via PDK cells to decrease their pathogenicity [29].

Table 1. List of companies with their international agreement in brief.

S. No.	Company Name	Vaccines	Purpose	Year	International Agreement
01	Bavarian Nordic	Vaxchora	Cholera	2022	With US and Europe
02	Bharat Biotech	COVAXIN®	COVID-19	2021	WithMX, IND, UAE, PHIL, BR, and US
03	Merck Pharmaceuticals	Heplisav-B	Hepatitis B	2022	With US, IND, CA, EU, BR, SA, JPN, and CN [30]
04	Pfizer-BioNTech	Comirnaty	SARS-CoV-2	2020	With US, EU, BR, AU, UK, CH and ZA [31]
05	Moderna	Spikevax	COVID-19	2022	With US, EU, CA, UK, CH, and JPN [32]
06	Johnson & Johnson (Janssen)	Janssen	COVID-19	2020	With US, EU, CA, and UK [33]
07	AstraZeneca	Vaxzevria	COVID-19	2021	With US, UK, IND, EU, and AU [34]
08	AstraZeneca	Covishield	COVID-19	2021	With US, UK, IND, EU, and AU [34]
09	Sanofi	Ipol®	Polio		
10	Merck	M-M-R® II	Measles, Mumps, Rubella	1996	With US, EU, CA, JPN, AU, BR, SA, and CN [35]
11	GlaxoSmithKline	RabAvert®	Rabies	2018	With US, and EU [36]
12	Sanofi	Imovax® Rabies	Rabies	2003	With US, UK, GER, ESP, ITLY and FR [37]
13	Pfizer	Prevnar 13®	Pneumococcal	2020	With US, CA, EU, and AU [31]
14	Emergent BioSolutions	BioThrax®	Anthrax	2008	With US, EU, and UN [38, 39]

(Table 1) cont.....

S. No.	Company Name	Vaccines	Purpose	Year	International Agreement
15	GlaxoSmithKline	Shingrix®	Herpes Zoster (Shingles)	2017	With EU, and US [36]
16	Merck Sharp & Dohme (MSD)	Gardasil®	Cervical cancer	2006	With EU, US, and CA [30]
17	PaxVax	Vivotif®	Typhoid	1989	With US, EU, SEA, IND, WHO, and Gavi [38, 39]
18	Serum Institute of India Ltd.	NASOVAC™	Pandemic (H1N1) Influenza	2012	With US, UK, EU, and IND [40]

NEW AGENDA OF WHO FOR IMMUNIZATION

An ambitious, comprehensive worldwide vision and strategy for vaccines and immunisation for the years 2021–2030 is outlined in the Immunisation Agenda 2030 (IA2030). It builds on past experiences, recognises the ongoing and emerging risks associated with infectious illnesses, and seizes fresh chances to address those threats. According to IA2030, vaccinations are essential to ensuring that everyone has access to the best possible physical and mental health and to a better, safer, and more prosperous future. They also serve as an investment in the future. IA2030 seeks to guarantee that we not only preserve the hard-earned gains but even surpass them, ensuring that no one is left behind in whatever circumstance or stage of life.

The goal of IA2030 is to mobilise and coordinate the efforts of local, national, regional, and international stakeholders, including academic and research institutions, corporations, civil society, national governments, regional organisations, international agencies, development partners, and healthcare providers. More effective and efficient use of resources, performance-enhancing innovation, and steps to achieve programmatic and financial sustainability will maximise its impact. To improve access to high-quality, affordable primary health care, achieve universal health coverage, and accelerate progress towards the 2030 Sustainable Development Goals (SDGs), success will depend on forming and fostering partnerships both inside and outside the health sector [41].

VACCINE DEVELOPMENT IN INDIAN SCENARIO

India's ability to do research and development on vaccinations is expanding, putting it in a position to significantly impact the creation of critically needed new vaccines. We are now positioned among the world's leading makers of vaccines. Listed below are a few vaccines that India has created thus far.

The Plague

The plague is an infectious disease that is brought on by the bacteria Yersinia pestis and is spread to people via rodent bites from infected fleas. A plague epidemic struck the nation in 1986. At Grant Medical College in Mumbai, Dr. Haffkine created a vaccine against the plague using a two-room setup that was given to him by the Indian government. The first vaccination to be developed in India was the plague vaccine created by Dr. Haffkine in 1897 [42].

The Polio

A contagious disease caused by the poliovirus is known as poliomyelitis or polio. Its infection results in nerve damage that can cause paralysis, breathing difficulties, and occasionally even death. In 1970, the Pasteur Institute of India, located in Coonoor, developed the first oral polio vaccine produced domestically in India, known as Sabin. A polio vaccine that was inactivated was also created in 1984, but it was eventually discontinued. India became polio-free in January 2011 and has remained so ever since [42].

The Rabies Virus

A lyssavirus that targets the central nervous system and causes convulsions, paralysis, and ultimately death is the deadly virus that causes rabies, which is spread from animals to people. Neural tissue anti-rabies vaccine was created at the Pasteur Institute of India (PII) in 1907. Later, the same institute created the technique to produce a human-useable rabies vaccine based on tissue culture and then purified DNA generated from Vero cells [42].

The Hepatitis B

The hepatitis B virus (HBV) is the known cause of hepatitis B, a liver illness. When the virus infects someone who is not affected and enters their body by blood, semen, or other bodily fluids from an infected individual, the infection spreads. At IISC, Bangalore, a domestic recombinant Hepatitis B vaccine was created in the late 1990s. Under the designations BEVAC and Elovac-B, respectively, Biological E Limited, and Indian Immunological Limited, Hyderabad, conducted the required clinical trials, secured the regulatory approvals, and released the vaccine in 2004 and 2006, respectively [42].

The Pig Influenza

Swine flu, often known as H1N1 influenza, is a highly contagious respiratory illness that affects pigs. Humans can contract this virus by coming into touch with infected pigs or swine influenza virus-contaminated settings. A vaccination against the H1N1 virus was created in 2009 to stop pandemic-related infections. The H1N1 vaccination prevents the flu by using viral particles that have been destroyed. Three Indian manufacturers—India Sanofi Pasteur, Serum Institute, and Bharat Biotech—manufacture and market the vaccine [42].

The Meningitis

Neisseria meningitidis bacteria primarily causes meningococcal meningitis, a bacterial infection of the meninges surrounding the brain and spinal cord. African Meningitis Belt successfully used MenAfriVac, a meningitis "A" vaccine produced by the Serum Institute of India, Pune. Meningococcal conjugate vaccines (MCVs) are currently approved for use in India for two different types: Menactra®, a quadrivalent vaccination from Sanofi Pasteur, and Serum Institute of India (SII)'s monovalent serogroup A vaccine [42].

The Cholera

A bacteria known as Vibrio cholerae taints food and water, resulting in the infectious disease cholera. It causes extremely watery diarrhoea, which, if left untreated, can occasionally result in dehydration and even death. The first domestically produced bivalent oral cholera vaccine, known as Shancol, was created by Shantha Biotechnics in Hyderabad in April 2009 and was granted a license for use in the nation. Shancol introduced the less expensive cholera vaccine [42].

The Japan Encephalitis

Japanese encephalitis (JE) is a virus that infects the brain and is spread by mosquitoes. Serious brain inflammation, a sharp headache, a high fever, and disorientation are possible side effects. The nation received its first "JENVAC" vaccine, which was created domestically, for Japanese encephalitis in October 2013. Scientists from Bharat Biotech International Ltd. and the Indian Council of Medical Research (ICMR) National Institute of Virology (NIV), Pune, collaborated to create the vaccine [42].

CONCLUDING REMARK

It can be concluded that international agreements and treaties play a crucial role in addressing vaccine-related challenges and promoting public health. These agreements, such as bilateral, multilateral, regional, and trade agreements, establish obligations, standards, and guidelines to ensure stability, collaboration, and resolution of conflicts among nations. The WTO is the main international organization dealing with trade regulations, and the TRIPS oversees minimum standards for intellectual property regulation, including vaccines and medical products. Additionally, it also highlights the standard regulatory process for vaccines, which includes preclinical studies, clinical studies, Biologics License Application, marketing authorization application, and regulatory review. It emphasizes the importance of rigorous and transparent planning, execution, analysis, and reporting of hypothesis testing studies to justify the clinical development of therapeutic targets. Prior to the COVID-19 pandemic, there were international agreements and initiatives such as GAVI, the Vaccine Alliance, and the WHO that aimed to address global health challenges. These agreements aimed to monitor, report, and address incidents that could endanger public health worldwide while minimizing interference with international trade and traffic. Overall, international cooperation and agreements are instrumental in ensuring the safety, efficacy, and accessibility of vaccines and promoting global public health.

REFERENCES

[1] "United Nations Treaty Collection." Accessed: Feb. 09, 2024. [Online]. Available from: https://treaties.un.org/Pages/Overview.aspx?path=overview/definition/page1_en.xml

[2] Accessed: Feb. 07, 2024. Available from: https://www.phe.gov/s3/law/Pages/International.aspx

[3] "Introduction - Researching Treaties and International Agreements - Research Guides at Library of Congress." 2024. Available from: https://guides.loc.gov/researching-treaties-and-internatio-al-agreements

[4] "WTO | intellectual property - overview of TRIPS Agreement." Accessed: Feb. 07, 2024. Available from: https://www.wto.org/english/tratop_e/trips_e/intel2_e.htm

[5] Singh K, Mehta S. The clinical development process for a novel preventive vaccine. J Postgrad Med 2016; 62(1): 4-11. [http://dx.doi.org/10.4103/0022-3859.173187] [PMID: 26732191]

[6] Huang W, Percie Du Sert N, Vollert J, Rice ASC. "General Principles of Preclinical Study Design," in Good Research Practice in Non-Clinical Pharmacology and Biomedicine, vol. 257, Bespalov A, Michel MC, Steckler T, Eds. Handbook of Experimental Pharmacology, vol. 257. , Cham: Springer International Publishing, 2019, pp. 55–69. [http://dx.doi.org/10.1007/164_2019_277]

[7] Kandi V, Vadakedath S. Clinical Trials and Clinical Research: A Comprehensive Review. Cureus 2023; 15(2): e35077. [http://dx.doi.org/10.7759/cureus.35077] [PMID: 36938261]

[8] Patil SB, Vaishnav HA, Mundada AS. Preparation of Biologics License Application (BLA) for USFDA: An Overview. Int J Pharm Sci Rev Res 2023; 79(2) [http://dx.doi.org/10.47583/ijpsrr.2023.v79i02.022]

[9] da Costa Gonçalves F, Demirci E, Zwiers A. A detailed analysis of expedited regulatory review time of marketing authorization applications for new anticancer drugs in the US and EU. Clin Transl Sci 2022; 15(8): 1959-67. [http://dx.doi.org/10.1111/cts.13308] [PMID: 35561071]

[10] "Gavi, the Vaccine Alliance." Accessed: Feb. 09, 2024. Available from: https://www.gavi.org/

[11] "GAVI Alliance." Accessed: Feb. 09, 2024. Available from: https://www.who.int/europe/about-us/partnerships/partners/global-health-partnerships/gavi-alliance

[12] "About the International Coordinating Group (ICG) on Vaccine Provision." Accessed: Feb. 09, 2024. Available from: https://www.who.int/groups/icg/about

[13] "First GAVI-eligible country marks official introduction of rotavirus vaccine." Accessed: Feb. 09, 2024. Available from: https://www.path.org/our-impact/media-center/first-gavi-eligible-contry-marks-official-introduction-of-rotavirus-vaccine/

[14] "Measles & Rubella Initiative," Wikipedia. Aug. 26, 2022. Accessed: Feb. 09, 2024. Available from: https://en.wikipedia.org/w/index.php?title=Measles_%26_Rubella_Initiative&oldid=1106860861

[15] "COVAX Facility." Accessed: Feb. 09, 2024. Available from: https://www.gavi.org/covax-facility

[16] "'No Regrets' Purchasing in a pandemic: making the most of advance purchase agreements | Globalization and Health | Full Text." Accessed: Feb. 09, 2024. Available from: https://globalizationandhealth.biomedcentral.com/articles/10.1186/s12992-022-00851-3

[17] Bown CP, Bollyky TJ. How COVID-19 vaccine supply chains emerged in the midst of a pandemic. World Econ 2022; 45(2): 468-522.
[http://dx.doi.org/10.1111/twec.13183] [PMID: 34548749]

[18] Singh B, Kaur J, Chattu VK. Global vaccine inequities and multilateralism amid COVID-19: Reconnaissance of Global Health Diplomacy as a panacea? Health Promot Perspect 2022; 12(4): 315-24.
[http://dx.doi.org/10.34172/hpp.2022.41] [PMID: 36852205]

[19] "2.pdf." Accessed: Feb. 09, 2024. Available from: https://crsreports.congress.gov/product/pdf/R/R47231/2

[20] "2014-2021: Bilateral guideline – Annex 6: Partnership agreement template | EEA Grants." Accessed: Feb. 09, 2024. Available from: https://eeagrants.org/resources/2014-2021-bilateral-guideline-annex-6-partnership-agreement-template

[21] Okereke M. Towards vaccine equity: Should big pharma waive intellectual property rights for COVID-19 vaccines? Public Health in Practice 2021; 2: 100165.
[http://dx.doi.org/10.1016/j.puhip.2021.100165] [PMID: 34345873]

[22] Songane M, Grossmann V. The patent buyout price for human papilloma virus (HPV) vaccine and the ratio of R&D costs to the patent value. PLoS One 2021; 16(1): e0244722.
[http://dx.doi.org/10.1371/journal.pone.0244722] [PMID: 33428667]

[23] Rodgers GL, Whitney CG, Klugman KP. Triumph of Pneumococcal Conjugate Vaccines: Overcoming a Common Foe, J. Infect. Dis 2021; 224(4): S352–S359.
[http://dx.doi.org/10.1093/infdis/jiaa535]

[24] "influenza.pdf." Accessed: Feb. 07, 2024. Available from: https://www.wipo.int/export/sites/www/policy/es/global_health/pdf/influenza.pdf

[25] "Vaccines and immunization." Accessed: Feb. 06, 2024. Available from: https://www.who.int/health-topics/vaccines-and-immunization

[26] Ertl HCJ. New Rabies Vaccines for Use in Humans. Vaccines (Basel) 2019; 7(2): 54.
[http://dx.doi.org/10.3390/vaccines7020054] [PMID: 31226750]

[27] Scriba TJ, Netea MG, Ginsberg AM. Key recent advances in TB vaccine development and understanding of protective immune responses against Mycobacterium tuberculosis. Semin Immunol 2020; 50: 101431.
[http://dx.doi.org/10.1016/j.smim.2020.101431] [PMID: 33279383]

[28] Wang SC, Rai CI, Chen YC. Challenges and Recent Advancements in COVID-19 Vaccines. Microorganisms 2023; 11(3): 787.
[http://dx.doi.org/10.3390/microorganisms11030787] [PMID: 36985360]

[29] Pintado Silva J, Fernandez-Sesma A. Challenges on the development of a dengue vaccine: a

comprehensive review of the state of the art. J Gen Virol 2023; 104(3): 001831. [http://dx.doi.org/10.1099/jgv.0.001831] [PMID: 36857199]

[30] "Merck Announces Fourth-Quarter and Full-Year 2023 Financial Results," Merck.com. Accessed: Feb. 09, 2024. Available from: https://www.merck.com/news/merck-announces-fourth-quarter-and-full-year-2023-financial-results/

[31] "Pfizer–BioNTech COVID-19 vaccine," Wikipedia. Feb. 04, 2024. Available from: https://en.wikipedia.org/w/index.php?title=Pfizer%E2%80%93BioNTech_COVID-19_vaccine&oldid=1203264137

[32] "Moderna Announces New Supply Contract With The U.S. Government For An Initial 66 Million Doses Of A Moderna Bivalent COVID-19 Booster Vaccine With Options For U.S. Government To Purchase Up To An Additional 234 Million Doses." Accessed: Feb. 09, 2024. Available from: https://investors.modernatx.com/news/news-details/2022/Moderna-Announces-New-Su-ply-Contract-With-The-U.S.-Government-For-An-Initial-66-Million-Doses-Of-A-M-derna-Bivalent-COVID-19-Booster-Vaccine-With-Options-For-U.S.-Government-To-Purchase-Up-To-An-Additional-234-Million-Doses/default.aspx

[33] Available from: https://www.jnj.com/press-releases/johnson-johnson-announces-landmark-agreement-to-enable-its-COVID-19-vaccine-to-be- manufactured-and-made-available-by-an-african-company-for-people-living-in-africa

[34] "Press corner," European Commission - European Commission. Accessed: Feb. 09, 2024. Available from: https://ec.europa.eu/commission/presscorner/home/en

[35] "termsAndConditionsOfSale.pdf." Accessed: Feb. 09, 2024. Available from: https://www.merckvaccines.com/wp-content/uploads/sites/8/2019/12/termsAndConditionsOfSale.pdf

[36] "GSK and Vir Biotechnology announce United States government agreement to purchase additional supply of sotrovimab, authorised for the early treatment of COVID-19 | GSK." Accessed: Feb. 09, 2024. Available from: https://www.gsk.com/en-gb/media/press-releases/gsk-and-vir-biotechn-logy-announce-united-states-government-agreement-to-purchase-additional-supply-of-sotrovimab/

[37] "Janssen Enters into Agreement with Sanofi to Advance Potential First-In-Class Vaccine Program," Janssen. Accessed: Feb. 09, 2024. Available from: https://www.janssen.com/janssen-enter--agreement-sanofi-advance-potential-first-class-vaccine-program

[38] "Emergent BioSolutions Signs Five-Year Agreement for Large-Scale Drug Substance Manufacturing for Johnson & Johnson's Lead COVID-19 Vaccine Candidate," Emergent BioSolutions. Accessed: Feb. 09, 2024. Available from: https://www.emergentbiosolutions.com/press/news-release-detai-s-emergent-biosolutions-signs-five-year-agreement-large-scale-drug/

[39] "EX-10.5." Accessed: Feb. 09, 2024. Available from: https://www.sec.gov/Archives/edgar/data/1682852/000119312518323562/d577473dex105.htm

[40] "Serum Institute Of India - News." Accessed: Feb. 09, 2024. Available from: https://www.seruminstitute.com/news_novavax-signs-COVID-19-vaccine-s-pply-deal-with-indias-serum-institute.php

[41] "Immunization Agenda 2030: A Global Strategy To Leave No One Behind." Accessed: Feb. 07, 2024. Available from: https://www.who.int/publications/m/item/immunization-agenda-2030-a-gl-bal-strategy-to-leave-no-one-behind

[42] "Indian contribution in Vaccine development | India Science, Technology & Innovation - ISTI Portal." Accessed: Feb. 06, 2024. Available from: https://www.indiascienceandtechnology.gov.in/COVID-1--vaccine/indian-contribution-vaccine-development

CHAPTER 7

COVID-19 and the Role of IP Rights in Vaccine Development

Shikha Jaiswal[1,*], **Sudha Vengurlekar**[2], **Sachin Kumar Jain**[1] and **Umesh K. Patil**[3]

[1] *Department of Pharmaceutics, Oriental University, Near Aurobindo Hospital, Sanwer Road, Indore 453555, MP, India*

[2] *Department of Pharmaceutical Chemistry, Oriental University, Near Aurobindo Hospital, Sanwer Road, Indore 453555, MP, India*

[3] *Department of Pharmaceutical Science, Dr. Hari Singh Gaur Vishwavidhyalaya, Sagar, MP, India*

Abstract: The pandemic sparked many discussions on IP rights and compulsory licensing was the first solution that many governments turned to, as it was widely believed that existing patent rights were the only obstacles preventing the world from obtaining a cure for COVID-19. However, the reality was quite different. When the pandemic first hit, there was simply no medicine or vaccine that was being blocked by a patent right because no treatment or vaccine existed. This mindset meant that innovators and researchers were expected to develop a cure in the shadow of the threat of compulsory licensing. What happened was that many innovators and pharma companies combined patent tools, opened up their intellectual property and know-how, and shared their knowledge for the sake of humanity.

Keywords: COVID-19, Coronaviruses, Intellectual property rights, Patent tools, SARS.

INTRODUCTION

What is Coronavirus?

Coronaviruses are a family of viruses that can cause respiratory illness in humans. They are called “corona” because of crown-like spikes on the surface of the virus. Severe acute respiratory syndrome (SARS), Middle East respiratory syndrome (MERS) and the common cold are examples of coronaviruses that cause illness in humans.

* **Corresponding author Shikha Jaiswal:** Department of Pharmaceutics, Oriental University, Near Aurobindo Hospital, Sanwer Road, Indore 453555, MP, India; E-mail: shikhajaiswal@orientaluniversity.in

Sachin Kumar Jain, Ravikant Gupta, Sudha Vengurlekar, Nidhi Bais & Gajendra P. Choudhary (Eds.)

The new strain of coronavirus — SARS-CoV-2 — was first reported in Wuhan, China in December 2019. It has since spread to every country around the world.

The coronavirus, specifically SARS-CoV-2, gained significant worldwide attention starting in early 2020 due to the rapid spread of COVID-19. In December 2019, cases of a mysterious pneumonia-like illness were reported in Wuhan, China. By January 2020, Chinese authorities identified the cause as a novel coronavirus, later named SARS-CoV-2, which is the virus responsible for COVID-19 (Fig. **1**).

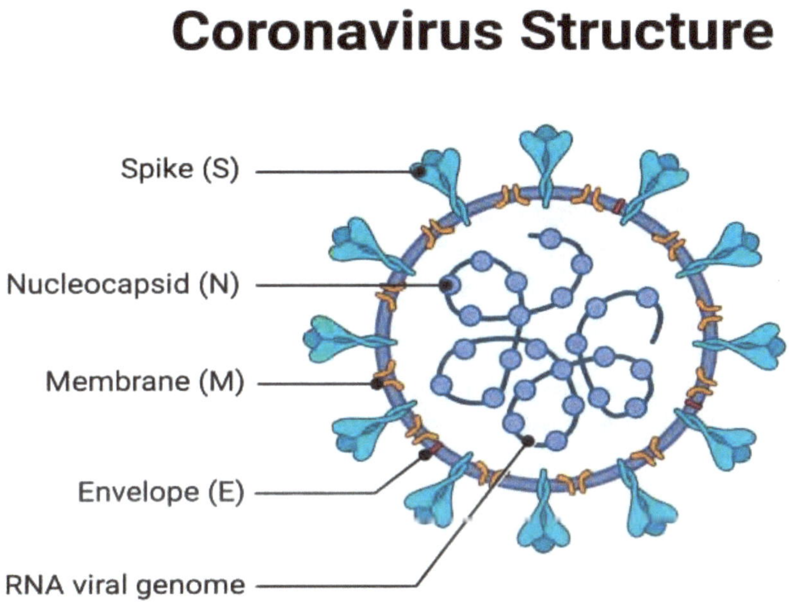

Fig. (1). Structure of corona virus.

The rapid spread of COVID-19 beyond China's borders, coupled with its high transmission rate and potential for severe illness in vulnerable populations, prompted global concern and response. The World Health Organization (WHO) declared COVID-19 a Public Health Emergency of International Concern on January 30, 2020, and later declared it a pandemic on March 11, 2020 [1 - 6].

What is the Incubation Period for COVID-19?

The incubation period for COVID-19, caused by the virus SARS-CoV-2, typically ranges from 2 to 14 days after exposure. However, most commonly, symptoms appear around 4-5 days after exposure to the virus. During this incubation period, an infected person may not show any symptoms but can still spread the virus to others, which is a significant factor contributing to the rapid spread of COVID-19 [7 - 10].

The Incubation Period for the New Coronavirus

The median incubation period, or the time at which half of the infected individuals will develop symptoms, is around 4-5 days. It is important to note that during this incubation period, infected individuals can spread the virus to others, even if they themselves do not yet show symptoms. This characteristic of the virus has contributed significantly to its rapid spread worldwide [11, 12].

The entry of SARS-CoV-2 into host cells primarily involves several key steps:

- **Attachment:** The spike protein (S protein) on the surface of SARS-CoV-2 binds to a specific receptor on the host cell surface. This receptor is angiotensin-converting enzyme 2 (ACE2), which is expressed in various human tissues, including the respiratory tract, lungs, heart, kidneys, and intestines.
- **Primed for Entry:** After the initial attachment, the spike protein must be primed by cellular proteases. This priming step involves cleaving the spike protein into two subunits (S1 and S2), which activates it for fusion with the host cell membrane (Fig. **2**).
- **Fusion and Entry:** Once primed, the viral membrane fuses with the host cell membrane. This fusion allows the viral genetic material (RNA) to enter the host cell cytoplasm.
- **Release of RNA:** Once inside the host cell, the viral RNA is released and used as a template for replication and transcription of new viral components.
- **Assembly and Release:** New viral particles are assembled within the host cell and then released to infect new cells or individuals [13 - 16].

What are the Symptoms of Coronavirus?

The symptoms of coronavirus, specifically referring to COVID-19 caused by SARS-CoV-2, can vary widely in severity and presentation. Common symptoms include:

Respiratory Symptoms

o Dry cough

o Sore throat

o Shortness of breath or difficulty breathing

Fever

Often accompanied by chills or sweating.

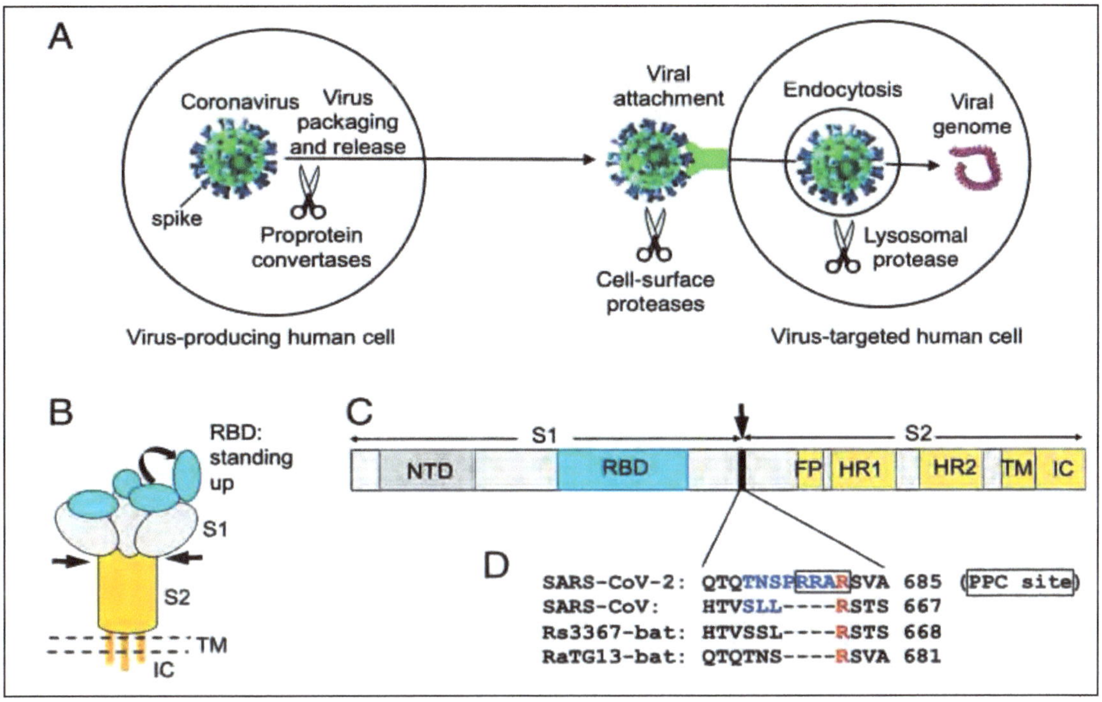

Fig. (2). Cell mechanism entry of SARS-CoV-2.

Fatigue

Feeling unusually tired or exhausted.

Muscle or Body Aches

Generalized pain or discomfort in muscles and joints.

Headache

Persistent or severe headaches.

Loss of Taste or Smell

An unusual or sudden loss of the ability to taste or smell (anosmia).

Gastrointestinal Symptoms

Some people may experience symptoms like nausea, vomiting, or diarrhea, though these are less common.

It is important to note that symptoms can range from mild to severe, and some individuals may be asymptomatic (showing no symptoms at all) despite being infected with the virus. Severe cases of COVID-19 can lead to pneumonia, acute respiratory distress syndrome (ARDS), multi-organ failure, and death, especially in older adults and those with underlying health conditions (Fig. **3**).

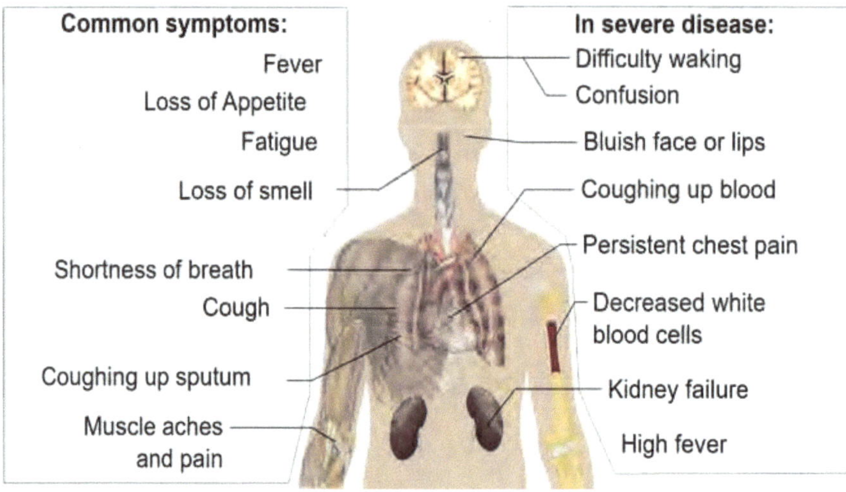

Fig. (3). Symptoms of corona virus [19, 20].

If you or someone you know develops symptoms suggestive of COVID-19, it is important to seek medical advice and follow local health guidelines for testing, isolation, and treatment [17, 18].

Where do Coronaviruses Come From?

Coronaviruses are often found in bats, cats, and camels. The viruses live in but don't infect the animals. Sometimes these viruses then spread to different animal species. The viruses may change (mutate) as they transfer to other species. Eventually, the virus can jump from animal species and begin to infect humans. In case of SARS-CoV-19, the first people infected are thought to have contracted the virus at a food market that sold meat, fish, and live animals [20 - 24].

How Severe is COVID-19 Infection?

Some people infected with SARS-CoV-2 will experience mild to moderate respiratory illness and most will recover without requiring special treatment.

COVID-19 can sometimes be a severe disease with respiratory insufficiency requiring intensive care and potentially leading to death. Older people and those with underlying medical conditions such as heart disease, diabetes, chronic respiratory disease, and cancer are more likely to develop serious illnesses. Vaccinated individuals are less likely to have a severe disease or be hospitalized. The severity of COVID-19 also varies according to variant and pre-existing immunity, developed after vaccination or recovery from a prior infection [25, 26].

What is IP in Vaccines?

In the context of vaccines, "IP" typically stands for "Intellectual Property." Intellectual Property refers to creations of the mind, such as inventions, designs, symbols, names, and images used in commerce. In case of vaccines, intellectual property often pertains to the unique processes, technologies, and formulations developed by pharmaceutical companies or research institutions to create and produce specific vaccines [27].

Vaccine development involves significant research and innovation, and the resulting intellectual property is crucial for the companies or organizations involved. It allows them to protect their investments, recoup development costs, and have exclusive rights to manufacture and distribute the vaccine [27, 28].

Issues related to intellectual property in the context of vaccines have gained attention during the COVID-19 pandemic. Some argue that temporarily waiving certain intellectual property rights could help increase global vaccine production and distribution, thereby addressing the challenges of vaccine availability on a global scale. These discussions are part of broader efforts to ensure widespread access to vaccines during public health emergencies [29].

Why is IP Rights Important?

Intellectual Property (IP) rights are important for several reasons, serving as a foundation for encouraging innovation, creativity, and economic development. Here are some key reasons why IP rights are considered crucial:

Incentive for Innovation: IP rights, such as patents, copyrights, and trademarks, provide inventors, creators, and innovators with exclusive rights to their creations for a limited period. This exclusivity serves as an incentive for individuals and companies to invest time, resources, and efforts into developing new technologies, products, and creative works.

Encouragement of Creativity: Copyrights protect literary, artistic, and musical works, fostering a creative environment by granting creators exclusive rights to their creations. This protection encourages artists, writers, musicians, and other creators to produce and share their work without the fear of unauthorized copying or use.

Economic Growth: IP rights contribute to economic growth by stimulating innovation, which, in turn, can lead to the development of new industries, job creation, and increased competitiveness. Strong IP systems are often associated with thriving economies and technological advancements.

Protection of Investments: Companies invest significant resources in research, development, and marketing. IP rights, particularly patents and trade secrets, protect these investments by granting exclusive rights and preventing others from using, selling, or reproducing the same innovations without permission.

Consumer Protection: Trademarks and other IP rights help consumers identify and differentiate products and services. By protecting brands, IP rights ensure that consumers can trust the quality and origin of the goods they purchase.

Transfer of Technology: IP rights can be licensed or sold, facilitating the transfer of technology and knowledge between entities. This can lead to collaborations, joint ventures, and the spread of innovations across industries and borders.

Legal Framework: IP rights provide a legal framework for resolving disputes related to the unauthorized use or infringement of intellectual creations. This framework helps maintain order in the marketplace and encourages fair competition [30 - 32].

While IP rights play a vital role in fostering innovation and economic development, there are ongoing discussions about finding a balance between protecting these rights and ensuring that essential innovations, particularly in fields like healthcare, are accessible to a broader population, especially during public health emergencies. Striking the right balance is crucial for addressing global challenges while still fostering innovation and creativity [32].

What are IP Rights as Basic Human Rights?

Intellectual Property (IP) rights are not typically considered basic human rights in the same way as fundamental rights like freedom of speech or the right to a fair trial. Instead, IP rights are legal constructs designed to incentivize innovation, creativity, and economic development, as mentioned earlier.

However, there are arguments that connect certain aspects of IP rights to broader human rights principles [30 - 33]. Here are some perspectives on how IP rights may intersect with human rights:

Right to Benefit from Scientific Progress: IP rights, particularly patents, are seen by some as a means to encourage scientific and technological progress by providing inventors with temporary exclusivity.

Right to Cultural Participation: IP rights, such as copyrights, can be linked to the right to participate in cultural life (International Covcnant on Economic, Social and Cultural Rights, Article 15). Copyright protection is often viewed as a way to encourage the creation and dissemination of cultural works, ensuring that artists and creators can benefit from their contributions to culture.

Economic and Social Rights: Some argue that IP rights, by encouraging innovation and economic development, indirectly contribute to the realization of economic and social rights, such as the right to work, the right to education, and the right to an adequate standard of living.

However, it is important to note that the relationship between IP rights and human rights is complex, and there are ongoing debates about how to strike the right balance. There are concerns about the potential impact of IP rights on access to essential goods and services, particularly in areas like healthcare, where issues of affordability and accessibility can intersect with public health considerations.

In discussions about global health emergencies, like the COVID-19 pandemic, there have been calls to balance IP rights with the need for widespread access to life-saving technologies. This reflects a tension between incentivizing innovation through IP rights and ensuring that critical advancements are accessible to those who need them [34 - 36].

What are the Advantages of Intellectual Property Rights?

Intellectual Property (IP) rights offer several advantages that contribute to fostering innovation, creativity, and economic development. Here are some key advantages:

Business Protection. Anybody can easily recognise the business.

Promote Innovativeness.

Increase in Profit.

Great Export Opportunities.

Preference in the Market.

Complicated Process.

High Cost.

Time-Consuming [37, 38].

Incentive for Innovation: IP rights, particularly patents, provide inventors and innovators with exclusive rights to their creations for a limited period. This exclusivity serves as a powerful incentive for individuals and companies to invest in research and development, fostering continuous innovation.

Protection of Investments: Companies invest significant resources in developing new technologies, products, and creative works. IP rights, such as patents and trade secrets, protect these investments by granting exclusive rights and preventing competitors from using or reproducing the same innovations without permission.

Market Competition: IP rights contribute to fair competition by ensuring that businesses can compete based on the quality and uniqueness of their products or services. Trademarks, for example, allow consumers to identify and choose products based on brand recognition.

Economic Growth: A strong IP system is associated with economic growth. By incentivizing innovation and creativity, IP rights contribute to the development of new industries, job creation, and increased competitiveness on a national and global scale.

Transfer of Technology: IP rights can be licensed or sold, facilitating the transfer of technology and knowledge between entities. This can lead to collaborations, joint ventures, and the spread of innovations across industries and borders.

Consumer Protection: Trademarks and other IP rights help consumers identify and differentiate products and services. By protecting brands, IP rights ensure that consumers can trust the quality and origin of the goods they purchase.

Cultural and Artistic Expression: Copyright protection encourages the creation and dissemination of cultural and artistic works by granting creators exclusive rights. This helps support the livelihoods of artists and fosters a vibrant cultural environment.

Research and Development Funding: IP rights can serve as a mechanism for companies and individuals to secure funding for research and development. Investors are more likely to support projects with the potential for exclusive rights and returns on investment through IP protection.

While these advantages are significant, it is important to note that the balance between IP rights and the broader public interest is a subject of ongoing debate. Striking the right balance is crucial for ensuring that innovation is incentivized while also addressing concerns related to access to essential technologies, particularly in fields like healthcare [39 - 42].

What is the Role of IP Rights in Vaccine Develtopment?

Inellectual property rights (IPR) refers to the legal rights given to the inventor or creator to protect his invention or creation for a certain period of time. These legal rights confer an exclusive right to the inventor/creator or his assignee to fully utilize his invention/creation for a given period of time [43 - 45].

This innovation triumph has been matched in manufacturing. By December 2021, around 12 billion doses of vaccines had been manufactured, enough to vaccinate the world's population. Currently, vaccine supply far exceeds the global distribution capacity. Africa's first COVID-19 vaccine manufacturing plant in South Africa recently announced that it may close due to lack of demand [46 - 48].

Intellectual Property (IP) rights play a crucial role in vaccine development by providing incentives for innovation, protecting investments, and facilitating the transfer of technology. Here are several ways in which IP rights contribute to the development of vaccines:

Incentivizing Innovation

IP rights, particularly patents, grant inventors and pharmaceutical companies exclusive rights to their vaccine-related innovations for a limited period (usually 20 years). This exclusivity serves as a powerful incentive for companies to invest in extensive research and development, as they can potentially recoup their investments through exclusive sales of the developed vaccine.

Protecting Investments

Developing a new vaccine is a complex and costly process that involves years of research, clinical trials, and regulatory approval. IP rights, such as patents and trade secrets, protect the unique processes, formulations, and technologies involved in vaccine development. This protection allows companies to safeguard their investments by preventing others from using or reproducing their innovations without permission.

Encouraging Collaboration and Licensing

Pharmaceutical companies often collaborate with research institutions, universities, and other companies in the development of vaccines. IP rights provide a legal framework for negotiating and establishing licensing agreements, allowing the transfer of technology and knowledge between entities. This collaboration can accelerate the vaccine development process.

Attracting Investment

Strong IP protection can attract investment from both private and public sectors. Investors are more likely to support vaccine development projects when they see the potential for exclusive rights and a return on their investment through IP protection.

Ensuring Quality and Safety

IP rights, particularly trademarks, allow companies to establish and protect their brands. This contributes to maintaining high-quality and safe vaccines, as companies have an interest in preserving the reputation associated with their brand.

While IP rights play a crucial role in incentivizing innovation and protecting investments, there are ongoing discussions about the balance between protecting these rights and ensuring broad and equitable access to vaccines, especially during global health emergencies [49 - 51].

Summary

The COVID-19 pandemic has brought significant attention to the role of Intellectual Property (IP) rights in vaccine development, sparking discussions about access, affordability, and the global distribution of vaccines. Here are some key points related to the role of IP rights in the development of COVID-19 vaccines:

Rapid Vaccine Development

The pandemic prompted an unprecedented global effort to develop and deploy COVID-19 vaccines quickly. IP rights, particularly patents, played a crucial role in incentivizing pharmaceutical companies and researchers to invest in the rapid development of vaccines.

Vaccine Innovation and Protection

Companies invested substantial resources in research, clinical trials, and manufacturing processes to bring effective vaccines to market. IP rights protected the innovations and technologies involved in the development of these vaccines, allowing companies to maintain exclusivity and potentially recoup their investments.

Licensing and Collaboration

Some pharmaceutical companies entered into licensing agreements or collaborations to enhance vaccine production and distribution. IP rights facilitated these partnerships, allowing for the transfer of technology and expertise between companies, research institutions, and manufacturers.

Global Access Challenges

The pandemic highlighted challenges related to global access to vaccines, particularly in low- and middle-income countries. Advocates for broader access argued that the temporary waiver of certain IP rights could help increase production and ensure more equitable distribution of vaccines.

Calls for IP Waivers

Various stakeholders, including some governments and public health organizations, advocated for the temporary waiver of certain IP rights, such as patents on COVID-19 vaccines, to enable increased manufacturing capacity and broader access. The World Trade Organization (WTO) has been a platform for discussions on these matters.

Differing Perspectives

While some argue that IP waivers are necessary to address the urgency of the pandemic and promote global health, others contend that strong IP protection is essential for future innovation, as it provides an incentive for companies to invest in research and development.

Voluntary Licensing and Technology Transfer

Some pharmaceutical companies engaged in voluntary licensing agreements and technology transfer initiatives to allow other manufacturers to produce COVID-19 vaccines. These efforts aimed to expand production capacity and improve global vaccine access.

It's important to note that the debate around the role of IP rights in vaccine development during the COVID-19 pandemic is ongoing, and perspectives vary among stakeholders, including governments, pharmaceutical companies, public health experts, and advocacy groups. The situation is dynamic, and discussions continue to evolve, with efforts focused on finding a balance between protecting IP rights and addressing global health needs [51 - 55].

CONCLUSION

The latest MERS epidemic in South Korea, which showed viral development in second and third-generation contacts, has rekindled public awareness of the threat posed by MERS-CoV, despite the virus's low incidence of documented human-t--human transmission. Since there is presently no viable therapy for MERS, creating a functional MERS vaccine to stop MERS-CoV infection is the best course of action. More research is being done on the subunit and viral vector-based vaccines out of the six vaccine types covered above. Only three possible MERS-CoV vaccine candidates have advanced to phase I clinical trials thus far, despite the fact that several encouraging vaccine candidates have been suggested and documented. These include two viral vector-based vaccines (MVA-MERS-S and MERS001) and a DNA vaccine (GLS-5300). It is still quite probable that there won't be a human MERS vaccination on the market anytime soon. In order to reduce delays in the execution of clinical trials, significant efforts should be made. This includes improving communication and coordination among sponsors, principal investigators, investigators, participants, and stakeholders.

REFERENCES

[1] John Heilprin, Advocates Mount New Initiative for WTO to Recognize 'Public Goods' in Trade Agreements – from Medicines to Forests, HEALTH POL'Y WATCH (Sept. 30, 2022).

[2] Canadian Patent Application No. 2,321,260, filed October 12, 2000.

[3] Patent Act, R.S.C. 1985, c P-4, s. 27(8); Harvard College v. Canada (Commissioner of Patents), [2002] 4 SCR 45; Monsanto Canada Inc. v. Schmeiser, [2004] 1 SCR 902.

[4] Morin E. Of mice and men: the ethics of patenting animals. Health Law J 1997; 5: 147-97. [PMID: 10569897]

[5] Plant Breeders' Rights Act, R.S.C. 1990, c. 20 at s. 4.

[6] Mahoney RT, Pablos-Mendez A, Ramachandran S. The introduction of new vaccines into developing countries. Vaccine 2004; 22(5-6): 786-92. [http://dx.doi.org/10.1016/j.vaccine.2003.04.001] [PMID: 14741174]

[7] Kaczynski A. Chaifetz S, Benkler Y, Katz Z. Addressing global health inequities: an open licensing approach for university innovations. Berkley Tech Law J 2005; 20: 1031.

[8] Mahoney RT, Maynard JE. The introduction of new vaccines into developing countries. Vaccine 1999; 17(7-8): 646-52. [http://dx.doi.org/10.1016/S0264-410X(98)00246-1] [PMID: 10067669]

[9] Morel C. Health innovation in developing countries to address diseases of the poor. Innov Strat Today

2005; 1: 1-15.

[10] Fedson DS, Preparing for pandemic vaccination: an international policy agenda for vaccine development. J Public Health Policy 26:4–29; and Barrett CL et al (2005) If smallpox strikes Portland.

[11] Ragavan S, Vanni A. Intellectual Property Law And Access To Medicines: Trips Agreement, Health, And Pharmaceuticals (Srividhya Ragavan & Amaka Vanni Eds., 2021.

[12] Chang L. A typology of intellectual property management for public health innovation and access: design considerations for policymakers. Open AIDS J 2010; 4(1): 4-24. [http://dx.doi.org/10.2174/1874120701004010004] [PMID: 20517487]

[13] Wenham C, Eccleston-Turner M, Voss M. The futility of the pandemic treaty: caught between globalism and statism, International Affairs, 2022; 98:(3) pp. 837–852.

[14] Mercurio B. WTO Waiver from Intellectual Property Protection for COVID-19 Vaccines and Treatments: A Critical Review, 62 VA. J. INT'L L. Online (Bergh) 2021; 9: 16.

[15] G.A. Res. 217 (III) A, Universal Declaration of Human Rights, at art. 25(1) (Dec. 10, 1948).

[16] G.A. Res. 2200 (XXI) A, International Covenant on Economic, Social and Cultural Rights, art. 12(1) (Dec. 16, 1966).

[17] Anand K, Karade S, Sen S, Gupta R. Coronaviruses; origin and evolution. Med J Armed Forces India 2020; 136-41. [http://dx.doi.org/10.1016/j.mjafi.2020.04.008] [PMID: 32341622]

[18] Ball T, Wace C, Smyth C, Brown D. Hunt for contacts of coronavirus-stricken pair in York. From the Times. 2020, January 31.

[19] Boseley S, Campbell D, Murphy S. The first British national to contract coronavirus had been in Singapore. From the Guardian.

[20] Chavez S, Long B, Koyfman A, Liang SY. Coronavirus Disease (COVID-19): a primer for emergency physicians, AJEM. Am J Emerg Med 2020; 1-10. [PMID: 32265065]

[21] Chen Y, Liu Q, Guo D. Emerging coronaviruses: Genome structure, replication, and pathogenesis. J Med Virol 2020, 92(4). 418-23. [http://dx.doi.org/10.1002/jmv.25681] [PMID: 31967327]

[22] Cheng ZJ, Shan J. 2019 Novel Coronavirus: where We Are and what We Know. Springer 2020.

[23] J. Corley. U.S. Government response to COVID-19 was slow. But how does it compare to other countries? From forbes.

[24] Coronavirus disease (COVID-19) advice for the public, From the World Health Organization, Available from: https://www.who.int/emergencies/diseases/novel-coronavirus-201 9/advice-for-public

[25] Coronavirus, People with Fever or 'continuous' Cough Told to Self-Isolate, From BBC News, 2020, March 12.

[26] Coronavirus, PM Says Everyone Should Avoid Office, Pubs, and Traveling, From BBC News, 2020, 16 March.

[27] COVID-19 Corona virus Real-Time Pcr Kit, From the World Health Organization. Available from: www.who.int/diagnostics_laboratory/eual/eul_0515_202_00_covid19_coronavirus_real_time_pcr_kit_ifu.pdf?ua=1

[28] COVID-19: guidance for staff in the transport sector, From GOV.UK, 2020.

[29] COVID-19, Non-essential Shops to Open from June 15 as the UK Eases Lockdown, From The Economic Times, 2020, May 26.

[30] De, COVID-19 Testing: what Are the Tests and Testing Procedures Being Carried Out in India? From Indian Express:, 2020, June 27.

[31] E. Desk, Explained: How the Antibody Test for COVID-19 Is Different from the PCR Test, From Indian Express:, 2020, March 28.

[32] Doremalen, N. Bushmaker, T. Morris, D.H. Holbrook, M.G. Gamble, A. Williamson, et al., Aerosol and surface stability of SARS-CoV-2 as compared with SARS-CoV-1, N. Engl. J. Med. 382 (2020) 1564–1567.

[33] Ete T, Fanai V, Bamon A, *et al.* Disease, drugs, and dilemma: a review of cardiovascular implications of novel COVID-19, Clin. Infect. Immun. (2020) 25–30.

[34] Fehr AR, Perlman S. Coronaviruses: an overview of their replication and pathogenesis. Methods Mol Biol 2015; 1282: 1-23.
[http://dx.doi.org/10.1007/978-1-4939-2438-7_1] [PMID: 25720466]

[35] Govt bans airlines from boarding passengers from China to India, From India Today: 2020, February 4.

[36] Guarner J. Three emerging corona viruses in two decades: the story of SARS, MERS, and now COVID-19. Am J Clin Pathol 2020; 420-1.
[http://dx.doi.org/10.1093/ajcp/aqaa029] [PMID: 32053148]

[37] Huang C, Wang Y, Li X, *et al.* Clinical features of patients infected with 2019 novel coronavirus in Wuhan, China. Lancet 2020; 395(10223): 497-506.
[http://dx.doi.org/10.1016/S0140-6736(20)30183-5] [PMID: 31986264]

[38] India May Run Out of ICU Beds for COVID-19 Patients by July End: Study, From The New Indian Express:, 2020, 06 12.

[39] Interim Clinical Guidance for Management of Patients with Confirmed Coronavirus Disease (COVID-19), Centre For Disease Control, 2020.

[40] Jha R. Sweden's 'Soft' COVID-19 Strategy: an Appraisal, ORF Occasional Paper, 2020.

[41] Jones, How did New Zealand become COVID-19 free? From BBC News.

[42] Krishnan S, Deo S, Manurkar S. 50 Days of Lockdown: Measuring India's Success in Arresting COVID-19. New Delhi: Observer Research Foundation 2020.

[43] Lauer SA, Grantz KH, Bi Q, *et al.* Grantz, Q. Bi, F.K. Jones, Q. Zheng, H.R. Meredith, J. Lessler, The incubation period of coronavirus disease 2019 (COVID-19) from publicly reported confirmed cases: estimation and application. Ann Intern Med 2020; 172(9): 577-82.
[http://dx.doi.org/10.7326/M20-0504] [PMID: 32150748]

[44] Zeng LK, Tao XW, Yuan WH, Wang J, Liu X, Liu ZS. [First case of neonate infected with novel coronavirus pneumonia in China]. Zhonghua Er Ke Za Zhi 2020; 58(0): E009.
[PMID: 32065520]

[45] K.S. M,). Explained: How Rapid Antigen Test Detects COVID-19, where it Will Be Used, From Indian Express:, 2020, June 19.

[46] Malik YS, Sircar S, Bhat S, Sharun K, Dhama k, Dadar M, *et al.* Emerging novel Corona virus (2019-nCoV)—current scenario, evolutionary perspective based on genome analysis and recent developments, J. Vet. Q. (2020) 68–76.

[47] Middle East Respiratory Syndrome Corona virus (MERS-CoV), From the World Health Organization, 2020.

[48] Versalovic J, Carroll KC, Funke G, Jorgensen JH, Landry ML, Warnock DW. Manual of Clinical Biology, ASM Press, Washington DC, 2019.

[49] Peeri NC, Shrestha N, Rahman MS, *et al.* The SARS, MERS and novel coronavirus (COVID-19) epidemics, the newest and biggest global health threats: what lessons have we learned? Int J Epidemiol 2020; 49(3): 717-26.
[http://dx.doi.org/10.1093/ije/dyaa033] [PMID: 32086938]

[50] Kira PB, Angrist N, Hale T, Phillips T. Variation. Government Responses To COVID-19. Blavatnik School Of Government 2020.

[51] Petrosillo N, Viceconte G, Ergonul O, Ippolito G, Petersen E. COVID-19, SARS and MERS: are they closely related? Clin Microbiol Infect 2020; 26(6): 729-34. [http://dx.doi.org/10.1016/j.cmi.2020.03.026] [PMID: 32234451]

[52] Police can issue 'unlimited fines' to those flouting coronavirus social distancing rules, says Health Secretary, From ITV News:, 2020, March 24.

[53] Richman DD, Whitley RJ, Hayden FG. Clinical Virology, Wiley, 2016. [http://dx.doi.org/10.1128/9781555819439]

[54] Roser M, Ritchie H, Ortiz-Ospina E, Hasell J. OurWorldInData.org. From coronavirus pandemic (COVID-19). Available from: https://ourworldindata.org/coronavirus

[55] Roser M, Ritchie H, Ortiz-Ospina E, Hasell J. Coronavirus pandemic (COVID-19). From OurWorldInData.org.

CHAPTER 8

The Future of Vaccine IP Right

Vaishali Raghuwanshi[1], **Sachin Kumar Jain**[2] and **Simran Soni**[1,*]

[1] *Sri Aurobindo Institute of Pharmacy, Indore 453555, MP, India*

[2] *Oriental College of Pharmacy & Research Oriental University, Near Aurobindo Hospital, Sanwer Road, Indore 453555, MP, India*

Abstract: It took a while for new vaccines that specifically target the requirements of poor nations to be developed. To solve this issue, several new public-sector vaccine development and research programs have been started. These new initiatives discover that they frequently want to work with the commercial sector and that, in doing so, they have to deal with the problem of managing intellectual property (IP). The significance of intellectual property management and the most effective ways for public sector organizations to manage it are not widely known. Because the regulatory process drives vaccine research and development, intellectual property management has become crucial. The cost of developing vaccines has skyrocketed due to the regulatory procedure, particularly for the extremely complex new vaccines that are currently being developed. For the necessary big investments, investors thus look for IP protection. On the other hand, we contend that, in light of this new perspective, intellectual property rights are crucial for raising the significant sums of money required to satisfy legal obligations. As a result, the general public as well as investors appreciate intellectual property rights. In the lack of public sector processes for carrying out the duties that the private industry currently performs, the public sector needs to boost its level of expertise in handling intellectual property and develop and execute tactics that will assist the public sector in achieving its public health goals, particularly for the poor and, among these individuals, the poor in developing countries.

Keywords: COVID-19, Compulsory licensing, Global health equity, Health diplomacy, Intellectual property, Next-generation vaccines, Public health, Pandemics, Technology transfer, Vaccine IP rights, Vaccines.

INTRODUCTION

The pace at which new vaccinations that target illnesses of particular concern in underdeveloped nations are being developed and introduced is extremely slow. In

* **Corresponding author Simran Soni:** Sri Aurobindo Institute of Pharmacy, Indore 453555, MP, India; E-mail: Simran.soni@saip.ac.in

Sachin Kumar Jain, Ravikant Gupta, Sudha Vengurlekar, Nidhi Bais & Gajendra P. Choudhary (Eds.)

poor nations, there has never been a rotavirus vaccination. The manufacturer withdrew it due to a link between vaccination and intussusception. Even in the absence of these safety concerns, there was worry over the product's comparatively high price, which was an unconnected issue. Even though a safe and efficient vaccination against S. pneumoniae infection was recently developed, it is not being used widely in underdeveloped nations due to its high cost and inability to protect against certain pneumococcal strains that are common in these areas [1].

World leaders have talked about the possibility of a worldwide waiver of the patent rights related to the COVID-19 vaccines in an attempt to get rid of some of these prohibitive obstacles that prevent the vaccine's benefits from being distributed internationally. The Agreement on Trade-Related Aspects of Intellectual Property Rights ("TRIPS Agreement") submitted to the World Trade Organization (WTO) may theoretically be amended to achieve such a patent waiver [1, 2]. Research believes that because patents keep information about how to make vaccines from being used by other pharmaceutical companies worldwide, they constitute an obstacle to a proposed three-step method that could produce a fairer distribution of vaccines.

A decision has been made regarding the proposed Trade-Related Aspects of Intellectual Property Rights (TRIPS) waiver for COVID-19 vaccines, medicines, and diagnostics by the World Trade Organization (WTO) Ministerial Conference. The Conference voted to partially waive TRIPS, but only for vaccines, in a contentious decision [3].

IP RIGHTS IN VACCINE DEVELOPMENT: INCENTIVES AND INNOVATION

The establishment of novel approaches aimed at enhancing worldwide health holds significant humanitarian and financial significance. The COVID-19 pandemic, which has already destroyed trillions of dollars worth of market value from U.S. stock indices and has the potential to kill over a million people in the country alone, serves as a striking example of this issue. Furthermore, COVID-19 is just one of several risks to world health. A startling 25% of deaths worldwide and more than two-thirds of mortality in children under five are attributable to infectious diseases, which include HIV, TB, hepatitis, and malaria. Nearly 150,000 Americans lost their lives to infectious diseases in 2014, and it is now acknowledged that global health is both a national security concern for the United States and a factor in the expansion of the world economy.

Among the global industries with the highest concentration is the vaccination sector. Before 2019, Pfizer, Sanofi, GSK, and Novartis accounted for more than

80% of global vaccination sales. Nonetheless, their vaccines mostly benefited the richest 20% of the global population, who zealously defended their monopoly rents with the use of patents and other tools related to intellectual property rights. Clinical trial results and other significant documents, for instance, are protected as confidential information, making a patent waiver essentially ineffective. Not only are vaccines essential, but so are many other pharmacological items [2, 3].

The COVID-19 pandemic's patent race victors were handsomely compensated by the stringent enforcement of vaccination patents, but it is reasonable to wonder if this left nearly eight billion individuals at the mercy of a small number of profit-driven companies. This scepticism is justified given that, even a year and a half after the vaccine's launch, half of the world's population was still unvaccinated, the virus continued to mutate and diminish the effectiveness of vaccinations, and the NPI's widespread interference severely hindered global trade and production opportunities. Furthermore, the major vaccine companies have mostly disregarded the less wealthy potential customers, such as those in sub-Saharan Africa, while treating wealthier nations as preferred clients [4].

THE GLOBAL VACCINE LANDSCAPE

Until November 2021, several COVID-19 vaccinations were authorized, while more than 326 COVID-19 vaccine candidates were being developed. According to the WHO, 194 vaccines were in pre-clinical development in November 23, 2021, and 132 vaccine candidates are presently undergoing testing in clinical trials. Finding the genetic sequence of a virus is the first step in creating a vaccine for it. On December 31, 2019, the World Health Organisation did, however, issue a warning regarding a novel coronavirus strain that was affecting individuals in China [4]. Later, Chinese officials confirmed the identification of a novel coronavirus strain that infects humans, and on January 11, 2020, the first genomic sequencing for SARS-CoV-2 was made public.

In the absence of safe and highly effective vaccinations and treatment options, non-pharmacological treatments are utilized to minimize transmission and the burden of coronavirus disease 2019 (COVID-19), however, the majority of these interventions come with hefty financial expenses. We urgently need effective COVID-19 vaccinations to lessen the significant burden of COVID-19 morbidity and mortality. In order to guarantee appropriate safety and immunogenicity in a range of individuals (*i.e.*, different ages, medical problems, severity of attack, geographic location, *etc.*), vaccine development is a drawn-out procedure that requires multiple testing steps [5]. The National Centre for Biotechnology Information (NCBI) states that a vaccine must pass four phases of clinical studies before a license to manufacture it is granted. This process can take up to ten years.

Nevertheless, the COVID-19 vaccine research process was sped up to 12–18 months while maintaining safety and efficacy criteria because of the critical pandemic scenario worldwide. The COVID-19 vaccine development process has been incredibly compressed thanks to a variety of variables, including a significant advancement in molecular biology and biotechnology and a partnership between public and private research institutions.

As far as we are aware, no prior research has utilized interactive Exploratory Data Analysis (EDA) and visualizations to highlight the global advancements in COVID-19 vaccination. The current study looks at several factors that contribute to a successful vaccination to assess public engagement worldwide. The main goal of this investigation is to provide answers to various questions about the condition of vaccination today to comprehend the continuous safe vaccination program that is being carried out worldwide. To address all barriers to vaccine distribution in this situation, government and policymakers must take into account people's experiences, attitudes, and perceptions regarding COVID-19 vaccination programs [6].

THE IMPACT OF THE COVID-19 PANDEMIC

The global pandemic caused by the highly contagious SARS-CoV-2 virus has spread. About 2% of carriers are thought to be in perfect health. Nevertheless, it was expected that 5-10% would get acute respiratory distress syndrome (ARDS). The pandemic's impacts could burden the healthcare system and hurt society. Six clinical manifestations might be modest or asymptomatic, severe, or even fatal. Fever, dry cough, sore throat, nasal congestion, malaise, headache, muscle discomfort, loss of taste and/or smell, diarrhea, and vomiting are among the illness's milder symptoms. Aside from respiratory symptoms like shortness of breath without any signs of severe pneumonia, serious clinical presentations include sepsis, ARDS, severe pneumonia, and septic shock. Numerous accounts exist of people whose mental health was negatively impacted by the virus. According to the study, SARS-CoV-2 patients had higher scores on the Hamilton Depression and Anxiety Scales than both healthy controls and patients with pneumonia from other causes [7]. The authors have put out several theories to explain these findings. In addition to the physical and psychological distress brought on by their infection, infected patients also suffer from media reports of deaths, uncertainty about the disease's characteristics, fear that family members may contract the infection, and restrictions on visiting that prevent friends and family from offering moral support [8].

According to a study that investigated the effects of face masks on the physical and mental health of populations in China and Poland, Poles used face masks less frequently than Chinese people did, and as a result, they experienced higher rates of infections, hospitalizations, and fatalities [7]. The same study found that Poles had much higher levels of stress, anxiety, and depression than Chinese people, likely due to their lower use of face masks. The COVID-19 pandemic has concerning effects on mental health, and medical professionals who are already overworked ought to keep an eye on their patient's emotional well-being and offer them social assistance [6, 9].

LEGAL AND ETHICAL CONSIDERATIONS IN VACCINE IP RIGHTS

Global Access and Equity

- Vaccine Nationalism: The COVID-19 pandemic underscored the concept of "vaccine nationalism," where countries prioritize their populations in vaccine distribution, potentially at the expense of global equity. This practice can exacerbate existing health disparities, leaving vulnerable populations in low-income countries without timely access to vaccines [10].
- COVAX Initiative: The Coalition for Epidemic Preparedness Innovations (CEPI), Gavi, the Vaccine Alliance, and the World Health Organization (WHO) established the COVAX initiative to address vaccine access issues globally. COVAX aims to ensure equitable access to COVID-19 vaccines by pooling resources and negotiating with manufacturers to supply doses to low- and middle-income countries [11].
- Health Diplomacy: Vaccine distribution has become a tool of health diplomacy, with countries using their vaccine supplies to strengthen diplomatic ties or gain geopolitical influence. This raises ethical questions about the instrumentalization of global health for political purposes and the potential consequences for equitable vaccine access [12].
- Vaccine Solidarity: Calls for vaccine solidarity emphasize the shared responsibility of the global community to address health crises collectively. This involves wealthier nations supporting the vaccination efforts of less affluent countries, acknowledging that controlling a pandemic requires a coordinated and inclusive approach [13].
- Intellectual Property Waivers: During the COVID-19 pandemic, there have been discussions about temporarily waiving intellectual property protections for COVID-19-related technologies, including vaccines. This proposal, initially put forward by some countries at the World Trade Organization (WTO), aims to facilitate the widespread production of vaccines and improve global access. However, this approach is subject to debate, with concerns about its effectiveness and potential impact on future innovation [14].
- Capacity Building: Building manufacturing and distribution capacity in low- and middle-income countries is crucial for long-term global health equity. This

involves technology transfer, knowledge sharing, and financial support to enable these countries to produce vaccines and other essential medicines independently [15].

- Community Engagement: Ethical considerations also extend to community engagement and empowerment. Inclusive decision-making processes that involve local communities and respect their perspectives can contribute to more effective and equitable vaccine distribution strategies [16].
- Monitoring and Accountability: Establishing mechanisms to monitor vaccine distribution and holding stakeholders accountable for their commitments is essential. This includes tracking the allocation of doses, ensuring transparency in procurement and distribution processes, and addressing any discrepancies that may arise [17].
- Post-Pandemic Preparedness: The experience of the COVID-19 pandemic highlights the need for a more robust and equitable global health infrastructure. Efforts to improve vaccine access should be part of broader initiatives focused on strengthening healthcare systems, addressing health disparities, and preparing for future pandemics [18].

In summary, global access and equity in vaccine distribution involve navigating legal frameworks, addressing ethical imperatives, and implementing practical measures to ensure that vaccines are distributed fairly across the world. The COVID-19 pandemic has brought these issues to the forefront, prompting discussions and actions to build a more resilient and inclusive global health system.

Compulsory Licensing

- Flexibilities in TRIPS Agreement: The Trade-Related Aspects of Intellectual Property Rights (TRIPS) Agreement, administered by the World Trade Organization (WTO), allows member countries to implement compulsory licensing under specific conditions. This includes cases of national emergencies, public non-commercial use, and anti-competitive practices. TRIPS provides a legal framework for countries to balance intellectual property rights with public health needs [19].
- Public Health Emergencies: The COVID-19 pandemic has highlighted the relevance of compulsory licensing during public health emergencies. In the face of a global crisis, some countries considered or implemented compulsory licensing to ensure widespread and affordable access to essential medical technologies, including vaccines, diagnostics, and treatments [20].
- Differential Pricing and Access: Compulsory licensing can be a tool to address concerns about high drug prices, especially in developing countries. By allowing the production of generic versions of patented medicines, countries may be able

to negotiate lower prices and improve accessibility, particularly for populations with limited financial resources. Compulsory licensing aligns with the ethical principle of equitable distribution of healthcare resources. It enables countries to take measures to ensure that patented technologies are accessible to their populations, particularly in situations where the high cost of patented medicines might otherwise limit access for a significant portion of the population [21].

- Industry Response: The prospect of compulsory licensing can incentivize pharmaceutical companies to engage in voluntary licensing agreements, technology transfer, or pricing negotiations. In some cases, the threat of compulsory licensing has led to collaborations between patent holders and generic manufacturers, resulting in more extensive access to medicines [21].
- Ethical Considerations for Patent Holders: The ethical challenge lies in striking a balance between the need to incentivize innovation through patent protection and the imperative to ensure widespread access to essential medicines. Policymakers, legal experts, and global health organizations must continually evaluate and refine the use of compulsory licensing as a mechanism to achieve this delicate equilibrium. Companies investing in research and development argue that the potential for compulsory licensing may undermine their incentives to innovate, as it may reduce the returns on their investments [22].
- Global Collaboration: The use of compulsory licensing requires global collaboration and adherence to international agreements. While countries have the sovereign right to issue compulsory licenses, navigating diplomatic relationships and potential trade repercussions requires careful consideration. Multilateral efforts and agreements can contribute to a more coordinated and cooperative approach to addressing global health challenges [23].

In conclusion, compulsory licensing represents a legal mechanism that countries can use to address ethical concerns related to access to medicines. It requires careful consideration of both the rights of patent holders and the broader public health imperatives, with the ultimate goal of ensuring that essential healthcare technologies are available to those who need them, especially in times of crises.`

CHALLENGES AND CONCERNS IN REFORMING VACCINE IP RIGHTS

The reform of vaccine intellectual property (IP) rights poses a significant challenge marked by complicated concerns requiring careful consideration. A primary worry is the potential decrease in incentives for innovation in the pharmaceutical industry [24]. Reducing or waiving IP protections discourages pharmaceutical companies from investing in vaccine research and development, historically seen as a way to reward innovation and recover extensive research and development costs. This concern extends to fears about the broader impact on future research, raising unsettling notions that altered IP rights could impede innovation not only for the current pandemic but also for future diseases.

The landscape is further complicated by the interplay of lobbying and political pressure. Pharmaceutical companies and stakeholders hold substantial political influence, which could be used against changes to IP rights. This challenging political environment complicates the process of enacting reforms. Trade-related issues are also a concern, acknowledging potential disruptions to established trade agreements and international relations due to alterations in IP rights [25].

The financial aspect of the debate is crucial. Intellectual property, a cornerstone asset for pharmaceutical companies, becomes a point of contention. Weakening these rights raises concerns about potential financial implications and the subsequent impact on investor confidence [26]. Investors and shareholders, concerned about potential losses in the industry, become increasingly uneasy in this uncertain landscape.

Quality control becomes a critical consideration, with companies emphasizing that maintaining control over IP rights is crucial for ensuring the quality and safety of their products [27]. Fears of fragmentation and a lack of coordination underscore the importance of a unified, global approach to reform efforts to prevent a fragmented system with varying rules in different regions, potentially hindering vaccine development and distribution.

The specter of counterfeiting and safety concerns takes the spotlight when contemplating weakened IP protections. The ease of entry for counterfeit or substandard vaccines poses significant risks to public health, necessitating robust regulatory measures [28]. Technology transfer challenges, a practical dimension of the concerns, come into focus, recognizing that even if IP rights are waived or shared, the transfer of vaccine manufacturing technology can be complex, especially in less-developed countries lacking the necessary infrastructure and expertise [29].

Legal and ethical considerations are pervasive in the discourse, acknowledging the complexity of changing IP rights. Questions related to existing agreements and the fundamental principle of rewarding innovation come to the forefront [30]. Small and medium enterprises (SMEs) emerge as particularly vulnerable entities, heavily reliant on IP protection to attract investment and partners, adding complexity to the reform debate. Investor confidence is a critical consideration, recognizing that alterations to IP rights can have repercussions throughout the pharmaceutical sector, potentially leading to reduced funding for vital research and development initiatives [31].

Challenges extend to monitoring and enforcement, with valid concerns about the logistical challenges of enforcing changes to IP rights and ensuring fair and effective vaccine distribution, especially in low-resource settings. Public-private partnerships, crucial to collaborative vaccine development, face potential viability and willingness concerns from pharmaceutical companies if IP rights are weakened. Health diplomacy also plays a role, recognizing that reforming IP rights may have far-reaching implications for international relations, requiring countries to balance their interests in public health against diplomatic considerations [32]. Navigating these challenges demands that stakeholders carefully balance fostering innovation, ensuring global health equity, and addressing the intricate interplay of economic, political, and ethical considerations [28].

TECHNOLOGICAL ADVANCES AND NEXT-GENERATION VACCINES

Technological advances are paving the way for a new generation of vaccines that have the potential to address challenges such as effectiveness and safer vaccines, particularly for infectious diseases that are difficult to prevent or treat.

Technological Advances in Vaccine Development

In addition to new vaccine technologies, technological advances are also improving the development of traditional vaccines. For example, scientists are now able to use computer-aided designs to create new vaccines [33, 34], and they are also developing new methods for delivering vaccines, such as through the skin or nose [35 - 38].

Next-generation Vaccines have the Potential to

- Be more effective against a wider range of pathogens
- Be safer and have fewer side effects
- Be more affordable and accessible
- Be easier to store and transport

Next generation of vaccines includes:

mRNA Vaccines

mRNA vaccines are a revolutionary new type of vaccine that uses messenger RNA (mRNA) to instruct cells to produce a protein that can trigger an immune response. This is in contrast to traditional vaccines, which contain a weakened or inactive form of a virus or bacteria. mRNA vaccines are highly effective and can be rapidly developed and produced [39].

mRNA vaccines work by introducing a piece of mRNA that corresponds to a viral protein, usually a small piece of a protein found on the virus's outer membrane. The mRNA enters cells and is used to make a protein that is identical to the viral protein [40]. The immune system then recognizes the protein as foreign and produces antibodies to it. These antibodies can then protect the body from infection if it is exposed to the virus in the future [41].

mRNA vaccines are currently being used to vaccinate against COVID-19 [42]. They are also being studied for use in vaccinating against other diseases, such as influenza, Zika virus, and rabies.

DNA Vaccine

DNA vaccines, a promising branch of gene therapy, have emerged as a novel approach to immunization against infectious diseases. Unlike traditional vaccines that introduce an inactive or weakened form of a pathogen, DNA vaccines utilize engineered DNA encoding a specific antigen to instruct the body's cells to produce the desired immune response [43].

DNA vaccines rely on the remarkable ability of DNA molecules to enter cells and incorporate themselves into the cellular machinery. Once inside, the plasmid DNA carrying the antigen gene directs the synthesis of the corresponding antigen protein. This intracellular production of the antigen mimics a natural infection, prompting the immune system to generate antibodies and activate memory cells that can provide long-lasting protection against the pathogen [44].

Here are some examples of DNA vaccines:

- Human Papillomavirus (HPV): DNA vaccines are being evaluated for their potential to prevent HPV-associated cancers, such as cervical, head and neck, and anal cancers [45].
- Influenza: DNA vaccines are being developed to provide broader protection against influenza viruses, including potential pandemic strains [46].
- Hepatitis B: DNA vaccines are showing promise in eliciting robust immune responses against hepatitis B virus, reducing the risk of chronic liver disease and liver cancer [47].
- HIV/AIDS: DNA vaccines are being explored as potential therapeutic options for HIV/AIDS, aiming to stimulate the immune system to control the virus and prevent disease progression [48].

Subunit Vaccines

Subunit vaccines, also known as acellular vaccines, are a type of vaccine that contains only purified parts of a pathogen, such as proteins, carbohydrates, or lipids. These purified components, termed subunits, are carefully selected to elicit a strong and effective immune response without causing the symptoms associated with the whole pathogen [49]. Subunit vaccines offer several advantages over traditional whole-cell vaccines, making them a valuable tool in the prevention of infectious diseases.

Here are some examples of Subunit vaccines:

- Hepatitis B: The hepatitis B vaccine, composed of the surface antigen of the hepatitis B virus, is one of the most effective vaccines, preventing liver cancer and other liver diseases caused by the virus [50].
- Human Papillomavirus (HPV): The HPV vaccine, containing the capsid protein of HPV, protects against HPV-associated cancers, including cervical, head and neck, and anal cancers [51].
- Influenza: Several influenza vaccines utilize subunit technology, specifically targeting the surface proteins of the influenza virus to provide protection against seasonal and pandemic influenza strains [52].
- Pertussis: The acellular pertussis vaccine, a component of the DTaP vaccine, contains purified pertussis toxins and surface antigens, protecting against whooping cough [53].

Attenuated Vaccines

Attenuated vaccines are a type of vaccine that contains a weakened or inactive form of a pathogen, such as a virus or bacteria. This weakened form of the pathogen is still able to trigger an immune response, but it is not strong enough to cause disease. Attenuated vaccines have been used for many years and are generally safe and effective.

Attenuated vaccines work by introducing the body to a weakened form of the pathogen. This weakened pathogen is able to replicate in the body, but it cannot cause disease because it is not strong enough. As the weakened pathogen replicates, it triggers the immune system to produce antibodies and other immune cells. These antibodies and immune cells will then be able to protect the body from the disease-causing form of the pathogen [54].

Some of the most common attenuated vaccines include [55]:

- The measles, mumps, and rubella (MMR) vaccine

- The chickenpox (varicella) vaccine
- The yellow fever vaccine

Inactivated Vaccines

Inactivated vaccines, also known as killed vaccines, are a type of vaccine that contains a non-viable form of a pathogen, such as a virus or bacteria. The pathogen is rendered inactive through various methods, such as heat or chemical treatment, ensuring that it cannot cause disease but can still trigger an immune response. Inactivated vaccines have been a cornerstone of immunization strategies for decades, effectively preventing infectious diseases by utilizing inactivated or killed forms of pathogens.

Inactivated vaccines work by introducing the body to an inactive form of the pathogen. This inactive pathogen is unable to replicate or cause disease, but it still retains the surface proteins or antigens that the immune system recognizes. As the inactive pathogen is presented to immune cells, they activate and produce antibodies and memory cells specifically tailored to the pathogen. These antibodies and memory cells will then be able to protect the body from the disease-causing form of the pathogen [55].

Some of the most common inactivated vaccines include:

- The rabies vaccine
- The hepatitis A vaccine
- The influenza vaccine
- The polio vaccine
- The pertussis vaccine

Viral Vector Vaccine

Viral vector vaccines have emerged as a promising new approach to immunization, utilizing engineered viruses to deliver genetic material encoding specific antigens into host cells. Unlike traditional vaccines that introduce an inactive or weakened form of a pathogen, viral vector vaccines harness the replication machinery of viruses to effectively stimulate an immune response against a designated target [56, 57].

Here are some examples of Viral vector vaccines:

- Adenovirus-vectored COVID-19 vaccine (ChAdOx1 nCoV-19): Developed by AstraZeneca and the University of Oxford, this vaccine utilizes a modified chimpanzee adenovirus vector to deliver the SARS-CoV-2 spike protein gene [58].

- Recombinant adenovirus type 5 vector-based Ebola vaccine (rAd5-ZEBOV): Approved by the European Medicines Agency, this vaccine protects against Ebola virus disease using a modified adenovirus type 5 vector [59].
- MVA-BN vaccine: Developed by Bavarian Nordic, this vaccine targets smallpox and monkeypox and utilizes a modified vaccinia Ankara (MVA) vector [60].

These vaccines have the potential to address the challenges of preventing and treating infectious diseases, and they could lead to a healthier future for millions of people around the world.

Technological advancements in vaccine development are rapidly evolving, leading to the creation of more effective, safer, and more accessible vaccines. These advancements are also having a significant impact on the intellectual property (IP) landscape surrounding vaccines.

IMPACT ON IP RIGHTS

One of the most significant impacts of technological advancements on vaccine IP is the increasing complexity of vaccine patents. As vaccines become more sophisticated, the inventions underlying them become more complex and difficult to protect with traditional patent claims. This can lead to disputes over patent infringement and make it more challenging for companies to enforce their IP rights.

The development of next-generation vaccines is also raising new IP issues, such as the question of who owns the rights to data generated during vaccine development. This data can be extremely valuable for developing new vaccines and treatments, and companies and researchers are increasingly competing for access to it [61].

The IP landscape surrounding vaccines is becoming increasingly complex as a result of technological advancements. It is important to find a balance between protecting innovation and ensuring that everyone has access to affordable and effective vaccines [62].

There are several potential solutions to the challenges posed by the changing IP landscape surrounding vaccines. These include:

- Developing new models for sharing data and collaborating on vaccine development.
- Creating more flexible patent licensing agreements.

- Establishing new guidelines for protecting and sharing IP rights in the context of public health emergencies.

CASE STUDIES AND EXAMPLES

Several real-world examples and case studies provide insights into how different entities are navigating vaccine intellectual property (IP) rights, particularly in the context of the COVID-19 pandemic. These examples showcase a range of approaches and strategies:

Medicines Patent Pool (MPP): The MPP is an example of a voluntary licensing mechanism that has been used in the past to increase access to essential medicines and, more recently, for COVID-19 therapies. It negotiates licenses with pharmaceutical companies to allow generic manufacturers in low- and middle-income countries to produce and distribute medicines.
BNT162b2 mRNA Vaccine Technology: Pfizer-BioNTech announced in 2021 that they would make the BNT162b2 mRNA vaccine technology available for third-party manufacturers through a licensing strategy. This step aimed to expand global vaccine production [63].
AstraZeneca and Oxford University: AstraZeneca, in collaboration with the University of Oxford, pledged to provide the COVID-19 vaccine at no profit during the pandemic. They have also engaged in partnerships with other manufacturers to enable mass production and equitable access. While they have maintained certain IP rights, they have made licensing agreements to allow production by various companies in different parts of the world.
Bharat Biotech and COVAXIN: Bharat Biotech, an Indian biopharmaceutical company, developed COVAXIN, an indigenous COVID-19 vaccine. Despite owning IP rights, Bharat Biotech collaborated with international organizations and governments to promote global access. They have transferred technology to other manufacturers, allowing them to produce the vaccine.
COVAX Initiative: COVAX, co-led by Gavi, the Vaccine Alliance, WHO, and CEPI, is a global initiative aimed at ensuring equitable access to COVID-19 vaccines. It relies on contributions from wealthier nations to support access for lower-income countries. The initiative focuses on procurement and distribution of vaccines, including those that are developed with IP protection.
Johnson & Johnson: Johnson & Johnson pledged not to profit from its COVID-19 vaccine during the pandemic. They also committed to making the vaccine available on a not-for-profit basis for emergency pandemic use. While they retained certain IP rights, they have licensed their technology to other manufacturers to boost production.
Pfizer and BioNTech: Pfizer and BioNTech, which developed one of the first authorized COVID-19 vaccines, have not waived IP rights but have pursued an aggressive manufacturing and distribution strategy to increase vaccine supply. They have expanded production and sought regulatory approvals worldwide to facilitate access.
Waiving TRIPS for COVID-19 Vaccines: Several countries, led by India and South Africa, proposed a temporary waiver of certain provisions of the TRIPS Agreement at the World Trade Organization (WTO) to facilitate broader access to COVID-19 vaccines. This proposal garnered support from many countries and organizations, but it faced opposition from some high-income countries and pharmaceutical industry groups [64].

CONCLUSION

The future of vaccine intellectual property (IP) rights is at a crossroads, with complex challenges and opportunities shaping the landscape. The slow development and introduction of vaccinations targeting illnesses in underdeveloped nations highlight the urgent need for reform. The COVID-19 pandemic has magnified the shortcomings of the existing system, prompting discussions about a global waiver of patent rights for COVID-19 vaccines. The recent decision to partially waive Trade-Related Aspects of Intellectual Property Rights (TRIPS) for vaccines underscores the global effort to balance innovation incentives with the imperative of equitable vaccine access. The vaccination sector, dominated by a few major companies, has raised concerns about profit-driven practices that favor wealthier nations. The quest for a more inclusive global vaccine landscape necessitates international collaboration, transparency, and alternative models like compulsory licensing and technology transfer. Examining the challenges in reforming vaccine IP rights reveals a delicate balance between fostering innovation and ensuring global health equity. Political pressures, trade-related concerns, and financial implications pose hurdles to change. Quality control, the specter of counterfeiting, and technology transfer challenges are practical considerations that must be addressed. Legal and ethical considerations, especially for small and medium enterprises (SMEs), highlight the need for a nuanced approach. Technological advances are paving the way for next-generation vaccines, offering hope for more effective, safer, and accessible immunization. The emergence of mRNA, DNA, subunit, attenuated, and viral vector vaccines reflects a dynamic landscape. These advancements, however, bring about new challenges in patent complexity and data ownership, requiring flexible solutions to balance innovation protection and public health. In navigating the evolving terrain of vaccine IP rights, the focus must remain on global access and equity. Initiatives like the COVAX program, vaccine solidarity, and capacity building in low- and middle-income countries are crucial components of a comprehensive strategy. Monitoring, accountability, and post-pandemic preparedness underscore the lessons learned from the COVID-19 crisis. As we look to the future, the path forward demands a careful balance of legal, ethical, and practical considerations. It requires a commitment to fostering innovation while ensuring that the benefits of scientific progress are shared equitably across the globe. The challenges are immense, but with collaborative efforts, transparency, and a dedication to the fundamental principle of health for all, we can shape a future where vaccines are accessible tools of global solidarity, protecting all populations from the threats of infectious diseases.

CONSENT FOR PUBLICATIONS

We hereby grant the editors and publishers of "Intellectual Property Right: Role in Current Scenario for Vaccines" and Bentham Science the exclusive right to publish the chapter titled "The Future of Vaccine IP Rights" which we have authored. We understand that this right includes the right to reproduce, distribute, and transmit the chapter in any form or medium, now known or hereafter developed, throughout the world and in perpetuity.

We also confirm that all necessary permissions have been obtained for the inclusion of any copyrighted material (such as tables) in the chapter.

ACKNOWLEDGEMENTS

We would like to express our deepest gratitude to all those who have contributed to the creation of this chapter. This endeavor has been a collaborative effort, and we are truly thankful for the support and encouragement received. We extend our heartfelt appreciation to all whose guidance and mentorship have been invaluable throughout the process. Your insights and expertise have shaped this chapter into a more comprehensive and insightful piece.

We are also indebted to our colleagues, whose thoughtful feedback and constructive criticism have played a crucial role in refining the ideas presented here. Their diverse perspectives have enriched the content and made it more robust. Lastly, we want to express our gratitude to our families and friends for their unwavering support and understanding during the demanding periods of this project. Your encouragement has been a source of strength and motivation. This chapter is the result of the collective effort and collaboration of many, and we are grateful to every individual who has played a role, no matter how small. Thank you for being part of this journey.

REFERENCES

[1] Mitchell AD, Taubman AS, Samlidis T. Intellectual Property and Vaccine Manufacturing: Utilising Existing TRIPS Agreement Flexibilities for COVID-19 and other Public Health Crises. Tulane Journal of Technology & Intellectual Property 2023; 25..

[2] Mahoney RT, Pablos-Mendez A, Ramachandran S. The introduction of new vaccines into developing countries. Vaccine 2004; 22(5-6): 786-92.
[http://dx.doi.org/10.1016/j.vaccine.2003.04.001] [PMID: 14741174]

[3] Boschiero N. COVID-19 Vaccines as Global Common Goods: An Integrated Approach of Ethical, Economic Policy and Intellectual Property Management. Global Jurist 2022; 22(2): 177-230.
[http://dx.doi.org/10.1515/gj-2021-0042]

[4] Hilty R, Batista PHD, Carls S, Kim D, Lamping M, Slowinski PR. COVID-19 and the role of intellectual property: position statement of the Max Planck Institute for innovation and competition of 7 May 2021 2021.
[http://dx.doi.org/10.2139/ssrn.3841549]

[5] Cozzi G, Galli S. COVID-19 Vaccines, Innovation, and Intellectual Property Rights. Handbook of Labor, Human Resources and Population Economics. Springer 2023; pp. 1-31.

[6] Raynaud M, Goutaudier V, Louis K, *et al.*, Impact of the COVID-19 pandemic on publication dynamics and non-COVID-19 research production, BMC Medical Research Methodology, 21(1): p. 255, 2021/11/22 2021,
[http://dx.doi.org/10.1186/s12874-021-01404-9]

[7] Heitzman J. Impact of COVID-19 pandemic on mental health. Psychiatr Pol 2020; 54(2): 187-98.
[http://dx.doi.org/10.12740/PP/120373] [PMID: 32772053]

[8] Xiong J, Lipsitz O, Nasri F, *et al.* Impact of COVID-19 pandemic on mental health in the general population: A systematic review. J Affect Disord 2020; 277: 55-64.
[http://dx.doi.org/10.1016/j.jad.2020.08.001] [PMID: 32799105]

[9] Sharma O, Sultan AA, Ding H, Triggle CR. A Review of the Progress and Challenges of Developing a Vaccine for COVID-19. Front Immunol 2020; 11: 585354.
[http://dx.doi.org/10.3389/fimmu.2020.585354] [PMID: 33163000]

[10] Hafner M, Yerushalmi E, Fays C, Dufresne E, Van Stolk C. COVID-19 and the Cost of Vaccine Nationalism. Rand Health Q 2022; 9(4): 1.
[PMID: 36238007]

[11] Manriquez Roa T, Holzer F, Luna F, Biller-Andorno N. Expert Views on COVAX and Equitable Global Access to COVID-19 Vaccines. Int J Public Health 2021; 66: 1604236.
[http://dx.doi.org/10.3389/ijph.2021.1604236] [PMID: 35035347]

[12] Katz R, Kornblet S, Arnold G, Lief E, Fischer J. Defining health diplomacy: changing demands in the era of globalization. Milbank Q 2011; 89(3): 503-23.
[http://dx.doi.org/10.1111/j.1468-0009.2011.00637.x] [PMID: 21933277]

[13] Leuffen D, Mounchid PM, Heermann M, Koos S. Mobilizing domestic support for international vaccine solidarity – recommendations for health crisis communication, npj Vaccines, 8(1): p. 28, 2023/02/28 2023,
[http://dx.doi.org/10.1038/s41541-023-00625-x]

[14] Amin T, Kesselheim AS. A Global Intellectual Property Waiver is Still Needed to Address the Inequities of COVID-19 and Future Pandemic Preparedness. Inquiry 2022; 59: 00469580221124821.
[http://dx.doi.org/10.1177/00469580221124821] [PMID: 36124939]

[15] Maani N, Abdalla SM, Ettman CK, *et al.* Global Health Equity Requires Global Equity. Health Equity 2023; 7(1): 192-6.
[http://dx.doi.org/10.1089/heq.2022.0169] [PMID: 36960163]

[16] Hopkins KL, Underwood T, Iddrisu I, *et al.*, Community-Based Approaches to Increase COVID-19 Vaccine Uptake and Demand: Lessons Learned from Four UNICEF-Supported Interventions, Vaccines, 11(7), p. 1180, 2023. Available from: https://www.mdpi.com/2076-393X/11/7/1180
[http://dx.doi.org/10.3390/vaccines11071180]

[17] Cherian T, Arora N, MacDonald NE. The global vaccine action plan monitoring and evaluation/accountability framework: Perspective. Vaccine 2020; 38(33): 5384-6.
[http://dx.doi.org/10.1016/j.vaccine.2020.04.036] [PMID: 32381481]

[18] Leach M, MacGregor H, Scoones I, Wilkinson A. Post-pandemic transformations: How and why COVID-19 requires us to rethink development. World Dev 2021; 138: 105233.
[http://dx.doi.org/10.1016/j.worlddev.2020.105233] [PMID: 33100478]

[19] Correa CM. Interpreting the Flexibilities Under the TRIPS Agreement, Cham, 2022: Springer International Publishing, in Access to Medicines and Vaccines, pp. 1-30.
[http://dx.doi.org/10.1007/978-3-030-83114-1_1]

[20] Nelson C, Lurie N, Wasserman J, Zakowski S. Conceptualizing and defining public health emergency

preparedness, (in eng), Am J Public Health, 97(1), no. Suppl 1, pp. S9-11, 2007. [http://dx.doi.org/10.2105/AJPH.2007.114496]

[21] Lee BY, McGlone SM. Pricing of new vaccines. Hum Vaccin 2010; 6(8): 619-26. [http://dx.doi.org/10.4161/hv.6.8.11563] [PMID: 20861678]

[22] McMahon A. Patents, Governance and Control: Ethics and the Patentability of Novel Beings and Advanced Biotechnologies in Europe. Camb Q Healthc Ethics 2021; 30(3): 529-42. [http://dx.doi.org/10.1017/S0963180120001073] [PMID: 34109920]

[23] Druedahl LC, Minssen T, Price WN. Collaboration in times of crisis: A study on COVID-19 vaccine R&D partnerships. Vaccine 2021; 39(42): 6291-5. [http://dx.doi.org/10.1016/j.vaccine.2021.08.101] [PMID: 34556366]

[24] Xue QC, Ouellette LL. Innovation policy and the market for vaccines. J Law Biosci 2020; 7(1): lsaa026. [http://dx.doi.org/10.1093/jlb/lsaa026] [PMID: 32733687]

[25] Albrecht D. Vaccination, politics and COVID-19 impacts, BMC Public Health, 22(1): p. 96, 2022/01/14 2022. [http://dx.doi.org/10.1186/s12889-021-12432-x]

[26] David DC, Bloom E, Daniel L. Tortorice. An Ounce of Prevention. Available from: https://www.imf.org/en/Publications/fandd/issues/2020/09/vaccine-financ--epidemics-and-prevention-bloom

[27] Mao Q, Xu M, He Q, *et al.*, COVID-19 vaccines: progress and understanding on quality control and evaluation, Signal Transduction and Targeted Therapy, 6(1): p. 199, 2021/05/18 2021. [http://dx.doi.org/10.1038/s41392-021-00621-4]

[28] Yarlagadda H, Patel MA, Gupta V, *et al.* COVID-19 Vaccine Challenges in Developing and Developed Countries. Cureus 2022; 14(4): e23951. [http://dx.doi.org/10.7759/cureus.23951] [PMID: 35547442]

[29] Fonseca EM, Shadlen KC, Achcar HM. Vaccine technology transfer in a global health crisis: Actors, capabilities, and institutions. Res Policy 2023; 52(4): 104739. [http://dx.doi.org/10.1016/j.respol.2023.104739] [PMID: 36785560]

[30] Jalilian H, Amraei M, Javanshir E, Jamebozorgi K, Faraji-Khiavi F. Ethical considerations of the vaccine development process and vaccination: a scoping review. BMC Health Serv Res 2023; 23(1): 255. [http://dx.doi.org/10.1186/s12913-023-09237-6] [PMID: 36918888]

[31] Jalilian H, Amraei M, Javanshir E, Jamebozorgi K, Faraji-Khiavi F. Ethical considerations of the vaccine development process and vaccination: a scoping review, BMC Health Services Research, vol. 23, no. 1, p. 255, 2023/03/14 2023. [http://dx.doi.org/10.1186/s12913-023-09237-6]

[32] Kennedy RB, Ovsyannikova IG, Palese P, Poland GA. Current Challenges in Vaccinology. Front Immunol 2020; 11: 1181. [http://dx.doi.org/10.3389/fimmu.2020.01181] [PMID: 32670279]

[33] Flower DR. Computer-Aided Vaccine Design. Hum Vaccin Immunother 2014; 10(1): 241-3. [http://dx.doi.org/10.4161/hv.26687] [PMID: 24100661]

[34] Tong JC, Ranganathan S. Computer-Aided Vaccine Design. Computer-Aided Vaccine Design 2013; 07(01): 1-135.

[35] Xu H, Cai L, Hufnagel S, Cui Z. Intranasal vaccine: Factors to consider in research and development, International Journal of Pharmaceutics, vol. 609, p. 121180, 2021/11/20/ 2021. [http://dx.doi.org/10.1016/j.ijpharm.2021.121180]

[36] Kim YC, Prausnitz MR. Enabling skin vaccination using new delivery technologies, Drug Delivery

and Translational Research, vol. 1, no. 1, pp. 7-12, 2011/02/01 2011.
[http://dx.doi.org/10.1007/s13346-010-0005-z]

[37] Ascher MS, Berman MA, Ruppanner R. Initial clinical and immunologic evaluation of a new phase I Q fever vaccine and skin test in humans. J Infect Dis 1983; 148(2): 214-22.
[http://dx.doi.org/10.1093/infdis/148.2.214] [PMID: 6350491]

[38] Yusuf H, Kett V. Current prospects and future challenges for nasal vaccine delivery, Human Vaccines & Immunotherapeutics, vol. 13, no. 1, pp. 34-45, 2017/01/02 2017.
[http://dx.doi.org/10.1080/21645515.2016.1239668]

[39] Jain S, Venkataraman A, Wechsler ME, Peppas NA. Messenger RNA-based vaccines: Past, present, and future directions in the context of the COVID-19 pandemic. Adv Drug Deliv Rev 2021; 179: 114000.
[http://dx.doi.org/10.1016/j.addr.2021.114000] [PMID: 34637846]

[40] Schlake T, Thess A, Fotin-Mleczek M, Kallen KJ. Developing mRNA-vaccine technologies. RNA Biol 2012; 9(11): 1319-30.
[http://dx.doi.org/10.4161/rna.22269] [PMID: 23064118]

[41] Pardi N, Hogan MJ, Porter FW, Weissman D. mRNA vaccines — a new era in vaccinology, Nature Reviews Drug Discovery, vol. 17, no. 4, pp. 261-279, 2018/04/01 2018.
[http://dx.doi.org/10.1038/nrd.2017.243]

[42] Fang E, Liu X, Li M, *et al.* Advances in COVID-19 mRNA vaccine development. Signal Transduct Target Ther 2022; 7(1): 94.
[http://dx.doi.org/10.1038/s41392-022-00950-y] [PMID: 35322018]

[43] Kutzler MA, Weiner DB. DNA vaccines: ready for prime time?, Nature Reviews Genetics, vol. 9, no. 10, pp. 776-788, 2008/10/01 2008.
[http://dx.doi.org/10.1038/nrg2432]

[44] Hobernik D, Bros M. DNA Vaccines—How Far From Clinical Use? Int J Mol Sci 2018; 19(11): 3605.
[http://dx.doi.org/10.3390/ijms19113605] [PMID: 30445702]

[45] Cheng MA, Farmer E, Huang C, Lin J, Hung CF, Wu TC. Therapeutic DNA Vaccines for Human Papillomavirus and Associated Diseases. Hum Gene Ther 2018; 29(9): 971-96.
[http://dx.doi.org/10.1089/hum.2017.197] [PMID: 29316817]

[46] Werninghaus IC, Hinke DM, Fossum E, Bogen B, Braathen R. Neuraminidase delivered as an APC-targeted DNA vaccine induces protective antibodies against influenza. Mol Ther 2023; 31(7): 2188-205.
[http://dx.doi.org/10.1016/j.ymthe.2023.03.012] [PMID: 36926694]

[47] De Pooter D, Van Gulck E, Chen A, *et al.* A Therapeutic Hepatitis B Virus DNA Vaccine Induces Specific Immune Responses in Mice and Non-Human Primates. Vaccines (Basel) 2021; 9(9): 969.
[http://dx.doi.org/10.3390/vaccines9090969] [PMID: 34579206]

[48] Letvin NL, Montefiori DC, Yasutomi Y, *et al.* Potent, protective anti-HIV immune responses generated by bimodal HIV envelope DNA plus protein vaccination. Proc Natl Acad Sci USA 1997; 94(17): 9378-83.
[http://dx.doi.org/10.1073/pnas.94.17.9378] [PMID: 9256490]

[49] Young A, Isaacs A, Scott CAP, *et al.* A platform technology for generating subunit vaccines against diverse viral pathogens. Front Immunol 2022; 13: 963023.
[http://dx.doi.org/10.3389/fimmu.2022.963023] [PMID: 36059532]

[50] Pattyn J, Hendrickx G, Vorsters A, Van Damme P. Hepatitis B Vaccines. J Infect Dis 2021; 224(12) (Suppl. 4): S343-51.
[http://dx.doi.org/10.1093/infdis/jiaa668] [PMID: 34590138]

[51] N. C. INSTITUTE. Human Papillomavirus (HPV) Vaccines. Available from: https://www.cancer.gov/about-cancer/causes-prevention/risk/infectious-agents/hpv-vaccine-fact-sheet#:~:text=The%20

current%20HPV%20vaccines%20are,activity%20against%20the%20natural%20virus

[52] Zhang N, Zheng BJ, Lu L, Zhou Y, Jiang S, Du L. Advancements in the development of subunit influenza vaccines. Microbes Infect 2015; 17(2): 123-34. [http://dx.doi.org/10.1016/j.micinf.2014.12.006] [PMID: 25529753]

[53] Schmitt P, Borkner L, Jazayeri SD, McCarthy KN, Mills KHG. Nasal vaccines for pertussis, Current Opinion in Immunology, vol. 84, p. 102355, 2023/10/01/ 2023. [http://dx.doi.org/10.1016/j.coi.2023.102355]

[54] Lauring AS, Jones JO, Andino R. Rationalizing the development of live attenuated virus vaccines. Nat Biotechnol 2010; 28(6): 573-9. [http://dx.doi.org/10.1038/nbt.1635] [PMID: 20531338]

[55] Minor PD. Live attenuated vaccines: Historical successes and current challenges, Virology, vol. 479-480, pp. 379-392, 2015/05/01/ 2015. [http://dx.doi.org/10.1016/j.virol.2015.03.032]

[56] Deng S, Liang H, Chen P, *et al.* Viral Vector Vaccine Development and Application during the COVID-19 Pandemic. Microorganisms 2022; 10(7): 1450. [http://dx.doi.org/10.3390/microorganisms10071450] [PMID: 35889169]

[57] S. Wang *et al.*, "Viral vectored vaccines: design, development, preventive and therapeutic applications in human diseases," Signal Transduction and Targeted Therapy, vol. 8, no. 1, p. 149, 2023/04/07 2023. [http://dx.doi.org/10.1038/s41392-023-01408-5]

[58] S. A. Mendonça SA, R. Lorincz, P. Boucher, and D. T. Curiel, Adenoviral vector vaccine platforms in the SARS-CoV-2 pandemic, npj Vaccines, vol. 6, no. 1, p. 97, 2021/08/05 2021. [http://dx.doi.org/10.1038/s41541-021-00356-x]

[59] Li JX, Hou LH, Meng FY, *et al.* Immunity duration of a recombinant adenovirus type-5 vector-based Ebola vaccine and a homologous prime-boost immunisation in healthy adults in China: final report of a randomised, double-blind, placebo-controlled, phase 1 trial. Lancet Glob Health 2017; 5(3): e324-34. [http://dx.doi.org/10.1016/S2214-109X(16)30367-9] [PMID: 28017642]

[60] Turtle L, Subramaniam K. Modified vaccinia Ankara–Bavarian Nordic vaccine against mpox in children. Lancet Infect Dis 2023; 23(9): 989-90. [http://dx.doi.org/10.1016/S1473-3099(23)00345-6] [PMID: 37336223]

[61] A. N. I. Property, in How the Technological Era Has Changed the Global Intellectual Property Ecosystem, ed, 2023.

[62] Woo S, Jang P, Kim Y. Effects of intellectual property rights and patented knowledge in innovation and industry value added: A multinational empirical analysis of different industries," Technovation, vol. 43-44, pp. 49-63, 2015/09/01/ 2015, [http://dx.doi.org/10.1016/j.technovation.2015.03.003]

[63] P. S. Arunachalam *et al.*, "Systems vaccinology of the BNT162b2 mRNA vaccine in humans," Nature, vol. 596, no. 7872, pp. 410-416, 2021/08/01 2021. [http://dx.doi.org/10.1038/s41586-021-03791-x]

[64] Kohler J, Wong A, Tailor L. Improving Access to COVID-19 Vaccines: An Analysis of TRIPS Waiver Discourse among WTO Members, Civil Society Organizations, and Pharmaceutical Industry Stakeholders. Health Hum Rights 2022; 24(2): 159-75. [PMID: 36579316]

CHAPTER 9

Case Studies: Ip Rights and Specific Vaccines

V. Raghuwanshi[1], **P. Bhide**[1], **Y. Bhandari**[2,*] and **Sachin Kumar Jain**[3]

[1] *Department of Pharmaceutics, Sri Aurobindo Institute of Pharmacy, Indore 453555, MP, India*

[2] *Department of Pharmaceutical Chemistry, Sri Aurobindo Institute of Pharmacy, Indore 453555, MP, India*

[3] *Department of Pharmacognosy, Oriental University, Oriental University, Near Aurobindo Hospital, Sanwer Road, Indore 453555, MP, India*

Abstract: Numerous intellectual property rights apply to vaccines. Vaccines may be covered by patents, copyrights, trademarks, and trade secrets. In response to various diseases including the pandemic, there have been debates regarding intellectual rights on vaccines. In the end, the federal government only placed an order for 3.2 million pills, fewer than 80,000 of which were filled by February 2023. The exact amount of government financing committed to one of India's companies has not been made public by the US government. A case study of global companies was unable to create a COVID-19 vaccine that was approved. Long before the COVID-19 pandemic, the global pharmaceutical company was awarded funding from the Gates Foundation for a project called "mRNA vaccine platform for rapid response in case of pandemic preparedness." Some companies mentioned in its German government development support were disclosed in regulatory filings, along with the government's "transferable and nonexclusive right to utilize any intellectual property created during the sponsored project, in the case of a special public interest." The Biopharmaceutical company has an in-licensing agreement with a Canadian company and important components for their patented LNP technology, which involves milestone and royalty payments. Additionally, a global biopharmaceutical company signed many contracts to enable the expansion of its vaccine production. The company has a sizable portfolio of patents covering its vaccination technique.

Keywords: BioNTech, COVID-19, HPV vaccines, Killed pathogen, Moderna, Polio vaccines, Pfizer, Rotashield, Technology Transfer, Vaccines, WHO.

INTRODUCTION

The significantly rapid development of various coronavirus disease 2019 (COVID-19) vaccines is the outcome of special cooperation between businesses,

* **Corresponding author Y. Bhandari:** Department of Pharmaceutical Chemistry, Sri Aurobindo Institute of Pharmacy, Indore 453555, MP, India; E-mail: yb1231998@gmail.com

government health organizations, and academic labs. New vaccines have been introduced, but there are also worries about how they will be made available in adequate amounts and dispersed equitably over the world [1, 2]. A waiver from certain of the terms of the World Trade Organization's Agreement on Trade-Related Aspects of Intellectual Property Rights (TRIPS) that would enable developing nations to manufacture their vaccines was suggested in October 2020 by Eswatini, India, Kenya, and South Africa. However, the European Union (EU), the United Kingdom, the United States, and some other countries have resisted the waiver since it has been viewed with skepticism, particularly by high-income countries [3, 4].

There are numerous vaccination forms and components, including distinct formulations, delivery methods, parts, and distribution networks. Similarly, there are numerous intellectual property (IP) rights that apply to vaccines. Vaccines may be covered by intellectual property rights such as patents, copyrights, trademarks, plant breeders' rights, and trade secrets. Therefore, discussing IP rights and vaccines should not start and stop with a single IP right being applied to a vaccination [5 - 7]. Multiple intellectual property rights that apply to vaccines should be discussed, as well as how to use them in concert to create a strategy that supports vaccine development and distribution. With this approach to IP rights for vaccines, the integrated rights can be taken into account alongside the reasons for using IP rights to protect vaccines and the issues surrounding specific IP rights for vaccines, like available IP credits for humanitarian purposes and mandatory licensing schemes. Although it requires attention, seeing vaccines as the target of several IP rights can have a big impact on vaccine distribution and development [8, 9].

The burden of IPRs and Licenses makes a difference for the nations who have forced IPRs on the generation of immunizations but hampers the 'less created countries" too. Topical investigation tends to appear that the "developed countries" have forced IPRs and Licenses on their antibodies that permit them to offer the antibodies at a better cost as IPRs and Licenses guarantee that the antibodies are one of a kind and are exceptionally compelling in treating the illness and hence strengthening the "underdeveloped countries" to buy the immunizations at a better cost (Fig. **1**) [10, 11].

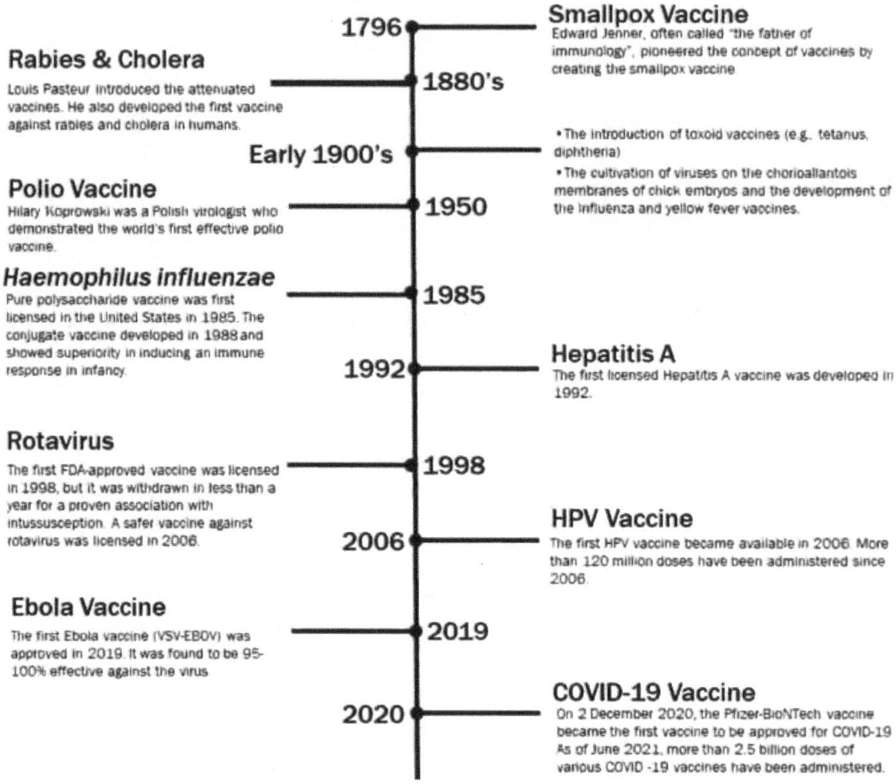

Fig. (1). Vaccine history timeline [55].
(COVID-19, coronavirus disease 2019; FDA, U.S. Food and Drug Administration; HPV, human papillomavirus).

COVID-19 VACCINES AND PATENT WAIVERS

Considering the COVID-19 pandemic, there have been debates regarding intellectual property rights on COVID-19 vaccines. Developing countries and public health advocates have called for waiving intellectual property rights on COVID-19 vaccines to increase global access and accelerate production [12, 13]. They argue that this would allow more manufacturers to produce vaccines, thereby addressing the global vaccine shortage. However, some pharmaceutical companies and countries with strong pharmaceutical industries have opposed this move, citing concerns about disincentivizing innovation and the potential negative impact on future drug development. Governmental awards of intellectual property rights, particularly patent rights, are ingrained in national legal systems worldwide for practical purposes. The foundation of long-standing intellectual property theory and policy is the notion that participants will be motivated by the possibility of getting a patent [14, 15]. To allocate funds to areas that might not receive enough funding for research and development (R&D). This utilitarian approach continues to be the primary force behind modern patent systems, despite a large body of research showing that it is not generally relevant to all sorts of commodities (and particularly not to all types of health goods) [16, 17]. Patentees divulge vital information regarding the invention covered by the patent in return for this specific kind of intellectual property rights. On the one hand, a patent allows the owner of the patent to have a lead time on the market for a sizable amount of time (officially 20 years, but in reality, much shorter, particularly for products like vaccines that need to be reviewed and approved by drug authorities). However, the patent system encourages the dissemination of scientific and technological knowledge that other innovators in the field might utilize by forcing the patent applicant to submit information about the invention that is then published by the patent office [18, 19].

After imposing a legal framework that bestows patent rights on any invention that satisfies the substantive requirements outlined in both international and national patent laws—a criterion that many of the presently pending COVID-19 patent applications will almost certainly meet—we now confront the inevitable fallout from this framework. In the absence of intervention in order, vaccine patent holders will be able to refuse to license their technology to third parties, even in the face of vaccine scarcity [20]. Thus, a waiver is presented as a way to get around the restrictive power that typically comes with a patent. Given the grave implications of our common public health issue, let us temporarily waive the exclusionary privilege so that other businesses will be able to start providing populations in the Global South with significantly more vaccination doses; two strategies need to be used: 1) duplicate current vaccines and 2) produce at scale [21, 22]. Consider patents as informational mechanisms similar to the data and instruments required to transform a recipe into an edible product to grasp the practical constraints of a waiver of intellectual property rights when vaccination is involved. A method or an ingredient required to make a vaccine will be revealed by one or more patents. However, similar to a cooking recipe, a patent's informational power does not grant access to the raw materials required to make a vaccine, nor does it cover any advice or guidelines that have not been documented in writing. Therefore, waivers eliminate exclusionary rights in the short term but do not address two major causes of the current vaccine shortage [23, 24].

THE JONAS SALK AND ALBERT SABIN POLIO VACCINES (CASE STUDY- I)

The development of the polio vaccine provides a historical case study in the intersection of vaccines and intellectual property. Both Jonas Salk and Albert Sabin developed polio vaccines independently. Salk's vaccine, based on inactivated poliovirus, was the first to be widely used, and he chose not to patent it. Instead, he believed that the vaccine belonged to humanity, famously stating, "Could you patent the sun?" In contrast, Sabin's vaccine, based on attenuated (weakened) live virus, was patented. Salk's decision not to patent his vaccine allowed it to be rapidly disseminated and contributed to the widespread eradication of polio [25, 26].

Dr. Albert Sabin created oral live attenuated poliovirus vaccine was first made available in 1962 and has been a childhood immunization staple since 1965. The yearly reported incidence of paralytic illness decreased from 0.8 cases per 100,000 people in 1961 to roughly 0.005 instances per 100,000 people in 1982 with the introduction of the Sabin vaccination. The fact that throughout the last ten years, just roughly 12 instances have been documented annually serves as an example of this [27]. The rates of OPV immunization have risen steadily since 1962. According to a small number of serologic surveys, up to 95% of infants aged 1 to 4 and 70% of children aged 10 to 14 were immunized against OPV up to 1981 [28, 29].

A thorough assessment of the epidemiological information gathered both before and following the extensive rate of decline in the frequency of paralytic poliomyelitis following the release of the Salk vaccine (1955) or the Sabin vaccine (1962) was strikingly similar, according to the use of the two polio vaccine types. In the United States, there have been two outbreaks of wild paralytic poliomyelitis since the Sabin vaccine was introduced in September–October 1972 and January–July 1979 [30, 31]. Both epidemics struck portions of a town that had not received any vaccination against polio in any form. The general public is largely immune, but no secondary occurrences of paralytic disease were seen despite repeated exposures to sick people. Therefore, when it comes to avoiding paralytic illness in children, IPV and OPV are equally beneficial [32, 33].

In the United States, approximately 225 cases of paralytic poliomyelitis had been reported over the previous 15 years (1969–1983). It is now feasible to determine with fair certainty that 80 or more of these instances were most likely connected to the vaccine strains of the virus included in the Sabin vaccination thanks to recent technological advancements that allow for the differentiation of poliovirus between wild (virulent) and vaccine strains. Based on the Sabin vaccination dosages distributed during this time, the total chance of developing paralytic poliomyelitis can be estimated to be between one case of the disease per 3.2 and 8 million doses of the vaccine; the first dosage of OPV has a higher risk [34, 35]. About one instance of paralytic illness is thought to occur for every 0.5 to 1.5 million vaccination doses administered at the initial dose. With the additional vaccination doses given, the risk of paralytic illness is incredibly minimal, with one incidence occurring for every 18 to 100 million doses given. About one case per million recipients of the first dose and one case per 22 million consecutive doses are expected to develop paralytic illness in contact with vaccines [36].

Additionally, there seems to be a larger risk among household contacts (one incidence every 4–5 million). Nonetheless, the risk seems to be incredibly low (one in 20 to 23 million) for contacts of vaccine recipients who are not household members. The majority of patients suffering from paralysis seem to have normal immune systems. Nonetheless, immunodeficiency has been discovered in 10-15% of patients with paralytic poliomyelitis linked to vaccination. These individuals appear to be 1000–10,000 times more at risk than members of the general population. Immune-compromised individuals seem to have an increased chance of contracting vaccine-induced paralysis as contacts or recipients. 30-60% of individuals with paralytic disease linked to vaccinations are adults. Most adult cases have family connections, such as parents of recently immunized children.

The Sabin vaccine was chosen as the preferred form of immunization against poliomyelitis in the United States, and the reasons for this are still as clear today as they were in 1962. The vaccine is widely accepted by the public because it is inexpensive and simple to administer. It is also thought to promote lifetime immunity and closely mimic immunologic responses seen following a real infection because of its mucosal proliferation. Through the simultaneous development of gut immunity, OVPV can halt the spread of wild viruses among the broader population. Lastly, a particularly effective method of immunizing or enhancing pre-existing immunity in close contact with the vaccination is the faecal shedding of the vaccine virus, a characteristic feature of the Sabin vaccine [37].

Despite OPV, the Salk vaccine has not been linked to any serious side effects. Several European countries, including Denmark, Finland, Holland, Ireland, and Sweden, have successfully adopted more potent variants of IPV as the preferred poliovirus vaccine, replacing the Salk vaccination that was used earlier in the United States. It is less acceptable because it is supplied by injection. To enhance the immunization procedure and public acceptance, several nations have paired it with diphtheria, tetanus, and pertussis vaccination as a single injection [15, 38].

THE ROTAVIRUS VACCINE AND TECHNOLOGY TRANSFER

When rotavirus was initially identified in 1973, it was determined to be the primary cause of childhood acute gastroenteritis. Since 1981, several phase I–III clinical trials have been carried out to provide a safe vaccination against Rotavirus. In 1998, the first vaccine to receive FDA approval was granted a license under the Rotashield® brand. However, it was removed in less than a year due to a confirmed link to intussusception. It took an additional eight years for the licensing of a safer rotavirus vaccine. In the USA, RotaTeq® (RV5: Pentavalent) was included in the immunization schedule in 2006. The FDA then granted a license for Rotarix® (RV1: Monovalent) in 2008. When evaluating the efficacy of several rotavirus vaccination types in the United States, a meta-analysis of several case-control studies did not find a statistically significant difference.

There are 29 patent applications submitted as PCTs or in the US that might be pertinent to the production of rotavirus vaccinations. Out of all three countries, GSK, the company that makes the vaccination Rotarix, had the most patent applications filed. It does not seem like Merck, the company that makes Rotateq, has any patents awarded in China, India, or Brazil. The United States National Institutes of Health (NIH) has patents on technologies used in the development of the bovine reassortant rotavirus vaccine (BRV). This patent was awarded in China and India, where it has been licensed to several developing country vaccine manufacturers (DCVMs). It was denied in Brazil; however, it is currently on appeal. Bharat Biotech and SII have submitted applications for their vaccine candidates as well.

A review of the patent landscape indicates that there don't seem to be any restrictions on patents in Brazil, China, or India that would prohibit the development of a BRV. Nonetheless, additional producers are attempting to produce upgraded versions of GSK's Rotarix vaccine. Depending on which markets they intend to sell their vaccines in, they could need to circumvent some of these patents. WHO representatives also brought up the possibility that patents on a liquid vaccine formulation for rotavirus could be a barrier. Merck has filed numerous patent applications in emerging nations for a liquid version of BRV. Even though this investigation was unable to locate any patents on liquid formulations granted to Merck in China, India, or Brazil, it is still feasible that Merck has based on the markets in which producers want to sell their vaccines, protection for this technique in other developing nations and the patent may be significant [39].

THE CASE STUDY OF PREVENTION (HPV VACCINE DEVELOPMENT)

The vaccination developed by Merck will be sold under the Gardasil™ brand. HPV strains 16, 18, 6, and 11 components are incorporated into L1 proteins and are included in the recombinant yeast medication Gardasil™.Therefore, the goal of this vaccine is to provide protection against the two most common strains of HPV that cause genital warts, which are implicated in 90% of cases that result in genital wart presentations, as well as against the two most common strains that cause cervical cancer, which are implicated in 70% of all cases that are identified. Phase 2 clinical research showed 90% effectiveness in lowering chronic infection or sickness associated with HPV types 6, 11, 16, 18 related conditions. Phase 3 trial data published in October 2005 showed that the vaccine was 100% effective for two years after administration in preventing infection with HPV 16 and HPV 18. During a pivotal Phase 3 study, 12,167 women aged 16 to 26 from 13 countries received Gardasil TM; 6,082 of these women received three doses at 0, 2, and 6 months, whereas 6,075 of these women received a placebo. In an intent-to-treat trial, efficacy decreased to 97% when women who had received fewer than the required three doses were included. On December 5, 2005, Merck submitted their biologics license application to the FDA for assessment. Pending approval, the company planned to commercialize the medicine in 2006. A decision might be made in as little as six to twelve months. Australia and the European Union (EU) filings are anticipated before the end of 2005 [24].

The vaccine developed by GSK will be sold under the Cervarix™ brand. Thanks to recombinant baculovirus technology, L1 proteins incorporating components from HPV types 16 and 18 are present in Cervarix™. Therefore, the purpose of this vaccine is to protect against only the two HPV kinds that are most common and cause cervical cancer. Cervarix™ has shown 100% efficacy in avoiding persistent infection and 92% efficacy in preventing transitory infection with HPV 16 and 18. These results were based on phase 2 clinical investigations. Phase 3 clinical trials are now in progress, and regulatory registration in the EU is anticipated to occur in 2006, followed by filing in the US, with an EU launch anticipated in 2007 [40].

The FDA's Centre for Biologics Evaluation and Research is responsible for approving and regulating vaccinations in the United States. The Office of Vaccines Research and Review collaborates with the Division of Vaccines and Related Product Applications to conduct reviews. The fundamental structure of the clinical development program for vaccines is the same as that of pharmaceuticals and biologics. Animal preclinical safety investigations are necessary. To begin human clinical trials, the vaccine maker must then apply an investigational new drug. There are three stages to conducting clinical trials. Phase 1 studies are the first conducted in a limited number of human volunteers to assess the safety and immunogenicity of the dosage regimen. The injection site and any systemic side effects will be evaluated clinically [41].

Many patients are being investigated at this stage of development in order to assess the safety and effectiveness of the suggested dosage schedule that is meant for commercial launch. The information obtained from these trials' extended follow-up allows one to estimate how long the immunity provided by the vaccination will last. The vaccine manufacturer will apply for a biologics license with the FDA after the clinical tests are finished to get permission to market the vaccine in the United States. To evaluate the data and decide whether the vaccine is sufficiently safe and efficacious for use in the target population, a multidisciplinary FDA review committee is assembled. One may request membership in the advisory committee council, which in the case of HPV vaccinations is the vaccinations and committee on biological products related to this subject [42].

There are now numerous approaches to boost HPV prevention rates from diverse perspectives. Scholars have been investigating strategies to lower the frequency of vaccinations, improve the half-life, and boost cross-protection against different forms of HPV. By combining Merck's current quadrivalent vaccination (HPV types 6, 11, 16, and 18) with the additional carcinogenic HPV types 31, 33, 45, 52, and 58, a novel non-valent vaccine currently undergoing a phase III clinical study aims to establish a 15-30% stronger anti-cancer impact. Nevertheless, the non-valent vaccine's usefulness as a next-generation HPV vaccine is questionable due to the lack of research analysing the novel vaccine's comparative performance and cost-effectiveness with existing vaccinations [29].

On the other hand, easier ways to administer the vaccine, like a nasal spray or patch, or better ways to store the vaccine could make it more easily and affordably accessible. By early 2012, the HPV vaccine was included in the national immunization programs (NIPs) of at least 40 nations. The United States, the United Kingdom, Canada, and Australia were the first of these nations to carry out the implementation. Just three European nations implemented the HPV vaccine into their national immunization programs in 2007. By the year 2008, that number had risen to twenty-two. Although early adolescent females are the primary target of most country programs, each country has its own set of established age groups. The disparities in healthcare systems and infrastructure give rise to these diverse implementation strategies (Table **1**).

Table 1. Main important vaccines and some important vaccine platforms [56].

Type of Vaccines	First Time Used	Advantages	Challenges
Live- attenuated pathogen	1798	Long lasting protecting	Safety and stability issues.
		Most do not require an adjuvant.	
Killed pathogen	1896	Most do not require an adjuvant.	

(Table 1) cont.....

<table>
<tr><th>Type of Vaccines</th><th>First Time Used</th><th>Advantages</th><th>Challenges</th></tr>
<tr><td>Toxoid</td><td>1923</td><td>-</td><td>-</td></tr>
<tr><td>Subunit (Protein, peptide, Polysaccharide</td><td>1970</td><td>Can be treated quickly.</td><td>Require an adjuvant.</td></tr>
<tr><td>Viruses like protein</td><td>1986</td><td>-</td><td rowspan="2">Require an adjuvant.
Preexisting immunity against the vector.
Potential challenges are still not completely known.</td></tr>
<tr><td>Viral vector</td><td>2019</td><td>Strong protection
Do not require an adjuvant.
Replicable manufacturing</td></tr>
<tr><td>Nucleic acid (DNA, RNA)</td><td>2020</td><td>Strong protection
Do not require an adjuvant.
Replicable manufacturing.</td><td>Potentially challenges still are not completely known.
Potentially challenges still are not completely known.</td></tr>
<tr><td>Antigen-presenting cells (dendritic cells),T cells</td><td>-</td><td>Approved by the United States Food and Drug Admiration for therapeutic use in cancer.</td><td>Potential challenges are still not completely known.</td></tr>
<tr><td>Bacterial vector</td><td>-</td><td>Lasting protection.
Stability.</td><td>Not yet approved for use in humans.</td></tr>
</table>

CASE STUDY OF MALARIA

Although malaria is a very challenging disease that has long defied contemporary science, recent developments show promise. Unlike research on pandemic influenza, which has been primarily sponsored by the public sector, malaria vaccine R&D is being carried out through public-private partnership (PDP) product development. The Bill and Melinda Gates Foundation's most recent donations have boomed the development of malaria vaccines. The Malaria Vaccine Initiative (MVI), a PATH-based PDP that labels malaria, was also consulted and is actively involved in the current effort.

Antibodies created utilizing the MSP-1 malaria antigen, from the merozoite arrangement of the Plasmodium life cycle and have produced promising outcomes, demonstrating strong immunogenicity and data from animal models. In any case, IP issues hinder access to this antigen. Numerous patents with overlapping claims make it not readily available. Obtaining it would require licenses from at least eight entities. The RTS,S vaccine consists of selected sequences from the circumsporozoite protein (sporozoite stage) fused to the hepatitis B virus surface antigen, co-expressed with unfused hepatitis B antigen in recombinant yeast cells. This vaccine has been shown to be safe, immunogenic, and effective. It is currently undergoing pediatric clinical trials and has demonstrated the ability to protect children for up to 18 months. A novel strategy involves using DNA constructs encoding multiple Plasmodium peptide epitopes and thrombospondin-related adhesion protein (known as 'DNA METRAP') to elicit T-cell mediated immune responses against the liver stage (hepatocytic stage) of malaria. By employing a 'prime-boost' technique, the immune response from the DNA vaccine can be significantly enhanced when followed by the administration of a modified vaccinia virus Ankara (MVA). Using radiation-attenuated sporozoites of Plasmodium falciparum and P. vivax as antigens may prevent diseases in 90% of those vaccinated for at least one year. However, this method is labor-intensive and requires the physical dissection of mosquitoes, mosquito salivary organs, and extraction of sporozoites. All things considered; this technology may have conceivable applications in developing countries. Malarial toxin glycosyl phosphatidyl inositol presents another potential route for vaccine development. This approach does not prevent infection but instead reduces the mortality and severity of the disease. It has shown promise as a candidate vaccine with encouraging results [43].

The process of developing vaccines: Regulatory approval, industrial scale-up, and research and development are the three primary phases needed to bring a vaccine to market. Preclinical development in the lab is the first step in research and development (R&D), which is increasingly the focus of patent applications. Following testing in animal models, clinical trials are conducted to test dosing and safety in humans (phase I), evaluate immunogenicity and efficacy (phase II), and further establish the efficacy and safety with increasing human sample sizes (phase III) if a preclinical candidate is found to have the potential for use against a specific disease. The business applies for registration and licensing if the product is found to be both safe and effective. Phase IV of continuous pharmacovigilance is the process that comes after this [44].

CASE STUDY OF PFIZER/ BIONTECH

Pfizer, an American company, effectively bargained to buy BioNTech's rights to the mRNA vaccine technology, a German company, at the beginning of the pandemic outbreak. Pfizer agreed to a 50/50 cut of gross revenue in exchange for BioNTech's rights, paying them over USD 1 billion in earnings from the subsequent vaccine's sales. Patents served as protection for BioNTech's technologies.

Pfizer would supply the majority of the world with its vaccine (Comirnaty), while BioNTech would hold the rights for Germany and Turkey. BioNTech would also maintain a licensing deal in which the PRC biotechnology business Fosun would pay up to USD 85 million in fees and a 35 percent share of gross earnings on behalf of the partners. For reasons that are yet unknown, the Pfizer BioNTech vaccine was only recently and in tiny numbers released in the PRC [45].

In a complex collaboration agreement, Pfizer and BioNTech agreed that Pfizer would make most decisions, including those regarding vaccine costs outside of Germany and Turkey.

The parties would jointly possess developed intellectual property (IP) while each party would continue to hold its exclusively developed IP. Prior to this, BioNTech had obtained an in-licensing agreement for mRNA technology from Acuitas and the University of Pennsylvania/Cellscript, both of which were compensated handsomely with sales proceeds from the vaccine.

When Pfizer entered the partnership, it had a highly developed American manufacturing and distribution network, and the majority of its production, at least in the early phases, was done there. Among the major vaccine makers, Pfizer is unique in that it did not obtain funding from the US government for technological development. However, the business did secure an order for 300 million doses of its vaccine in March 2021, with a dosage costing USD 19.90. Pfizer/BioNTech has received over USD 15 billion for over 655 million doses from the US government by December 2022.The US government was unable to acquire the customary Bayh-Dole "march-in" rights to Pfizer patents since there was no development funding [46].

In November 2020, the European Union (EU) and Pfizer/BioNTech also engaged in a large-scale APA for up to 300 million doses for EUR 19.5 a dosage. Pfizer/BioNTech signed several more contracts to supply Peru, Colombia, the Dominican Republic, and Albania, among other nations. Each of these contracts had a price per dose of USD 12 and no clear delivery date commitment. IP would remain owned by Pfizer/BioNTech. Be aware that Pfizer was not required to provide LMICs at favorable rates under the terms of its agreements with the US government.

Pfizer's CEO opposed the company's application for a WTO TRIPS waiver, arguing that Pfizer's supply capacity was being limited by component material shortages and that adding additional firms to the market for suppliers would exacerbate the issue.

He added that due to restrictions on cold chain storage, LMICs were hesitant to buy the mRNA vaccine. There is no evidence that Pfizer/BioNTech threatened to sue any business for patent infringement in order to force it to stop manufacturing during the epidemic.

It is presently engaged in legal disputes about rights to patented technologies, among other things, with Moderna. Forty Moderna filed the action against them, and it began in Germany and the US. Since then, it has moved to Belgium, Ireland, and the UK. BioNTech and Pfizer have made rebuttals.

CASE STUDY OF MODERNA

The development of mRNA therapeutic platforms has been the primary focus of American biotechnology business Moderna. In 2018, it carried out a profitable initial public offering of stock. The US government and Moderna agreed to a development and purchase deal shortly after the pandemic outbreak, with an initial purchase price of USD 498 million, which would increase to almost USD 10 billion by July 2022. This agreement eventually led to the creation of the Spikevax vaccine. During the first 200 million doses, the price per treatment was roughly USD16.80. Moderna was obligated by the terms of the arrangement with the US government to manufacture its vaccines domestically [47].

Moderna was obligated by the terms of the arrangement with the US government to manufacture its vaccines domestically. Based on US government assistance, the US government was granted "march-in" rights to patents, and ordinary federal government procurement procedures would grant it a nonexclusive license to employ the innovation for its objectives.

If Moderna failed to produce vaccinations on reasonable conditions, this granted the government the authority to provide technology to other parties. (Public interest groups have often asked the US government to use its legal authority to "march-in" over pharmaceuticals, including vaccines, but it has never done so.

The University of Pennsylvania will earn royalties for the in-licensed mRNA technology from Moderna by the end of 2021, valued at approximately USD 650 million, or around 3.5 percent.

Additionally, Moderna has agreed to pay the US National Institutes of Health, Dartmouth College, and Scripps Research USD 400 million (sometimes referred to as a "delayed licensing" price) in exchange for the right to use their patented technique for stabilizing spike proteins produced by mRNA. Moderna and the Swiss company Lonza, which has operations in both Switzerland and the US, have partnered on a significant contract manufacturing project [48, 49].

Moderna and Lonza, a Swiss company with US and Swiss production facilities, partnered on a large-scale contract manufacturing project. Moderna granted Lonza a license to use its intellectual property (IP) to produce the mRNA vaccine; all other parties kept ownership of their IP. In March 2022, Moderna updated its "access policy," which declared that it will solely defend its patents in 92 Gavi-COVAX Advanced Market Commitment countries against other parties in infringement lawsuits [50].

CASE STUDY ASTRAZENECA-OXFORD

Researchers at Oxford University created a vaccine candidate based on a modified simian adenovirus shortly after the COVID-19 pandemic. An Oxford organization that served as a vehicle for the commercialization of university-developed patents had previously patented the vaccine technique. The vaccine's creators started small-scale test manufacturing to make it available for nonexclusive licensing for accessible and reasonably priced vaccinations. Oxford was convinced that a respectable international pharmaceutical company should handle vaccine marketing. Oxford had received funding for its study from several organizations, including the Gates Foundation and the Wellcome Trust.

Oxford gave AstraZeneca an out-licensing agreement for its patents, and AstraZeneca took over future development and licensing of the vaccine (keeping Oxford to handle some clinical trial work). AstraZeneca and CEPI signed a financial agreement that obliged AstraZeneca to provide the vaccine, AZD1222 (Vaxzevria), to LMICs at reasonable and accessible costs. To manufacture the vaccine, AstraZeneca hired a European CMO, however, they encountered problems when the vaccine's early batches included the incorrect dosage, which also caused issues with how clinical studies were carried out. The vaccine's release was postponed as a result [51].

To maintain its position in the high-income market, and to manufacture and distribute the vaccine in India and other LMICs, AstraZeneca and the SII reached a licensing agreement.

Production was successfully started by the SII, which sold the vaccine for USD 3 per dosage (under the brand name Covishield). It served as the main provider for both the sizable Indian populace and the Indian government. In June 2020, CEPI agreed to pay the contract price of USD 750 million to buy 300 million doses from SII and deliver them to the COVAX plant. The vaccines were supplied by the SII to COVAX and LMICs; however, due to an export prohibition imposed by the Indian government during a peak COVID-19 outbreak, delivery was significantly delayed. The SII announced in November 2021 that it had generated over1.25 billion doses of Covishield [6].

CASE STUDY OF JOHNSON & JOHNSON/JANSSEN

Collaborating with Beth Israel Medical Centre (which seems to own several of the patents that were relied upon for the vaccine), Johnson & Johnson produced a vaccine (Jcovden) based on a modified adenovirus. Johnson & Johnson obtained a development deal for USD 456 million. A contract with the US government was signed to purchase the vaccine, plus an extra USD 1 billion for initial delivery. Intellectual property owned by Johnson & Johnson was maintained. It also had the right of patent protection for technologies developed during its development contract, but with a limited "march-in" privilege that favored the US government. Johnson & Johnson was required to provide its initial. The US government would receive 100 million doses, but they may also be sold to other parties. Initially, Johnson &Johnson depended on American-based Emergent Biosolutions to manufacture their vaccine. The US government stopped the contract manufacturer's output since it didn't follow GMP guidelines. Along with other alternative production agreements, Johnson & Johnson inked fill and finish agreements with Aspen Pharmacare 31 in South Africa.

The latter made an investment in constructing a new facility, but because there were not enough orders, the production line was shut down. Aspen agreed to create four more vaccines in the facility, with approval from CEPI/Gates and the SII [10, 52].

CASE STUDY OF NOVAVAX

The vaccine Nuvaxovid (Covovax in India), developed by the comparatively small US-based company Novavax, is based on the construction of polypeptides by recombinant DNA technology. In June 2020, the United States government granted USD 1.6 billion to Novavax, enabling the business to conduct phase 3 clinical studies and supply 100 million doses of its vaccine.

The bark of a tree that is mostly found in Chile is the source of the unique antigen (Matrix M) utilized by Novavax. Novavax maintains a substantial patent portfolio pertaining to its vaccine. As per the terms of the deal, Novavax offers the US government a license to use its intellectual property for the vaccine project while maintaining ownership rights over any technology generated under the development agreement.

The vaccine developed by Novavax had significant technological challenges throughout development, and the US FDA only approved it in July of 2022. In the end, the federal government only placed an order for 3.2 million pills, fewer than 80,000 of which were filled by February 2023. The exact amount of government financing committed to Novavax has not been made public by the US government or Novavax [53].

CASE STUDY OF CUREVAC

CureVac was unable to create a COVID-19 vaccine that was approved. Long before the COVID-19 pandemic, CureVac was awarded funding from the Gates Foundation for a project called "mRNA vaccine platform for the rapid response in case of epidemic preparedness."CureVac mentioned in its German government development support was disclosed in regulatory filings, along with the government's "nonexclusive and transferable right, in the event of a compelling public interest, to exploit intellectual property created during the sponsored project."CureVac has an in-licensing agreement with Arcturus and Acuitas for their patented LNP technology, which involves milestone and royalty payments. Additionally, CureVac signed many contracts to enable the expansion of its vaccine production. According to CureVac, the company has a sizable portfolio of patents covering its vaccination technique [54].

CONCLUSION

In conclusion, the rapid development of COVID-19 vaccines has sparked debates on intellectual property rights, with calls for patent waivers to increase global access. The historical case of the polio vaccines by Salk and Sabin highlights the impact of patent decisions on vaccine dissemination and eradication efforts. Additionally, the development of rotavirus vaccines underscores the importance of technology transfer and safety in vaccine approval processes. There are multiple patent applications related to the production of rotavirus and HPV vaccines, with different companies and organizations involved. The development of these vaccines involves various technologies and approaches, and there are ongoing efforts to improve their efficacy and accessibility.

REFERENCES

[1] Ranjan P. The case for waiving intellectual property protection for COVID-19 vaccines. Observer Research Foundation. 2021; 456.

[2] Thambisetty S, McMahon A, McDonagh L, Kang HY, Dutfield G. Addressing vaccine inequity during the COVID-19 pandemic: The trips intellectual property waiver proposal and beyond. Camb Law J 2022; 81(2): 384-416. [http://dx.doi.org/10.1017/S0008197322000241]

[3] Legge DG, Kim S. Equitable access to COVID-19 vaccines: cooperation around research and production capacity is critical. Journal for Peace and Nuclear Disarmament. 2021; 4(sup1): 73-134.

[4] Santos Rutschman A. Property and Intellectual Property in Vaccine Markets. Tex. A&M J. Prop L 2021; 7: 110.

[5] Baachus J. An unnecessary proposal: a WTO waiver of intellectual property rights for COVID-19 vaccines. Cato Institute, Free Trade Bulletin. 2020; (78).

[6] Scheibner J, Nielsen J, Nicol D. An ethico-legal assessment of intellectual property rights and their effect on COVID-19 vaccine distribution: an Australian case study. J Law Biosci 2022; 9(2): lsac020. [http://dx.doi.org/10.1093/jlb/lsac020] [PMID: 35855401]

[7] Mahoney RT, Pablos-Mendez A, Ramachandran S. The introduction of new vaccines into developing countries. Vaccine 2004; 22(5-6): 786-92. [http://dx.doi.org/10.1016/j.vaccine.2003.04.001] [PMID: 14741174]

[8] World Health Organization. Intellectual property rights and vaccines in developing countries: meeting report 19-20 April 2004. World Health Organization; 2004.

[9] Alqhaiwi JM, Rayyan IF, Alhasan TK, Almajali TA. The Effectiveness of Compulsory Licensing in Accessing Vaccines COVID-19 Case Study. Kurdish Studies 2023; 11(2): 365-82.

[10] Boschiero N. COVID-19 vaccines as global common goods: An integrated approach of ethical, economic policy and intellectual property management. Global Jurist 2022; 22(2): 177-230. [http://dx.doi.org/10.1515/gj-2021-0042]

[11] Eccleston-Turner M. Beyond patents: Scientific knowledge, and access to vaccine. Ethics Med Public Health 2017; 3(1): 64-73. [http://dx.doi.org/10.1016/j.jemep.2017.02.011]

[12] Mahoney RT. Product Development Partnerships: Case studies of a new mechanism for health technology innovation. Health Res Policy Syst 2011; 9(1): 33. [http://dx.doi.org/10.1186/1478-4505-9-33] [PMID: 21871103]

[13] Damjanović G. The role of intellectual property rights in the (un) availability of vaccines during the pandemic. Archibald Reiss Days. 2021; 11.

[14] Chimpango B. Vaccine nationalism and equitable access to COVID-19 pharmaceuticals: TRIPS Agreement under trial (again). J Int Trade Law Policy 2021; 20(3): 166-83. [http://dx.doi.org/10.1108/JITLP-03-2021-0012]

[15] Milstien JB, Gaulé P, Kaddar M. Access to vaccine technologies in developing countries: Brazil and India. Vaccine 2007; 25(44): 7610-9. [http://dx.doi.org/10.1016/j.vaccine.2007.09.007] [PMID: 17913312]

[16] Smith DR, Leggat PA. Albert Sabin: the development of an oral poliovirus vaccine. Pioneers Of Medicine Without A Nobel Prize. 2014: 75. [http://dx.doi.org/10.1142/9781783263851_0005]

[17] Smith DR, Leggat PA. Pioneering figures in medicine: Albert Bruce Sabin--inventor of the oral polio vaccine. Kurume Med J 2005; 52(3): 111-6. [http://dx.doi.org/10.2739/kurumemedj.52.111] [PMID: 16422178]

[18] Zimmermann J. War on Disease: Polio Eradication in the United States. historia. scribere. 2023; (15):263-80.

[19] Meldrum ML. The Salk polio vaccine field trial of 1954. The Oxford Textbook of Clinical Research Ethics. 2008: 61.

[20] Vashishtha VM, Kamath S. A Brief History of Vaccines Against Polio. Indian Pediatr 2016; 53 (Suppl. 1): S20-7. [PMID: 27771635]

[21] Hedley-Whyte J, Milamed DR. International contributions toward the conquest of polio. Ulster Med J 2019; 88(1): 47-54. [PMID: 30675080]

[22] Bhan MK, Glass RI, Ella KM, *et al.* Team science and the creation of a novel rotavirus vaccine in India: a new framework for vaccine development. Lancet 2014; 383(9935): 2180-3. [http://dx.doi.org/10.1016/S0140-6736(14)60191-4] [PMID: 24629993]

[23] Glass RI, Parashar UD, Bresee JS, *et al.* Rotavirus vaccines: current prospects and future challenges. Lancet 2006; 368(9532): 323-32. [http://dx.doi.org/10.1016/S0140-6736(06)68815-6] [PMID: 16860702]

[24] Salicrup LA, Fedorková L. Challenges and opportunities for enhancing biotechnology and technology transfer in developing countries. Biotechnol Adv 2006; 24(1): 69-79. [http://dx.doi.org/10.1016/j.biotechadv.2005.06.004] [PMID: 16098701]

[25] Dennehy PH. Rotavirus vaccines: an overview. Clin Microbiol Rev 2008; 21(1): 198-208. [http://dx.doi.org/10.1128/CMR.00029-07] [PMID: 18202442]

[26] Kovac I, Maslac V, Horvatinovic T. Challenges of technology transfer in the vaccine development process. Economic and Social Development: Book of Proceedings. 2022: 424-34.

[27] Hamidi A, Hoeksema F, Velthof P, *et al.* Developing a manufacturing process to deliver a cost effective and stable liquid human rotavirus vaccine. Vaccine 2021; 39(15): 2048-59. [http://dx.doi.org/10.1016/j.vaccine.2021.03.033] [PMID: 33744044]

[28] Friede M, Palkonyay L, Alfonso C, *et al.* WHO initiative to increase global and equitable access to influenza vaccine in the event of a pandemic: Supporting developing country production capacity through technology transfer. Vaccine 2011; 29 (Suppl. 1): A2-7. [http://dx.doi.org/10.1016/j.vaccine.2011.02.079] [PMID: 21684422]

[29] Salicrup LA, Harris RF, Rohrbaugh ML. Partnerships in technology transfer: An innovative program to move biomedical and health technologies from the laboratory to worldwide application. IP Strategy Today 2005; 12: 1-2.

[30] Javanbakht M, Moradi-Lakeh M, Yaghoubi M, *et al.* Cost-effectiveness analysis of the introduction of rotavirus vaccine in Iran. Vaccine 2015; 33 (Suppl. 1): A192-200. [http://dx.doi.org/10.1016/j.vaccine.2014.12.035] [PMID: 25919160]

[31] Song JM. Parenteral, non-live rotavirus vaccine: recent history and future perspective. Clin Exp Vaccine Res 2021; 10(3): 203-10. [http://dx.doi.org/10.7774/cevr.2021.10.3.203] [PMID: 34703802]

[32] Stéphenne J. Vaccines as a global imperative--a business perspective. Health Aff (Millwood) 2011; 30(6): 1042-8. [http://dx.doi.org/10.1377/hlthaff.2011.0338] [PMID: 21653955]

[33] Bisbas G. mRNA Technology Transfer Programme. Lancet Microbe 2023; 4(8): e578. [http://dx.doi.org/10.1016/S2666-5247(23)00183-0] [PMID: 37419132]

[34] Chen J, Grow S, Iturriza-Gómara M, Hausdorff WP, Fix A, Kirkwood CD. The Challenges and Opportunities of Next-Generation Rotavirus Vaccines: Summary of an Expert Meeting with Vaccine Developers. Viruses 2022; 14(11): 2565. [http://dx.doi.org/10.3390/v14112565] [PMID: 36423174]

[35] Madsen LB, Ustrup M, Fischer TK, Bygbjerg IC, Konradsen F. Reduced price on rotavirus vaccines: enough to facilitate access where most needed? Bull World Health Organ 2012; 90(7): 554-6. [http://dx.doi.org/10.2471/BLT.11.094656] [PMID: 22807602]

[36] Taneja D, Malik A. Burden of rotavirus in India - Is rotavirus vaccine an answer to it? Indian J Public Health 2012; 56(1): 17-21. [http://dx.doi.org/10.4103/0019-557X.96951] [PMID: 22684168]

[37] Connolly MP, Topachevskyi O, Standaert B, Ortega O, Postma M. The impact of rotavirus vaccination on discounted net tax revenue in Egypt: a government perspective analysis. PharmacoEconomics 2012; 30(8): 681-95. [http://dx.doi.org/10.2165/11597750-000000000-00000] [PMID: 22788259]

[38] Ward RL, Clark HF, Offit PA. Influence of potential protective mechanisms on the development of live rotavirus vaccines. J Infect Dis 2010; 202(S1) (Suppl.): S72-9.

[http://dx.doi.org/10.1086/653549] [PMID: 20684721]

[39] Chandrasekharan S, Amin T, Kim J, *et al.* Intellectual property rights and challenges for development of affordable human papillomavirus, rotavirus and pneumococcal vaccines: Patent landscaping and perspectives of developing country vaccine manufacturers. Vaccine 2015; 33(46): 6366-70. [http://dx.doi.org/10.1016/j.vaccine.2015.08.063] [PMID: 26368398]

[40] Stevens H, Debackere K, Goldman M, Mahoney RT, Stevens P, Huys I. Vaccines: accelerating innovation and access. Global Challenges Report, World Intellectual Property Organization (WIPO). 2017 Nov 7.

[41] World Health Organization. Intellectual property rights and vaccines in developing countries: meeting report 19-20 April 2004. World Health Organization; 2004.

[42] Kovac I, Maslac V, Horvatinovic T. Challenges of technology transfer in the vaccine development process. Economic and Social Development: Book of Proceedings. 2022 Apr 1:424-34.

[43] Thambisetty S, McMahon A, McDonagh L, Kang HY, Dutfield G. The trips intellectual property Waiver proposal: creating the right incentives in patent law and politics to end the COVID-19 pandemic. [http://dx.doi.org/10.2139/ssrn.3851737]

[44] Krattiger, Anatole, et al. "Intellectual property management strategies to accelerate the development and access of vaccines and diagnostics: case studies on pandemic influenza, malaria and SARS." (2006).

[45] Krattiger A, Kowalski SP, Eiss R, Taubman A. Intellectual property management strategies to accelerate the development and access of vaccines and diagnostics: case studies on pandemic influenza, malaria and SARS.

[46] Willcox M, Diallo D, Sanogo R, Giani S, Graz B, Falquet J, Bodeker G. Intellectual property rights, benefit-sharing and development of "improved traditional medicines": A new approach. Journal of ethnopharmacology. 2015 Dec 24;176:281-5.7

[47] Luiza VL, Chaves GC, Barboza TMT, Gonçalves LPB, Stobbaerts EG. Challenges in a product development partnership: a malaria treatment case study. Cien Saude Colet 2017; 22(7): 2197-211. [http://dx.doi.org/10.1590/1413-81232017227.04042017] [PMID: 28724002]

[48] Allarakhia M, Strandburg KJ. A Cultural Commons Study of New Approaches to Drug Development: Case Studies from the Fight Against Malaria.

[49] Gupta R, Gabrielsen B, Ferguson S. Nature's medicines: traditional knowledge and intellectual property management. Case studies from the National Institutes of Health (NIH), USA. Curr Drug Discov Technol 2005; 2(4): 203-19. [http://dx.doi.org/10.2174/157016305775202937] [PMID: 16475917]

[50] Taylor S, Berridge V. Medicinal plants and malaria: an historical case study of research at the London School of Hygiene and Tropical Medicine in the twentieth century. Trans R Soc Trop Med Hyg 2006; 100(8): 707-14. [http://dx.doi.org/10.1016/j.trstmh.2005.11.017] [PMID: 16546230]

[51] Azam M. Intellectual property and public health in the developing world. Open Book Publishers 2016. [http://dx.doi.org/10.11647/OBP.0093]

[52] Tisi A. Patent rights or patient rights? An assessment of intellectual property and right to health within the COVID-19 pandemic (Doctoral dissertation).

[53] Thambisetty S, McMahon A, McDonagh L, Kang HY, Dutfield G. The trips intellectual property Waiver proposal: creating the right incentives in patent law and politics to end the COVID-19 pandemic. [http://dx.doi.org/10.2139/ssrn.3851737]

[54] Durell K. Vaccines and IP rights: a multifaceted relationship. Vaccine Design: Methods and Protocols,

Volume 2: Vaccines for Veterinary Diseases. 2016:791-811.
[http://dx.doi.org/10.1007/978-1-4939-3389-1_52]

[55] Saleh A, Qamar S, Tekin A, Singh R, Kashyap R. Vaccine development throughout history. Cureus 2021; 13(7): e16635.
[PMID: 34462676]

[56] Pollard AJ, Bijker EM. A guide to vaccinology: from basic principles to new developments. Nat Rev Immunol 2021; 21(2): 83-100.
[http://dx.doi.org/10.1038/s41577-020-00479-7] [PMID: 33353987]

CHAPTER 10

Recommendations for Policymakers, Pharmaceutical Companies, and the Global Community

Dakshesh Goel[1], **Sonika Shrivastav**[1] and **Kamal Singh Rathore**[2,*]

[1] *SGT College of Pharmacy, SGT University, Gurugram, Haryana, India*

[2] *B.N. College of Pharmacy, B.N. University, Udaipur, Rajasthan, India*

Abstract: The pharmaceutical industry plays a crucial role in global healthcare, with policymakers, pharmaceutical companies, and communities working together to ensure access to safe and effective medicines. This document provides insights and recommendations for policymakers, pharma companies, and global communities to navigate the evolving landscape of pharmaceutical regulations, quality control, and access to essential medicines.

Key themes include the impact of regulatory policies on drug marketing, the importance of regulatory quality control in the pharmaceutical industry, and the evaluation of collaborative medicines registration initiatives. The document also highlights new approaches to regulatory innovation emerging during the COVID-19 pandemic and emphasizes the need for cleaner production quality regulation strategies.

Furthermore, the document addresses challenges faced by pharmaceutical industries, such as intellectual property rights protection, meeting global requirements during crises like the COVID-19 pandemic, and transforming pharmaceutical curricula to align with industry needs. It also discusses the professional competency and challenges faced by clinical pharmacists in India, quality management techniques for pharmacy institutions, and bridging the gap between academia and practice.

Overall, the recommendations presented in this document aim to enhance the efficiency, effectiveness, and equity of pharmaceutical systems worldwide, ultimately improving access to essential medicines and promoting better health outcomes for all.

Keywords: COVID-19, Pharmaceutical curriculum, Pharmaceutical industries, Regulatory policy, Regulatory framework.

* **Corresponding author Kamal Singh Rathore:** B.N. College of Pharmacy, B.N. University, Udaipur, Rajasthan, India; E-mail: profkamal@bnuniversity.ac.in

Sachin Kumar Jain, Ravikant Gupta, Sudha Vengurlekar, Nidhi Bais & Gajendra P. Choudhary (Eds.)

INTRODUCTION

The pharmaceutical sector occupies a central and indispensable role in the vast landscape of global healthcare. As a cornerstone of medical progress, it serves as the driving force behind the development of life-changing treatments and therapeutic breakthroughs, contributing significantly to the well-being of individuals worldwide. The intricate interplay of innovation, regulatory frameworks, and societal well-being within the pharmaceutical domain necessitates a nuanced and collaborative approach. Achieving excellence in the sector demands concerted efforts from a spectrum of stakeholders, including policymakers, pharmaceutical companies, educational institutions, and the global community [1]. This essay embarks on a journey to explore the multifaceted challenges faced by the pharmaceutical sector and outlines a comprehensive, collaborative strategy to address them, offering tailored recommendations for each stakeholder group.

The dynamic nature of the pharmaceutical landscape underscores the need for a visionary approach from policymakers. Positioned at the intersection of scientific advancement, patient safety, and economic growth, policymakers play a pivotal role in shaping the regulatory environment that governs the industry. A critical aspect of this is the imperative for comprehensive regulatory reforms that strike a delicate balance between fostering innovation and ensuring the safety and efficacy of pharmaceutical products [2]. Streamlining approval processes and staying abreast of technological advancements become essential components of a regulatory framework that is not just robust but agile, capable of adapting to the rapidly evolving landscape of pharmaceutical innovation [3].

In tandem with regulatory reforms, policymakers must recognize the foundational importance of education in propelling the pharmaceutical sector forward. Allocating resources for the development of state-of-the-art pharmaceutical education infrastructure becomes imperative. This includes the constant evolution of laboratories, the establishment of cutting-edge research facilities, and the implementation of faculty training programs to ensure that educators remain at the forefront of industry trends. By doing so, policymakers contribute to the cultivation of a skilled workforce that is not only knowledgeable but also adaptive to the dynamic demands of the pharmaceutical industry [4].

Moreover, policymakers can play a crucial role in fostering collaborations between pharmaceutical companies and educational institutions. Such partnerships create symbiotic relationships, enriching academic curricula with real-world insights and ensuring that educational programs align seamlessly with industry needs. By facilitating these industry-academia collaborations, policymakers contribute to the holistic development of pharmaceutical professionals, nurturing a workforce that is not only academically sound but also practically adept [4].

Skill development initiatives stand as another pillar of policymaker interventions. In a rapidly evolving industry, ensuring the employability of pharmacy graduates requires proactive measures. Policymakers can champion targeted programs that promote industry-relevant skills such as data analytics, regulatory affairs, and quality control. By doing so, they align the skill sets of graduates with the evolving needs of the pharmaceutical sector, creating a workforce that is not only job-ready but also capable of driving innovation within the industry.

As the torchbearers of innovation and economic growth within the pharmaceutical sector, pharmaceutical companies form the bedrock of progress. Their role extends beyond the development of life-saving drugs; they are instrumental in shaping the industry's trajectory through strategic initiatives that balance short-term gains with long-term sustainability.

Internship and training programs emerge as a linchpin for bridging the gap between academic learning and practical application. Pharmaceutical companies should take the lead in establishing robust internship and training programs, providing students with hands-on experience and facilitating a seamless transition from academia to the pharmaceutical industry. These initiatives not only contribute to the professional development of individuals but also foster a pipeline of skilled professionals ready to tackle the industry's evolving challenges.

Furthermore, the commitment to research and development becomes non-negotiable for pharmaceutical companies aspiring to lead the industry. Allocating substantial resources to fuel innovation, the development of new drugs, and the exploration of cutting-edge technologies is not merely an investment in the company's future but a commitment to addressing the ever-changing healthcare needs of the global population. Long-term investments in R&D position companies as innovators, ensuring they stay competitive in a landscape defined by scientific advancements and breakthrough discoveries.

Employee training and development represent another dimension of corporate responsibility. With the rapid pace of pharmaceutical advancements, companies must invest in continuous training programs for their existing workforce. This commitment to ongoing education ensures that employees remain well-versed in the latest technologies, methodologies, and industry trends, contributing to the overall adaptability and resilience of the pharmaceutical workforce [4, 5].

Corporate Social Responsibility (CSR) takes on a more profound meaning when intertwined with education and skill development. By integrating these elements into CSR initiatives, pharmaceutical companies extend their impact beyond the realm of drug development. Contributing to community development and nurturing local talent not only aligns with ethical business practices but also addresses the broader societal needs tied to healthcare and education.

As the pharmaceutical sector transcends geographical boundaries, the global community assumes a pivotal role in shaping its trajectory. Collaborative efforts on an international scale become imperative to address shared challenges, foster innovation, and ensure equitable access to healthcare solutions. The global community serves as the catalyst for positive change, leveraging its collective wisdom and resources to elevate the pharmaceutical sector to new heights.

Encouraging collaborative research initiatives emerges as a cornerstone of the global community's role. By fostering international collaborations in research and development, the global community facilitates the exchange of knowledge and expertise, driving innovation and addressing global health challenges [6]. This collaborative approach recognizes that solutions to complex health issues often require a collective effort that spans continents and transcends individual capabilities [6, 7].

Knowledge-sharing platforms become instrumental in breaking down silos within the pharmaceutical industry. Establishing global platforms for sharing best practices, research findings, and innovations creates a network that accelerates progress in drug development and healthcare solutions. This interconnectedness enables stakeholders to learn from each other's successes and challenges, fostering an environment of continuous improvement and collaboration [8].

Support for developing nations emerges as a moral and strategic imperative for the global community. Providing financial and technical support to these nations is critical for improving their pharmaceutical education systems and industry standards. This assistance contributes to building a more robust global pharmaceutical ecosystem, ensuring that progress is not confined to certain regions but is inclusive and sustainable on a global scale [9].

Mentorship programs, when encouraged on a global scale, become a powerful tool for connecting experienced professionals with young talents. This mentorship approach facilitates knowledge transfer, career guidance, and the development of a well-rounded pharmaceutical workforce worldwide. By creating avenues for mentorship, the global community contributes to the nurturing of talent and the establishment of a collaborative culture within the pharmaceutical sector [10].

While policymakers, pharmaceutical companies, and the global community set the stage for industry advancement, educational institutions serve as the breeding ground for the future workforce. Their adaptability and responsiveness to industry demands are pivotal in ensuring that graduates emerge from their programs well-equipped with the skills and knowledge needed to drive innovation in the pharmaceutical sector. Educational institutions must act as dynamic entities, continuously updating their pharmacy curriculum to align with industry needs and technological advancements [11]. This commitment ensures that graduates are not only academically proficient but also possess the skills demanded by the pharmaceutical industry. By keeping their programs relevant, educational institutions contribute to the creation of a workforce that can seamlessly integrate into the ever-evolving landscape of pharmaceutical advancements.

Bridging the gap between theory and practice is essential for preparing students for the workforce. Educational institutions should take an active role in facilitating industry visits, hosting guest lectures, and promoting internships to provide students with real-world exposure. These experiences are instrumental in shaping well-rounded professionals, ready to contribute meaningfully to the pharmaceutical sector from day one [11, 12].

Moreover, encouraging collaborations between academia and industry in research projects becomes vital. Such partnerships not only contribute to the development of practical solutions but also foster a symbiotic relationship between educational institutions and the pharmaceutical sector. By engaging in collaborative research, institutions not only enhance the quality of education but also contribute to the industry's innovation ecosystem.

POLICYMAKERS

Key focus areas for policymakers are mentioned in Fig. (**1**).

Fig. (1). Key focus areas for policymakers in advancing pharmaceutical education and innovation.

Regulatory Reforms

It stands as a cornerstone in shaping the trajectory of the pharmaceutical sector, and policymakers bear a crucial responsibility in sculpting an environment that fosters innovation while upholding stringent safety and efficacy standards. In the ever-evolving landscape of healthcare, a comprehensive approach to regulatory reforms is imperative to ensure the industry's sustained growth and its ability to meet the evolving needs of global health. This section explores the key components of regulatory reforms and outlines a strategic framework that policymakers should undertake for the advancement of the pharmaceutical sector [13].

Dynamic and Adaptive Regulatory Framework

At the forefront of regulatory reforms lies the need for a dynamic and adaptive framework. Policymakers should prioritize the continuous evaluation and enhancement of existing regulations to keep pace with the rapidly evolving nature of the pharmaceutical industry (Table **1**). An agile framework allows for the incorporation of innovative technologies, cutting-edge research methodologies, and emerging therapeutic approaches without compromising safety and efficacy standards [14].

Table 1. Regulatory support frameworks.

Regulatory Aspect	Best Practices	Implementation Challenges
Streamlined Processes	Clear guidelines for joint projects.	Data-sharing compliance issues.
Data-Sharing Compliance	Ensuring data security and privacy.	Regulatory complexity.
Collaborative Guidelines	Framework for industry-academia partnerships.	Regulatory oversight challenges.

Streamlining Approval Processes

A critical aspect of regulatory reforms is the streamlining of approval processes. Cumbersome and lengthy approval timelines can hinder the timely introduction of life-saving drugs to the market [14]. Policymakers must champion efforts to simplify and expedite regulatory pathways, leveraging modern technologies, data analytics, and real-time monitoring mechanisms to enhance the efficiency of the approval process without compromising safety [15].

International Collaboration and Harmonization

Recognizing the global nature of the pharmaceutical industry, policymakers should actively pursue international collaboration and harmonization of regulatory standards. Aligning regulatory requirements across borders minimizes redundancies, accelerates the approval process, and facilitates the global distribution of pharmaceutical products [16]. Bilateral and multilateral agreements for mutual recognition of regulatory decisions strengthen international cooperation.

Proactive Response to Technological Advancements

The advent of transformative technologies, such as gene therapies and personalized medicine, necessitates a proactive response from regulatory bodies. Policymakers should lead efforts to assess and adapt regulatory frameworks to accommodate these innovations. Staying ahead of technological advancements ensures that regulatory guidelines remain relevant, fostering an environment that encourages innovation and the development of groundbreaking therapies.

Transparency and Communication

Transparency is a cornerstone of effective regulatory reforms. Policymakers should prioritize clear and transparent communication regarding regulatory decisions, guidelines, and updates. Transparent processes build trust among stakeholders, including pharmaceutical companies, healthcare professionals, and the public. Clear communication also aids in compliance, fostering a collaborative atmosphere within the industry [17, 18].

Post-Marketing Surveillance and Feedback Mechanisms

Regulatory reforms extend beyond the initial approval phase to encompass robust post-marketing surveillance. Policymakers should establish effective monitoring systems to track the real-world safety and efficacy of pharmaceutical products. Implementing feedback mechanisms allows for continuous evaluation, enabling regulatory bodies to make data-driven decisions and respond promptly to emerging concerns or unforeseen adverse effects [19].

Incentives for Innovation

Regulatory reforms should be complemented by incentives that stimulate pharmaceutical innovation. Policymakers can explore mechanisms such as expedited approval pathways for breakthrough therapies, extended patent protections, and targeted research grants [20]. These incentives not only encourage research and development but also attract investment, positioning the pharmaceutical sector as a hub for groundbreaking discoveries [20].

Collaboration with Stakeholders

Informed regulatory decision-making requires active collaboration with a diverse set of stakeholders. Policymakers should engage with pharmaceutical companies, healthcare professionals, patient advocacy groups, and academic institutions [21]. Establishing regular consultations and collaborative mechanisms ensures that regulatory reforms are shaped by a collective understanding of industry needs and perspectives.

Investment in Education

Investment in education serves as a fundamental building block for the advancement of the pharmaceutical sector, with policymakers playing a pivotal role in shaping the educational landscape. A well-equipped and knowledgeable workforce is essential for driving innovation maintaining industry standards, and ensuring the sector's sustained growth. This section explores the critical components of educational investment and outlines a strategic framework that policymakers should undertake to elevate the quality of pharmaceutical education.

Infrastructure Development

At the core of educational investment is the development of state-of-the-art infrastructure for pharmaceutical education. Policymakers should allocate resources to ensure that educational institutions have modern laboratories, cutting-edge research facilities, and updated technology. A conducive learning environment not only enhances the educational experience but also facilitates hands-on training, preparing students for the practical challenges of the pharmaceutical industry.

Faculty Training Programs

Recognizing the dynamic nature of the pharmaceutical sector, policymakers should prioritize faculty training programs. These initiatives ensure that educators remain current with industry trends, research methodologies, and technological advancements [22]. Continuous professional development for faculty members enhances the quality of teaching and equips them to deliver relevant and up-t--date content to students [23].

Curriculum Enhancement

Investment in education should include a commitment to the continuous enhancement of the pharmaceutical curriculum. Policymakers should encourage educational institutions to regularly update their curricula to align with industry needs, technological advancements, and emerging trends. A dynamic curriculum ensures that graduates are well-equipped with the knowledge and skills demanded by the ever-evolving pharmaceutical landscape [24, 25].

Research Facilities and Collaboration

Policymakers should foster a culture of research within educational institutions by allocating resources for the establishment of research facilities. Encouraging collaboration between academia and industry in research projects is vital [26]. This collaboration not only enhances the practical relevance of research but also contributes to the development of innovative solutions, creating a symbiotic relationship between educational institutions and the pharmaceutical sector [26, 27].

Industry-Academia Collaboration

To bridge the gap between academic learning and industry requirements, policy makers should actively facilitate collaborations between pharmaceutical companies and educational institutions. These partnerships provide students with real-world exposure, internships, and opportunities to work on industry-relevant projects (Table **2**). Industry-academia collaboration ensures that academic programs align with the practical needs and expectations of the pharmaceutical sector [28].

Table 2. Comparison of industry-academia collaboration initiatives.

Initiative	Description	Benefits
Internship Programs	Incorporating practical training into the curriculum.	Real-world experience for students.
Research Collaborations	Joint projects between academia and industry.	Fosters innovation and knowledge exchange.
Skill Development Programs	Programs focusing on industry-specific skills.	Enhances employability of graduates.

Promotion of Specialized Programs

Recognizing the diverse nature of roles within the pharmaceutical sector, policymakers should promote the development of specialized programs. These programs could focus on areas such as regulatory affairs, data analytics, quality control, and other industry-specific skills. Tailoring education to meet specific industry demands enhances the employability of graduates and contributes to the overall skill development of the workforce [28].

Student Scholarships and Support Programs

To encourage enrollment in pharmaceutical education programs, policymakers should consider the implementation of student scholarships and support programs. Financial assistance reduces barriers to entry for aspiring pharmaceutical professionals and fosters a diverse and inclusive student body. Scholarships can be targeted towards those pursuing specialized fields, contributing to the development of a well-rounded workforce.

Continued Professional Development for Practitioners

Investment in education should extend beyond formal academic settings to include continued professional development for practitioners in the pharmaceutical sector. Policymakers can support ongoing education and training programs for professionals already in the workforce. This ensures that practitioners remain abreast of industry advancements, regulatory changes, and best practices, contributing to the overall adaptability and competence of the pharmaceutical workforce [29, 30].

Industry-Academia Collaboration

Industrial collaborations serve as a linchpin for the advancement of the pharmaceutical sector, providing a bridge between academic knowledge and real-world application. Policymakers play a crucial role in fostering an environment that encourages and facilitates meaningful partnerships between pharmaceutical companies and other stakeholders. This section explores the essential components of promoting industrial collaborations and outlines a strategic framework that policymakers should undertake to enhance synergies between academia and industry.

Facilitation of Partnerships

Policymakers should actively facilitate partnerships between pharmaceutical companies and educational institutions. This involves creating platforms for dialogue, networking events, and matchmaking initiatives that connect academia with industry. By acting as catalysts for collaboration, policymakers can foster an environment where industry players and academic institutions see the mutual benefits of working together [31].

Incentives for Collaboration

Policymakers can introduce incentives to encourage pharmaceutical companies to collaborate with educational institutions [31]. These incentives may include tax benefits, research grants, or other financial support for joint projects. By recognizing and rewarding collaborative efforts, policymakers send a clear signal about the value they place on partnerships between academia and industry [32, 33].

Joint Research Initiatives

Policymakers should actively promote joint research initiatives that bring together researchers from both academia and industry. Funding programs dedicated to collaborative research projects can stimulate innovation, address industry-specific challenges, and contribute to the development of practical solutions with real-world applications [33].

Internship and Training Programs

Establishing and supporting internship and training programs is crucial for nurturing collaboration between pharmaceutical companies and educational institutions. Policymakers can encourage companies to open their doors to students, providing them with hands-on experience and exposure to real-world challenges. This not only benefits students but also fosters a culture of knowledge exchange between academia and industry [33].

Coordinated Regulatory Support

Policymakers should work towards creating a regulatory framework that supports and encourages collaborative initiatives. Streamlining regulatory processes for joint projects, ensuring data-sharing compliance, and providing clear guidelines for collaborative ventures can remove obstacles that may hinder industrial-academic partnerships [31].

Industry Input in Curriculum Development

Policymakers can encourage closer ties between industry and educational institutions by involving industry professionals in curriculum development [34]. This ensures that academic programs align with industry needs, producing graduates with skills and knowledge directly applicable to the pharmaceutical sector. Industry input helps tailor educational offerings to the practical requirements of the workforce [35].

Technology Transfer Programs

Policymakers can play a pivotal role in establishing technology transfer programs that facilitate the seamless exchange of knowledge, innovations, and technologies between academia and industry. These programs promote the commercialization of academic research, fostering a culture where breakthroughs in research can translate into tangible products and processes within the pharmaceutical sector (Table **3**).

Table 3. Impacts of technology transfer programs.

Program Outcome	Description	Key Metrics
Knowledge Exchange	Facilitating seamless transfer of innovations.	Number of successful collaborations.
Commercialization Success	Converting research breakthroughs into products.	Revenue generated from academic research.

Encouraging Small and Medium Enterprises (SMEs)

Policymakers should pay attention to the involvement of small and medium enterprises in collaborative efforts. Offering targeted support, such as grants or incentives, can encourage SMEs to engage in partnerships with educational institutions. The inclusion of SMEs enhances diversity within collaborative projects and brings agility to the innovation ecosystem [36].

Skill Development Programs

Skill development programs are instrumental in enhancing the employability of graduates in the pharmaceutical sector, ensuring they possess the industry-specific skills demanded by evolving challenges. Policymakers play a pivotal role in shaping and promoting initiatives that focus on skill development. This section explores key components of skill development programs and outlines a strategic framework that policymakers should undertake to nurture a skilled and adaptable pharmaceutical workforce (Table **4**).

Table 4. Diversity and inclusivity in skill development programs.

Program Aspect	Description	Strategies for Inclusivity
Financial Support	Scholarships and grants for underrepresented groups.	Ensures accessibility for all individuals.
Geographical Accessibility	Programs available in diverse locations.	Remote learning options for inclusivity.
Mentorship Opportunities	Guidance and support for diverse participants.	Tailored support for different needs.

Identification of Industry-Relevant Skills

Policymakers should collaborate with industry experts to identify and understand the specific skills in demand within the pharmaceutical sector. This involves conducting regular skill gap analyses to ascertain the evolving needs of the industry. By staying attuned to industry requirements, policymakers can tailor skill development programs to address the most pressing needs of the pharmaceutical workforce [38, 39].

Targeted Training Initiatives

Developing targeted training initiatives is a critical aspect of skill development. Policymakers should champion programs that focus on key skills such as data analytics, regulatory affairs, quality control, and other industry-specific competencies. These initiatives can take the form of workshops, short courses, and certification programs designed to equip individuals with the precise skills sought by pharmaceutical employers [38, 39].

Collaboration with Industry for Program Design

Policymakers should actively involve pharmaceutical industry professionals in the design and development of skill development programs. By collaborating with industry stakeholders, policymakers can ensure that training initiatives are aligned with current industry practices and requirements. This collaborative approach enhances the relevance and effectiveness of skill development programs [38].

Flexible and Adaptive Curriculum

Skill development programs should feature a flexible and adaptive curriculum that can swiftly respond to changes in the pharmaceutical landscape. Policymakers should encourage educational institutions to design programs that incorporate the latest industry trends, emerging technologies, and regulatory updates. This ensures that graduates possess skills that are not only current but also future-proofed against industry advancements [39].

Promotion of Continuous Learning

Policymakers should instill a culture of continuous learning within the pharmaceutical workforce. This involves promoting ongoing education and professional development opportunities [39, 40]. Encouraging employees to engage in lifelong learning ensures that the workforce remains agile, adaptable, and capable of navigating the dynamic challenges presented by advancements in pharmaceutical research and development [40].

Monitoring and Evaluation Mechanisms

Establishing robust monitoring and evaluation mechanisms is crucial to ensuring the effectiveness of skill development programs. Policymakers should implement feedback loops, performance assessments, and outcome evaluations to gauge the impact of these initiatives. This data-driven approach cnablcs continuous improvement and refinement of skill development programs based on real-world outcomes.

Accessibility and Inclusivity

Policymakers should prioritize the accessibility and inclusivity of skill development programs. This involves making these initiatives available to a diverse range of individuals, including those from underrepresented groups. Providing financial support, and scholarships, and ensuring geographical accessibility enhance the inclusivity of skill development programs, contributing to a more diverse and talented pharmaceutical workforce [41].

PHARMACEUTICAL COMPANIES

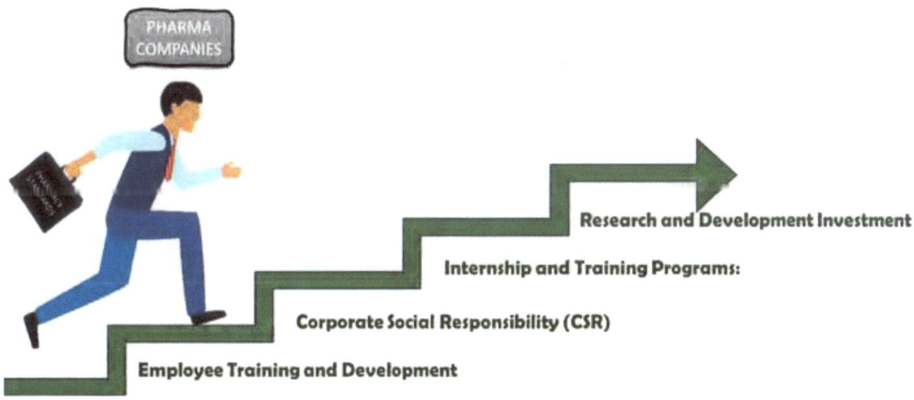

Fig. (2). Pharmaceutical companies: role in workforce skill development and innovation.

Internship and Training Programs

Internships and training programs are integral components of a pharmaceutical company's commitment to developing a skilled and knowledgeable workforce mentioned in Fig. (**2**). These initiatives not only bridge the gap between academic learning and practical application but also contribute to the professional growth of individuals entering the pharmaceutical industry. This section explores key elements of effective internship and training programs and outlines a strategic framework that pharmaceutical companies should adopt to nurture talent and promote seamless transitions from academia to industry (Table **5**).

Table 5. Key elements of effective internship programs in the pharmaceutical industry.

Program Component	Description	Benefits
Cross-Functional Exposure	Rotations across departments for a holistic view.	Diverse skill development and insights.
Mentorship Opportunities	Pairing with experienced professionals.	Guidance, career advice, and integration.
Training on Industry Practices	Sessions on best practices and regulations.	Foundation for success in the sector.

Structured Internship Programs

Pharmaceutical companies should establish structured internship programs designed to provide students with hands-on experience in a real-world pharmaceutical setting. These programs should be well-defined, incorporating clear objectives, project-based assignments, and mentorship opportunities. By structuring internships, companies ensure that students gain a comprehensive understanding of the industry while contributing meaningfully to ongoing projects.

Cross-Functional Exposure

Internship programs should offer cross-functional exposure to participants. Pharmaceutical companies should design rotations or projects that allow interns to work across various departments, such as research and development, regulatory affairs, marketing, and quality control. This approach provides a holistic view of the pharmaceutical landscape and helps interns discover their areas of interest and expertise [33].

Mentorship Opportunities

Establishing mentorship opportunities within internship programs is essential for the professional development of interns. Pharmaceutical companies should pair interns with experienced professionals who can provide guidance, share insights, and offer career advice. Mentorship fosters a supportive learning environment, accelerates the integration of interns into the company culture, and contributes to long-term professional growth [42].

Training on Industry Practices

Internship programs should include dedicated training sessions on industry best practices, regulatory requirements, and ethical standards. This ensures that interns not only gain practical experience but also develop a solid foundation of knowledge essential for success in the pharmaceutical sector. Training programs should cover topics relevant to the specific roles and responsibilities within the company [42].

Real-World Project Assignments

Interns should be assigned real-world projects that align with the company's objectives and challenges. Pharmaceutical companies can benefit from fresh perspectives and innovative ideas brought by interns. By integrating interns into ongoing projects, companies provide them with a sense of ownership and contribution, fostering a collaborative mindset and preparing them for the complexities of the pharmaceutical industry.

Networking Opportunities

Pharmaceutical companies should actively facilitate networking opportunities for interns. This includes interactions with professionals across different departments, participation in company events, and exposure to industry conferences. Networking allows interns to build connections, learn from experienced professionals, and gain insights into potential career paths within the pharmaceutical sector [43].

Performance Evaluation and Feedback

Implementing a robust performance evaluation system is crucial for internship programs. Pharmaceutical companies should provide regular feedback to interns, acknowledging their strengths and identifying areas for improvement. A transparent evaluation process contributes to interns' professional development, helps them understand their contributions, and assists companies in identifying high-potential individuals for future employment opportunities [44].

Research and Development Investment

Research and development (R&D) investment is a cornerstone of success for pharmaceutical companies, driving innovation, advancing medical knowledge, and shaping the future of healthcare. This section explores key elements of effective R&D investment and outlines a strategic framework that pharmaceutical companies should adopt to maintain competitiveness, address unmet medical needs, and contribute to the evolution of the pharmaceutical sector.

Strategic R&D Planning

Pharmaceutical companies should begin by developing a strategic R&D plan that aligns with the company's long-term goals and market demands. This plan should prioritize therapeutic areas, technology platforms, and innovative approaches that have the potential to make a significant impact. By mapping out a clear R&D strategy, companies can ensure focused and purposeful investment in areas with the greatest potential for success [37].

Allocation of Resources

Effective R&D investment involves allocating resources judiciously across different stages of the drug development pipeline. Pharmaceutical companies should balance investments in early-stage research, preclinical studies, clinical trials, and post-market surveillance. Strategic resource allocation ensures a comprehensive approach to drug development, from initial discovery to market approval and beyond [45, 46].

Emphasis on Translational Research

Translational research, which aims to bridge the gap between laboratory discoveries and practical applications in patient care, should be a focal point of R&D investment. Pharmaceutical companies should prioritize translational research initiatives that facilitate the transition of promising scientific discoveries into viable therapeutic solutions. This approach accelerates the development of new treatments and technologies [37].

Partnerships and Collaborations

Collaborative ventures with academic institutions, research organizations, and biotechnology companies can amplify the impact of R&D investment. Pharmaceutical companies should actively seek partnerships to share knowledge, access diverse expertise, and leverage complementary resources. Collaborations enhance the breadth and depth of R&D efforts, fostering innovation and accelerating the pace of drug discovery and development [32].

Investment in Cutting-Edge Technologies

Staying at the forefront of technological advancements is crucial for pharmaceutical R&D. Companies should invest in cutting-edge technologies such as artificial intelligence, machine learning, genomics, and precision medicine. Embracing these technologies enhances the efficiency of drug discovery, optimizes clinical trial design, and allows for more personalized and targeted therapeutic interventions [47].

Focus on Rare Diseases and Unmet Needs

R&D investment should strategically target rare diseases and unmet medical needs. By addressing these underserved areas, pharmaceutical companies contribute to the development of novel treatments that have a profound impact on patients' lives. Prioritizing rare diseases also offers regulatory advantages and market opportunities.

Employee Training and Development

Employee training and development are essential components for the success and sustainability of pharmaceutical companies. In an industry characterized by rapid advancements, evolving regulations, and complex research methodologies, investing in the continuous learning and professional growth of employees is paramount. This section explores key elements of effective employee training and development and outlines a strategic framework that pharmaceutical companies should adopt to cultivate a skilled and adaptable workforce.

Strategic Training Needs Analysis

Pharmaceutical companies should begin by conducting a comprehensive analysis of training needs across various departments. This strategic assessment identifies skill gaps, emerging industry trends, and specific training requirements for different roles. By understanding the unique needs of their workforce, companies can tailor training programs to address areas that directly contribute to organizational goals.

Customized Training Programs

Developing customized training programs allows pharmaceutical companies to address specific skill requirements and challenges within their workforce. Training initiatives should align with the company's strategic objectives, regulatory compliance needs, and technological advancements. Customization ensures that employees receive targeted and relevant content, maximizing the impact of training on job performance.

Integration of E-Learning Platforms

Leveraging e-learning platforms is crucial for the flexibility and scalability of training initiatives. Pharmaceutical companies should integrate digital learning tools that enable employees to access training materials remotely, at their own pace. E-learning platforms facilitate continuous learning, accommodate diverse learning styles, and provide a cost-effective means of delivering training content [48, 49].

Technical and Regulatory Training

Given the highly regulated nature of the pharmaceutical industry, companies should prioritize technical and regulatory training. This includes keeping employees abreast of the latest regulatory requirements, compliance standards, and industry best practices. Training programs should cover topics such as Good Manufacturing Practices (GMP), Good Clinical Practices (GCP), and other relevant regulations.

Leadership Development Programs

Investing in leadership development is crucial for building a strong organizational culture and ensuring the success of pharmaceutical companies. Leadership training programs should nurture the skills and qualities essential for effective management within the industry, including strategic thinking, communication, decision-making, and team building [50].

Cross-Functional Training Opportunities

Cross-functional training initiatives encourage employees to broaden their skill sets and gain a holistic understanding of the pharmaceutical business. Pharmaceutical companies should provide opportunities for employees to engage in cross-functional training, allowing them to collaborate across departments and contribute to multidisciplinary projects [33].

Continuous Learning Culture

Cultivating a culture of continuous learning is essential for employee development. Pharmaceutical companies should encourage employees to take ownership of their learning journey, providing resources, incentives, and recognition for ongoing professional development. A continuous learning culture fosters innovation, adaptability, and a motivated workforce [51].

Corporate Social Responsibility (CSR)

Corporate Social Responsibility (CSR) is a vital aspect of the pharmaceutical industry, reflecting a commitment to ethical practices, sustainability, and contributing to societal well-being. Pharmaceutical companies, as key stakeholders in global healthcare, have the responsibility to go beyond profit generation and actively engage in initiatives that address societal needs. This section explores key elements of effective CSR in the pharmaceutical sector and outlines a strategic framework that companies should adopt to make a positive impact on communities and the environment.

Access to Medicines and Affordability

One of the primary CSR focuses for pharmaceutical companies is ensuring access to medicines for underserved populations. Companies should adopt pricing strategies and collaboration models that facilitate affordable access to life-saving drugs, especially in low-income and developing regions. Initiatives such as differential pricing and partnerships with NGOs can contribute to making medicines more accessible [52].

Global Health Initiatives

Engaging in global health initiatives demonstrates a commitment to addressing broader healthcare challenges beyond product development. Pharmaceutical companies should actively participate in efforts to combat infectious diseases, support vaccination campaigns, and contribute to global health infrastructure development. Collaborating with international organizations and governments can amplify the impact of these initiatives [53].

Research and Development for Neglected Diseases

CSR efforts in the pharmaceutical sector should include a focus on research and development for neglected diseases that disproportionately affect vulnerable populations. Companies can allocate resources and expertise to discover and develop treatments for diseases that may not attract significant commercial interest. This commitment contributes to closing healthcare gaps and addressing unmet medical needs.

Environmental Sustainability

Adopting environmentally sustainable practices is a crucial aspect of CSR for pharmaceutical companies [53]. This involves implementing eco-friendly manufacturing processes, reducing carbon footprints, and minimizing waste generation. Companies should strive for sustainable supply chain practices, energy-efficient operations, and responsible waste disposal to contribute to a healthier planet [54].

Ethical Clinical Trials and Human Rights

CSR initiatives in the pharmaceutical industry should prioritize ethical conduct in clinical trials and respect for human rights. Companies must adhere to rigorous ethical standards in the design, conduct, and reporting of clinical trials, ensuring the well-being and rights of study participants. Transparent communication about trial outcomes also contributes to building trust with the broader community [55].

Health Education and Awareness Programs

Proactive engagement in health education and awareness programs is a vital CSR component for pharmaceutical companies. By supporting initiatives that promote health literacy, disease prevention, and healthy lifestyles, companies contribute to building healthier communities. Educational campaigns can focus on specific diseases, treatment adherence, and general health and well-being.

Community Engagement and Philanthropy

CSR efforts should extend to active community engagement and philanthropy. Pharmaceutical companies can establish community outreach programs, support local healthcare infrastructure, and contribute to charitable organizations. Strategic philanthropy aligned with community needs demonstrates a commitment to social responsibility and builds positive relationships with stakeholders [56, 57].

Disaster Relief and Humanitarian Aid

Responding to disasters and humanitarian crises is a critical aspect of CSR for pharmaceutical companies. These efforts involve providing emergency medical supplies, supporting healthcare infrastructure in affected areas, and collaborating with relief organizations. Timely and effective responses during crises showcase a company's commitment to global citizenship [58, 59].

Employee Volunteerism and Well-being

Encouraging employee volunteerism and well-being is an integral part of CSR within the pharmaceutical sector. Companies should support employees in participating in volunteer activities that contribute to societal well-being. Additionally, promoting a healthy work-life balance, mental health support, and employee well-being programs enhance the overall impact of CSR efforts.

GLOBAL COMMUNITY

Engaging with the global community is a pivotal aspect of corporate responsibility for pharmaceutical companies. As key players in the healthcare ecosystem, these companies have a unique opportunity and responsibility to contribute to global health, knowledge sharing, and sustainable development. This section explores key elements of effective engagement with the global community and outlines a strategic framework that pharmaceutical companies should adopt to foster collaboration and address global health challenges.

International Research Collaborations

Active participation in international research collaborations is essential for pharmaceutical companies to contribute to global health advancements. Collaborative efforts with researchers, institutions, and organizations worldwide facilitate the exchange of knowledge, expertise, and resourccs. Thcsc partncrships accelerate the pace of scientific discovery, leading to innovations that benefit global health [60].

Open Access to Research Findings

Pharmaceutical companies should prioritize open access to their research findings, publications, and clinical trial data. By making information widely available, companies contribute to the collective knowledge base of the global scientific community. Open access fosters transparency accelerates progress and allows researchers worldwide to build upon existing knowledge [61].

Support for Global Health Infrastructure

Investing in and supporting global health infrastructure is a critical component of corporate responsibility. Pharmaceutical companies can contribute to building healthcare systems, enhancing medical facilities, and improving access to quality healthcare in underserved regions [62, 63]. This support strengthens the resilience of healthcare systems, particularly in the face of global health challenges [63].

Collaborative Research Initiatives

Actively fostering collaborative research initiatives on a global scale is imperative. Pharmaceutical companies should seek opportunities to engage in joint research projects with international partners. These initiatives encourage the exchange of diverse perspectives, expertise, and resources, leading to breakthroughs that address global health issues and advance medical science [64].

Knowledge Sharing Platforms

Establishing and participating in knowledge-sharing platforms is vital for contributing to the global scientific community. Pharmaceutical companies should actively share best practices, research findings, and innovations through conferences, forums, and online platforms. This commitment to knowledge exchange fosters a culture of collaboration and accelerates progress in drug development and healthcare solutions.

Global Access to Medicines

Ensuring global access to medicines is a core responsibility for pharmaceutical companies. Companies should adopt strategies such as tiered pricing, voluntary licensing, and partnerships with international organizations to make essential medicines more accessible, particularly in low- and middle-income countries. This commitment reflects a dedication to addressing healthcare disparities on a global scale [65].

Support for Developing Nations

Providing financial and technical support to developing nations is crucial for improving pharmaceutical education systems and industry standards. Pharmaceutical companies can engage in capacity-building initiatives, offer training programs, and support local healthcare infrastructure projects. This support contributes to building a more robust and sustainable global pharmaceutical ecosystem.

Humanitarian Aid and Emergency Response

Pharmaceutical companies should be prepared to provide humanitarian aid and emergency response during global health crises, natural disasters, or public health emergencies [65]. This involves donating medicines, medical supplies, and financial resources to support affected communities. Quick and effective responses demonstrate a commitment to global citizenship and societal well-being [66].

EDUCATION INSTITUTIONS

Education institutions play a crucial role in shaping the future of the pharmaceutical sector by equipping students with the knowledge, skills, and mindset necessary for success in a rapidly evolving industry. This section explores key elements of effective collaboration between education institutions and the pharmaceutical sector, outlining a strategic framework for fostering industry-aligned education and preparing students for the dynamic challenges of the pharmaceutical field.

Continuous Curriculum Enhancement

Education institutions should prioritize continuous enhancement of the pharmacy curriculum to align with industry needs and technological advancements. Regular reviews and updates ensure that students are exposed to the latest developments in pharmaceutical research, regulations, and technology [67]. Collaboration with industry experts helps identify emerging trends and integrate relevant content into the curriculum [67, 68].

Industry Exposure Through Partnerships

Establishing strong partnerships with pharmaceutical companies is essential for providing students with industry exposure. Education institutions should actively collaborate with industry professionals to organize guest lectures, seminars, and industry visits. These initiatives allow students to gain insights into real-world practices, challenges, and innovations, bridging the gap between theoretical knowledge and practical application [69].

Research Collaboration with Pharmaceutical Companies

Collaboration between academia and the pharmaceutical industry in research projects is vital for fostering innovation. Education institutions should actively seek partnerships with pharmaceutical companies to conduct collaborative research. Joint research initiatives provide students with hands-on experience, expose them to cutting-edge advancements, and contribute to practical solutions that benefit both academia and industry [69].

Internship Programs and Practical Training

Incorporating internship programs into the academic curriculum is crucial for providing students with practical training and industry experience. Education institutions should establish partnerships with pharmaceutical companies to facilitate internships. These programs allow students to apply theoretical knowledge in real-world settings, develop practical skills, and gain a deeper understanding of industry operations [70].

Skill Development Initiatives

Education institutions should prioritize skill development initiatives that go beyond academic knowledge. Collaborating with industry stakeholders, institutions can design programs that focus on enhancing skills such as data analytics, regulatory affairs, and quality control [71]. Tailored skill development initiatives ensure that graduates are well-prepared to meet the specific demands of the pharmaceutical workforce (Table **6**).

Table 6. Metrics for monitoring and evaluation of skill development programs.

Evaluation Aspect	Measurement Criteria	Data Collection Methods
Participant Feedback	Satisfaction surveys and feedback mechanisms.	Surveys, focus groups, interviews.

(Table 6) cont.....

Evaluation Aspect	Measurement Criteria	Data Collection Methods
Performance Assessments	Skill proficiency and learning outcomes.	Assessments, tests, project reviews.
Outcome Evaluations	Program impact on employability and career growth.	Longitudinal studies, alumni surveys.

Industry-Relevant Certifications and Training

Offering industry-relevant certifications and training programs within educational institutions enhances the employability of graduates. Collaborating with pharmaceutical companies to design and deliver these programs ensures that students acquire skills and certifications recognized by the industry [72]. This collaboration also facilitates a seamless transition for graduates from academia to professional roles [72, 73].

Advisory Boards with Industry Experts

Establishing advisory boards comprising industry experts is a proactive approach for education institutions. These boards provide valuable insights into industry trends, skills in demand, and changing job market dynamics. Regular interactions with advisory boards help institutions tailor their programs to meet the evolving needs of the pharmaceutical sector [69].

Facilitating Industry-Academia Collaboration

Education institutions should actively facilitate collaboration between pharmaceutical companies and students. This can be achieved through industry-academia partnership programs, joint projects, and collaborative events. These initiatives create a symbiotic relationship where students gain practical experience, and companies have access to a pool of well-prepared graduates [33].

Global Collaboration in Education and Research

Encouraging global collaboration in education and research expands the horizons of students and faculty [74]. Education institutions should seek partnerships with international pharmaceutical institutions, facilitating student exchange programs, collaborative research projects, and joint educational initiatives. Global collaboration broadens perspectives, fosters cultural diversity, and enriches the educational experience [75].

CONCLUSION

In conclusion, the collaborative strategies proposed for advancing the pharmaceutical sector emphasize the critical role of policymakers, pharmaceutical companies, the global community, and education institutions in shaping the industry's future. The multifaceted approach outlined in this essay seeks to address challenges and capitalize on opportunities, fostering innovation, sustainability, and the development of a well-prepared workforce.

Policymakers are urged to undertake comprehensive regulatory reforms, ensuring a balance between fostering innovation and maintaining safety standards. Investment in education infrastructure and the facilitation of industry-academia collaborations are essential for producing graduates equipped with the skills demanded by the pharmaceutical sector. Skill development initiatives and streamlined approval processes contribute to enhancing the employability of pharmacy graduates. Pharmaceutical companies, as industry leaders, are encouraged to establish robust internship and training programs. These programs provide students with practical experience, easing their transition from academia to the dynamic pharmaceutical industry. Furthermore, research and development investment, employee training, and corporate social responsibility initiatives showcase the industry's commitment to innovation, ethical practices, and societal well-being. The global community is essential in fostering international collaboration through research initiatives and knowledge-sharing platforms. Support for developing nations, mentorship programs, and collaborative efforts to address global health challenges are pivotal for creating a cohesive and interconnected global pharmaceutical ecosystem. Education institutions play a foundational role in preparing future professionals by continuously enhancing curricula, fostering industry exposure, and facilitating research collaborations. Skill development, industry-relevant certifications, and global collaboration contribute to producing graduates who are not only academically proficient but also industry-ready. As stakeholders in the pharmaceutical sector adopt and implement these collaborative strategies, they contribute to elevating industry standards, fostering innovation, and creating a workforce that can effectively address the evolving challenges in healthcare. The recommendations presented offer a comprehensive roadmap for stakeholders to work together, ensuring the continued advancement and sustainability of the pharmaceutical sector on a global scale. Through collective efforts, the industry can navigate uncertainties, capitalize on opportunities, and remain at the forefront of healthcare advancements, ultimately benefitting societies worldwide.

REFERENCES

[1] Experts share collaborative strategies for easing pharmaceutical logistics [Internet]. Economic Times Health world. Available from: https://health.economictimes.indiatimes.com/news/pharma/pharma-industry/experts-share-collaborative-strategies-for-easing-pharmaceutical-logistics/108497065

[2] Fundamentals of the pharmaceutical supply chain [Internet]. Pharma News Intel; c2024 Available from: https://pharmanewsintel.com/news/fundamentals-of-the-pharmaceutical-supply-chain

[3] Pharma in 2022: Building trust, extending collaboration [Internet]. STAT; 2022. Available from: https://www.statnews.com/2022/02/17/pharma-in-2022-building-trust-extending-collaboration/

[4] Rojas-Méndez JI, Rivera-Camino J, Acosta-Prado JC. The role of social media and social networks in service innovation: A literature review and avenues for future research. J Bus Ind Mark 2021; 36(8): 1682-96.
[http://dx.doi.org/10.1108/JBIM-07-2020-0365]

[5] Pharma industry outlook: The challenges and opportunities [Internet]. DCAT Value Chain Insights. Available from: https://www.dcatvci.org/features/pharma-industry-outlook-the-challenges-and-opportunities

[6] Zhang X, Shao S, Li W, Huang W, Huang Q, Lin J, *et al.* Influence of a COVID-19 outbreak on pharmaceutical quality risk management: an empirical study of Chinese pharmaceutical companies. Glob Health Res Policy 2023; 8(1): 1-13.
[http://dx.doi.org/10.1186/s41256-023-00334-x] [PMID: 36650592]

[7] Gaitonde RB, Moore G. The pharmaceutical industry's use of data-driven drug discovery platforms: A review. Drug Dev Ind Pharm 2020; 46(4): 511-20.
[http://dx.doi.org/10.1177/8756479320976130]

[8] Lilleoere AM, Holme Hansen E. Knowledge-sharing enablers and barriers in pharmaceutical research and development. J Knowl Manage 2011; 15(1): 53-70.
[http://dx.doi.org/10.1108/13673271111108693]

[9] Fisher W, Okediji RL, Sampath PG. Fostering Production of Pharmaceutical Products in Developing Countries, 43 MICH. J INT'L 2022; L: 1.

[10] Regmi K, Kunwar A, Thapa P. Training needs assessment of pharmacy workforce in Nepal: a mixed-methods study. BMC Med Educ 2020; 20(1): 1-11.
[http://dx.doi.org/10.1186/s12909-020-02188-0] [PMID: 32228560]

[11] Gilmartin M. Development and validation of a survey instrument for assessing prescribers' perception of computerized drug-drug interaction alerts in England. Digit Health 2019; 5: 2055207619832927.
[http://dx.doi.org/10.1177/1757913919832927]

[12] Olsson S, *et al.* Education and Training in Pharmaceutical Medicine: Medicines Development and Regulation for Scientists Worldwide. Front Pharmacol 2023.
[http://dx.doi.org/10.3389/fphar.2023.59194]

[13] Joseph, Isaac. (2023, November 30). Importance of Compliance With Regulations in the Pharmaceutical Industry. SSRN. Available at SSRN: https://ssrn.com/abstract=4679812
[http://dx.doi.org/10.2139/ssrn.4679812]

[14] Weitzel J, Pappa H, Banik GM, *et al.* Understanding Quality Paradigm Shifts in the Evolving Pharmaceutical Landscape: Perspectives from the USP Quality Advisory Group. AAPS J 2021; 23(6): 112.
[http://dx.doi.org/10.1208/s12248-021-00634-5] [PMID: 34654974]

[15] Geigert J. Regulatory Pathways Impacting Biopharmaceuticals. The Challenge of CMC Regulatory Compliance for Biopharmaceuticals. Cham: Springer 2023.
[http://dx.doi.org/10.1007/978-3-031-31909-9_2]

[16] Ndomondo-Sigonda M, Miot J, Naidoo S, *et al.* Harmonization of medical products regulation: a key factor for improving regulatory capacity in the East African Community. BMC Public Health 2021; 21(1): 187.
[http://dx.doi.org/10.1186/s12889-021-10169-1] [PMID: 33478421]

[17] Modi ND, Kichenadasse G, Hoffmann TC, *et al.* A 10-year update to the principles for clinical trial data sharing by pharmaceutical companies: perspectives based on a decade of literature and policies. BMC Med 2023; 21(1): 400.
[http://dx.doi.org/10.1186/s12916-023-03113-0] [PMID: 37872545]

[18] Francer J, Izquierdo JZ, Music T, *et al.* Ethical pharmaceutical promotion and communications worldwide: codes and regulations. Philos Ethics Humanit Med 2014; 9(1): 7. [http://dx.doi.org/10.1186/1747-5341-9-7] [PMID: 24679064]

[19] Murray JA. Post-Marketing Surveillance in Pharmaceuticals: Reactions. J Public Policy Mark 1986; 5(1): 44-60. Available from: http://www.jstor.org/stable/30000214 [http://dx.doi.org/10.1177/074391568600500103]

[20] 20. Maier-Rigaud, Frank P. and Maier-Rigaud, Frank P. and Lauer, Robert and Robles, Laura, Innovation Incentives in the Pharmaceutical Sector: Re-thinking Competition and Public Policy? (May 13, 2021). World Competition - Law and Economics Review, 2021; 44(3); pp. 307-332. Available at SSRN: https://ssrn.com/abstract=3845568 [http://dx.doi.org/10.2139/ssrn.3845568]

[21] Bettanti A, Lanati A, Missoni A. Biopharmaceutical innovation ecosystems: a stakeholder model and the case of Lombardy. J Technol Transf 2022; 47(6): 1948-73. [http://dx.doi.org/10.1007/s10961-021-09890-1] [PMID: 34611378]

[22] Li J, Xiao C, Hou J, *et al.* Clinical pharmacy undergraduate education in China: a comparative analysis based on ten universities' training programs. BMC Med Educ 2023; 23(1): 83. [http://dx.doi.org/10.1186/s12909-023-04049-y] [PMID: 36732755]

[23] Huang Z, Zhang X, Wu L, *et al.* Progress on Pharmaceutical Sciences/Pharmacy Postgraduate Education: a Bibliometric Perspective. J Pharm Innov 2022; 17(4): 1360-72. [http://dx.doi.org/10.1007/s12247-021-09611-z] [PMID: 35096194]

[24] Yen KP, Sekar M, Ansari MT. Developing an Outcome-Based Pharmaceutical Science Curriculum: an Evaluation Based on Triangulation Method. Indian Journal of Pharmaceutical Education and Research 2016; 50(4): 534-41. [http://dx.doi.org/10.5530/ijper.50.4.5]

[25] Chisholm O. Curriculum Transformation: From Didactic to Competency-Based Programs in Pharmaceutical Medicine. Front Pharmacol 2019; 10: 278. [http://dx.doi.org/10.3389/fphar.2019.00278] [PMID: 30949056]

[26] Nouri AI, Hassali MA, Hashmi FK. Contribution of pharmacy education to pharmaceutical research and development: critical insights from educators. Perspect Public Health 2020; 140(1): 62-6. [http://dx.doi.org/10.1177/1757913919832927] [PMID: 31165671]

[27] Scahill SL, Akhlaq M, Garg S. A bibliometric review of pharmacy education literature in the context of low-to middle-income countries. Currents in Pharmacy Teaching and Learning. 2013 May 1; 5(3): 218-32.

[28] Gersdorf T, He VF, Schlesinger A, *et al.* Demystifying industry–academia collaboration. Nature Reviews Drug Discovery 2019; 18: 743-4. [http://dx.doi.org/10.1038/d41573-019-00001-2]

[29] Main PAE, Anderson S. Evidence for continuing professional development standards for regulated health practitioners in Australia: a systematic review. Hum Resour Health 2023; 21(1): 23. [http://dx.doi.org/10.1186/s12960-023-00803-x] [PMID: 36941655]

[30] Darwish RM, Ammar K, Rumman A, Jaddoua SM. Perception of the importance of continuing professional development among pharmacists in a middle east country: A cross-sectional study. PLoS One 2023; 18(4): e0283984. [http://dx.doi.org/10.1371/journal.pone.0283984] [PMID: 37058486]

[31] Nasto, B. (2015, October 23). Academic-industrial partnerships convey a cultural shift. Biopharma Dealmakers.

[32] New Models for Academic Partnerships. (2014, September 27). PharmaVoice. Available from: https://www.pharmavoice.com/news/academic-partnerships/613305/

[33] Almarsdottir AB, Traulsen JM. Multimethod research into policy changes in the pharmacy sector-the nordic case Research in Social and Administrative Pharmacy, 2009; 5(1), pp. 82 90. [http://dx.doi.org/10.1016/j.sapharm.2008.04.005]

[34] Collaborative programmes and industry-led research. Available from: https://www.ukri.org/what-w--do/commercialisation/collaborative-programmes-and-industry-led-research/

[35] Hobbs L, Kelly H. STEM into industry – brokering relationships between schools and local industry. Curric Perspect 2020; 40(2): 247-55. [http://dx.doi.org/10.1007/s41297-020-00111-7]

[36] Audretsch DB, Guenther C. SME research: SMEs' internationalization and collaborative innovation as two central topics in the field. J Bus Econ 2023; 93(6-7): 1213-29. [http://dx.doi.org/10.1007/s11573-023-01152-w]

[37] Romasanta AKS, van der Sijde P, van Muijlwijk-Koezen J. Innovation in pharmaceutical R&D: mapping the research landscape. Scientometrics 2020; 125(3): 1801-32. [http://dx.doi.org/10.1007/s11192-020-03707-y]

[38] Palsokar G, Tajne M. A Study on the Perceived Gap in Between Industry and Academia with Reference to the Curriculum of Post-Graduate Courses In Pharmaceutical Sciences in india. Indian Journal of Pharmaceutical Education and Research 2018; 52(1): 10-20. [http://dx.doi.org/10.5530/ijper.52.1.2]

[39] Steenhof N. Adaptive Expertise in Undergraduate Pharmacy Education. Pharmacy (Basel) 2023; 11(1): 32. [http://dx.doi.org/10.3390/pharmacy11010032] [PMID: 36827670]

[40] McHugh D, Yanik AJ, Mancini MR. An innovative pharmacology curriculum for medical students: promoting higher order cognition, learner-centered coaching, and constructive feedback through a social pedagogy framework. BMC Med Educ 2021; 21(1): 90. [http://dx.doi.org/10.1186/s12909-021-02516-y] [PMID: 33546690]

[41] Inclusive Skill Development: India and Differently-abled Livelihood. (2023, March 24). Smile Foundation. Available from: https://www.smilefoundationindia.org/blog/inclusive-skill-developme-t-india-and-differently-abled-livelihood/

[42] Thomas JR. Training Opportunities for a Career in the Pharmaceutical and Biomedical Industry. In: Thomas JR, Saso L, van Schravendijk C, Eds. Career Options in the Pharmaceutical and Biomedical Industry. Cham: Springer 2023. [http://dx.doi.org/10.1007/978-3-031-14911-5_19]

[43] Taylor LS. Networking in the Pharmaceutical Sciences. Mol Pharm 2024; 21(4): 1549-50. [http://dx.doi.org/10.1021/acs.molpharmaceut.4c00267] [PMID: 38512057]

[44] Yue JJ, Chen G. Competence of pharmacy mentors: a survey of the perceptions of pharmacy postgraduates and their mentors. BMC Med Educ 2020; 20(1): 265. [http://dx.doi.org/10.1186/s12909-020-02188-0] [PMID: 32787894]

[45] Rao, Anita, Strategic R&D Investment Decisions in the Pharmaceutical Industry (September 1, 2019). Available from: https://ssrn.com/abstract=2652755 [http://dx.doi.org/10.2139/ssrn.2652755]

[46] Chen R, Liu S, Han J, *et al.* Trends in rare disease drug development. Nat Rev Drug Discov 2024; 23(3): 168-9. [http://dx.doi.org/10.1038/d41573-023-00177-8] [PMID: 37932437]

[47] Xu Z, Biswas B, Li L, Amzal B. AI/ML in Precision Medicine: A Look Beyond the Hype. Ther Innov Regul Sci 2023; 57(5): 957-62. [http://dx.doi.org/10.1007/s43441-023-00541-1] [PMID: 37310669]

[48] Giannakos MN, Mikalef P, Pappas IO. Systematic Literature Review of E-Learning Capabilities to

Enhance Organizational Learning. Inf Syst Front 2022; 24(2): 619-35.
[http://dx.doi.org/10.1007/s10796-020-10097-2] [PMID: 33551669]

[49] Thakker SV, Parab J, Kaisare S. Systematic research of e-learning platforms for solving challenges faced by Indian engineering students. Asian Association of Open Universities Journal 2021; 16(1): 1-19.
[http://dx.doi.org/10.1108/AAOUJ-09-2020-0078]

[50] Oyenuga G, Law M, Parbat M, Tofade T. Implementing an Online Longitudinal Leadership Development Program Using a Leadership-Specific Continuing Professional Development (CPD) Tool. Pharmacy (Basel) 2020; 8(2): 79.
[http://dx.doi.org/10.3390/pharmacy8020079] [PMID: 32384604]

[51] Rierson B, Miller P. A question of leadership: What lessons can the corporate sector learn from the nonprofit sector about relational leadership—being in touch with the inter□ and intrarelationships that affect and influence an organization? Leadersh Action 2006; 26(5): 12-3.
[http://dx.doi.org/10.1002/lia.1179]

[52] Danzon PM, Towse A. Differential pricing for pharmaceuticals: reconciling access, R&D and patents. Int J Health Care Finance Econ 2003; 3(3): 183-205.
[http://dx.doi.org/10.1023/A:1025384819575] [PMID: 14625999]

[53] Gold ER, Sachs RA. Toward a moral consensus on pricing pharmaceuticals for global access. Kennedy Inst Ethics J 2017; 27(3): 343-74.

[54] Singh RP, *et al.* Green pharmaceutical manufacturing: A review. Green Chem Lett Rev 2015; 8(1): 3-22.

[55] McDiarmid MA, *et al.* Environmental sustainability in healthcare: the importance of getting the pharmaceutical sector right. J Clean Prod 2019; 228: 244-51.

[56] Whitehead M, Dahlgren G, Evans T. Equity and health sector reforms: can low-income countries escape the medical poverty trap? Lancet 2001; 358(9284): 833-6.
[http://dx.doi.org/10.1016/S0140-6736(01)05975-X] [PMID: 11564510]

[57] Smith C. Corporate social responsibility: Determinants of pharmaceutical industry participation in community-based initiatives. J Bus Res 2018; 90: 213-25.

[58] Altinay L, *et al.* Disaster relief operations: past, present and future. Ann Tour Res 2019; 77: 83-101.

[59] Noland RB, Linn JF. Aid, growth, and development: Have we come full circle? J Policy Model 2016; 38(4): 507-28.

[60] Wagner CS, Porter AE. The scientific impact of nations: what different countries get for their research spending. Nature 1995; 378(6553): 29-35.

[61] Suber P. Open access, impact, and demand. BMJ 2006; 333(7582): 1261-3.
[PMID: 15891208]

[62] Bossert TJ, *et al.* Health system strengthening: prospects and threats. Health Policy Plan 2007; 22(5): 325-8.

[63] Shiffman J, Smith S. Generation of political priority for global health initiatives: a framework and case study of maternal mortality. Lancet 2007; 370(9595): 1370-9.
[http://dx.doi.org/10.1016/S0140-6736(07)61579-7] [PMID: 17933652]

[64] Chakma, Justin, *et al.* International collaborative research partnerships: blending science with management and diplomacy. Science Translational Medicine 7.282 (2015): 282fs14-282fs14.

[65] 't Hoen, Ellen FM. To promote innovation and access to health technologies, countries should make effective use of the flexibilities in the WTO Agreement on Trade-Related Aspects of Intellectual Property Rights (TRIPS). Bulletin of the World Health Organization 92.12 (2014): 831-838.

[66] The effect of improved tuberculosis diagnosis on mortality on hospital admissions in rural Malawi.

Lancet 1993; 341(8846): 263-6.

[67] Medina MS, *et al.* Evaluating the Impact of an Innovative Curriculum to Teach Pre-professional Undergraduates Pharmacy and Medical Topics at a Minority Institution. J Health Dispar Res Pract 2019; 12(3): 120-34.

[68] Anderson, Claire, *et al.* Changing the Learning Landscape in Pharmacy Education: Strategies for Competency-Based Curricula. Pharmacy (Basel, Switzerland) 7.3 (2019): 106.

[69] Medina, Melissa S. An Innovative Partnership to Promote Diversity in the Pharmacist Workforce. American Journal of Pharmaceutical Education 82.9 (2018): 6346.

[70] Romanelli F, *et al.* Internship characteristics that influence the career decision of pharmacy interns. Am J Pharm Educ 2005; 69(2): 176-83.

[71] Fejzic, Jasmina, Moles R. Perceived importance of pharmaceutical quality assurance by pharmacy undergraduates and recent graduates. American Journal of Pharmaceutical Education 78.2 (2014): 37.

[72] Tofade, Toyin S., *et al.* Use of certification to assess student ability to perform pharmaceutical calculations. American Journal of Pharmaceutical Education 78.2 (2014): 38.

[73] Guirguis, Lisa M., *et al.* The impact of community pharmacy residency training on pharmacy practice faculty members' confidence in, attitudes toward, and use of evidence-based medicine skills." American Journal of Pharmaceutical Education 72.6 (2008): 138.

[74] Zlotos, Leon A., *et al.* "Meeting the Demand for Pharmaceutically Educated Global Health Professionals." Pharmacy (Basel, Switzerland) 8.4 (2020): 197.

[75] Anderson, Claire, *et al.* "Changing the Learning Landscape in Pharmacy Education: Strategies for Competency-Based Curricula." Pharmacy (Basel, Switzerland) 7.3 (2019): 106.

SUBJECT INDEX

A

B

C

D

E

F

G

H

J

K

L

P

Q

R

S

W

Z

www.ingramcontent.com/pod-product-compliance
Lightning Source LLC
LaVergne TN
LVHW070949210926
848482LV00002B/145